Among Friends

MFK FISHER

•

North Point Press
San Francisco
1983

Published by arrangement with the author and with
Alfred A. Knopf, Inc., New York
Printed in the United States of America
Library of Congress Catalogue Card Number: 83-061393
ISBN: 0-86547-116-9

"A Palace Incident," "Streets of Gold Foresworn," "The Best View,"
"Lightened Heart and Quickened Energies," "Love Blemished but
Abiding," and "Child of an Inner 'Ghetto'" (Under the title "The
Quiet and Kind") were first published in *The New Yorker.*

SECOND PRINTING

Contents

Part II

·

The Town

Part III

·

. . . And Beyond

Among Friends

Prologue

Child of an Inner "Ghetto"

There is a kind of withdrawal, courteous but cabalistic, that a person meets in trying to talk with Quakers about their faith, if he is not a member of the Society of Friends and is plainly not trying to become one. At the opposite end of the pole of discipline and self-control there is the dewy-eyed sentimentality of people of other Christian sects who think of Quakers as men of infinite brotherhood and patience, and of understanding and good will and everything basically to be desired but left unattained in modern life, at least by non-Quakers. Between these two extremes, which are no more so than those between a Sephardic Jew from Lisbon and a band of hippie poets who have served their time in the Haight-Ashbury, there are the kind of Quakers I grew up with, when I was a child in Whittier, California.

All children can be cruel, and all children mimic their elders, and I was often teased, indirectly for being a non-Quaker and directly for being of foreign descent, by the peers who walked amiably every morning to school with me, sat with me all day without a sneer or snub, and then often turned vicious on the way home. The interesting thing about their almost ritual tauntings, which faded and flared according to the moon and the seasons, was that I knew nothing of cruelty as such, and thought theirs was part of normal life. My friends, for such they were, were only saying mocking things they had heard at home, from the kind quiet lips of their Quaker parents.

I do not remember hearing anything at all about *them* from my own father and mother, except an occasional and gentle quip made by the banker, Amos Maple, which my father would repeat at luncheon with relish. These witticisms were usually based on the sly use of an Old Testament quotation, and there was nothing but admiration in my sire's enjoyment of them. They were what was new on the Rialto that morning, at the intersection of Greenleaf and Philadelphia in the little town, and therefore they could be savored in the ghettos by anyone privileged enough to have caught them. My parents enjoyed the play of human wit as deeply as did the Quaker moneylender. Perhaps this intimate attitude of awareness, in my family, contributed to my early acceptance of my schoolmates' conditioned teasings; perhaps my bland immunity was as cruel as theirs.

My father, Rex Kennedy, was an intruder in the predominantly Quaker settlement when we went there early in 1912. He was not a member of the Society of Friends, either birthright or convert, and it was told him directly by his relatives and indirectly by his new associates that in a small town founded by and for a religious group not his own, he could not long last . . . a year at best, before he would be gently frozen out. But Quakers accept with their deliberate philosophy the belief that men should live side by side as brothers, whenever racially and professionally agreeable to the community, and after a considered and cool look at my father he was allowed to stay. I doubt that he ever let himself be aware of this tacit "permission": *he chose* to be there, to run the *News* and raise his family there, and finally to die there, without any nod except from the Supreme Being. That is how it was, for him.

He appeared to be a decent young man, of seemly habits if somewhat overtall, and with an occasional wild gleam in his eye (which he soon learned to mask except at home). He had been born into newspapers, and at nine was setting type on a stolen tombstone (still the smoothest surface!) for his father in Iowa villages, while his mother filled up the empty columns of their weekly journal with poems based on Felicia Hemans, and taught Latin and Greek, and even Anglo-American, in whatever local high school her wandering husband settled near. He was the son of a circuit-rider printer who had been given to publishing excerpts from the sermons of his idol, Peter Cartwright. Grandfather was a giant, very beautiful and subject to violent moods, and after he "saw the light" in his early forties he started tearing down the houses of joy he had once known and building temples to the Lord in their place. So my father knew something of religious fervor when he settled in Whittier, built by a band of outcast Christians for their own peaceable survival.

He went there because the daily paper was for sale at a suspiciously low price. The money he had received for his half of the Albion (Michigan) *Recorder* from his older brother was running out, and so, concurrently, was his wish to leave the newspaper business forever. He had spent most of the cash on options for orange groves near Ventura that proved to be planted on hardpan. He had proved enjoyably that he could never support his family as a beachcomber on Puget Sound. He had discovered in one stint on a paper in San Diego that he was constitutionally unfitted to be anything but his own boss. The editor of the Whittier paper had disappeared, as all non-Quakers there were said to do, and Rex and his good wife Edith gave up their wanderings, which she had feared and secretly loathed, and sank all their money and borrowings into the *News*. Her rich disapproving relatives agreed with his local advisers that he could not possibly last in the town and that he was endangering the security of his family. It must have been hard for him to return to a profession he had so much hoped to escape, but after a long life in it he still had the same daring gleam in his eye that was there on his first day at his desk in Whittier. He was still a bungling amateur of orange groves, still superbly convinced of his divine right to be a small-town editor. He believed in predestination, and was a triumphant fatalist.

Edith, when they arrived in Whittier in 1912, seemed well-mannered according to the Quaker ladies who never called on her but managed to observe her closely. She was said to sing well, but unfortunately only at home and in the choir of her heathenish little Episcopal church. She kept having children, which proved that she was at least Christian by intent. But she was said to be of Irish descent. In fact, her mother lived in the same house with her, and although old Mrs. Holbrook dressed and behaved in a proper way, she admitted to having been born somewhere north of Dublin. In other words, both of the ladies living in the big house at the edge of the "nice" part of town must be either Northern Protestants or Southern Papists in their own foreign land and all Irish females in America were or at least had been cooks.

As for the new young fellow planning to run the *News,* he too bore a name either Irish or Scottish, and most men of his race and build, from what the gentle and withdrawn citizens of Whittier knew, were either cops or rowdy brawlers in saloons, just as fifty years later people with Italian names would be thought of as high-paid killers in things like the Mafia.

All this surmise, as my parents settled blandly or at least doggedly into the little community, was aired now and then at family tables other than ours, and the next day I would pay for it, as the gang of little girls and an occasional sex-hungry boy would trudge behind, while I walked home. We were then between six and ten years old. In the mornings they always stopped at our house, and we walked and hopped together through the quiet sweet-smelling streets, planted with bushes never seen today, and tall handsome trees brought as seedlings by the courageous homesick pioneers across the Great Desert. Mornings were nice. Afternoons sometimes were a little miserable, but I never let on that I would like to cry or yell. On a bad day, with classes over and the Penn Street Schoolyard deserted, I would walk home alone, with my friends of that morning tagging me, perhaps twenty paces behind, like a pack of suddenly captious taunting dogs.

"What does your big fat Irish mother do?" the litany might start.

"My mother takes care of us," I would call back, disdaining to reply to any of the adjectives.

"Oh, no, she doesn't! She's the cook. All Irish women are cooks."

Actually, my mother stayed out of the kitchen as much as possible, except for making divinity fudge perhaps once a year, or an occasional cake like the monument for Father's birthday called a Lady Baltimore, or patting together egg croquettes for the cook to fry in Lent. There was no use explaining this to the kids, especially since they kept their distance and it might sound foolish in a shout. So after another half-block, which I paced as fast as possible without seeming to run, and thus satisfy them, somebody would yell, "What does your big skinny Irish father do?"

Again I would let the adjectives slide past me, and yell back that he ran the *News,* and my day-long, year-long friends would howl with laughter, and shout, "Oh, *no,* he doesn't! He's a cop. All Irish men are cops."

It seems strange to me now, so twisted am I by prejudices and their effects, that this sporadic gibing never really angered me. It did not occur to me to speak of it at home. My friends plainly did not know what they were talking about and would be all right tomorrow. . . . I thought it was part of being there in Whittier, just as other kids in other kinds of ghettos have the same passive acceptance of a lot more of it . . . until they can leave.

There were less than five thousand people in the town then, and only a few of them were anything but Quakers. There were perhaps thirty Episcopalians like us, and then handfuls of other sects, and some Catholics who were mostly Mexican and therefore firmly put outside the city limits in Jim Town. There was one little store run by Jews, called the Bazaar. There was never a Negro, except for our Cynthia who could not long stand her aloneness, even with us to love her. But the people I went to school with were white and they were birthright Friends, and I knew that every morning, any morning, they would stop for me on the sidewalk in front of my house, and speak politely to Mother if she stood on the porch steps, and that then we would tag in a discreetly gamboling pack to the schoolyard, shying loquat or date seeds along the gutters, or green apricots, according to the seasons . . . hopping puddles amicably after it had rained on the lumpy sidewalks. It would be ridiculous to try to prove anything at all to them.

I am not sure what a doctor would say about the apparent passivity on my part, this lack of anger. The teasing was part of life there, completely unimportant as such, and certainly unworthy of my attention. I knew my mother was not a big fat cook and my father not an Irish cop, but our private life was so apart from my friends' that it seemed pointless to try to explain their misconceptions to them.

I think this is true of most children before they emerge from their birth-skins, their spiritual placentas, into active life in the world. I know some of them, now as I did then, from other "restricted areas" as was ours, and I believe that the early years are mostly full of warmth and innocence and love, and that what goes on in cult groups, or on the local Rialto, is mostly unheard, invisible, unjudged, by the little ones. It does not much matter if they are badly housed, nourished by chance, isolated in groups or even alone. It does not matter until later, when they begin to grow new skins to exist in. Myself, I was well and warmly lodged. But I feel that an equally vulnerable precitizen in much less cosy surroundings, and hounded more than I ever was on the sidewalks of no matter what city, will survive if he has love to return to, as I did.

This condition must be unquestioned. Mine was. If there is a confusion in the household or the cave, the child is shaken *there*, and not outside. I stayed unshaken, because my cave was orderly and loving. As I see it now, my father was a strong young man, knowingly plunging himself and his wife and his offspring into a foreign and presumably closed society. She was a tender woman, shaped by her strong Victorian environment, and perhaps as innocent of true ugliness all her life as her little children were for their first years. Together they gave us all we needed to stay unharmed, unpuzzled, for a time.

I never bothered to wonder where my friends heard what they sometimes felt impelled to yell at me, at my younger sister Anne, but it is plain that what they had learned came from the mouths of their parents, people whom many nonmembers of the Friends' Society deem almost saintlike. I knew a lot of them as I grew older. Some were sanctimonious bastards. Some were truly gentle and fine, almost worthy of my parents.

I was never asked inside a Friend's house, in the more than forty years I lived in Whittier. Instead, at least when I was little, all the girls and even a few boys came to our place, freely and often. If we were thirsty, we went through the back porch (Don't tramp into the house and wake Grandmother . . . or the new baby . . . or Mother) for long gasping slurps from a shared tumbler under the kitchen tap. On the way out, we each took an orange from the row of them that always stood on the ledge under the screened window, or an apple or pear in season. If I limited the party to four young ladies, and saw to it that everything was left tidy, I could serve cornflakes and milk on the long piano bench in the living room.

And twice while we lived on Painter Avenue, and then once soon after we moved down to the Ranch, Mother gracefully did something for little people she was literally incapable of doing for adults, and gave beautiful, balanced, exciting parties for us. The first was in honor of my birthday, and the last of my sister Anne's, and I forget what brought on the one in the middle, but they were fine routs, attended by all our Episcopal Sunday school associates and many nice Quaker children we knew. By now it is easy to wonder what Mother's motives were, if any. Perhaps she was saying flatly to the other ladies of the little town that we lived in such and such a way and were glad to share it? Certainly she produced the only children's parties in my own experience, and in an uncharacteristic way, and if there were other such celebrations going on in Whittier, we never knew of them.

Occasionally I heard a parent "thee-and-thou" one or another of my friends, but in general this leftover linguistic trait, which had already become a deliberate mannerism, was not used, at least in front of non-Quakers. Of course I was familiar with it, being an Anglican and on close terms with godly language, in which we could be more familiar with our Deity than our dogs. I liked it, and always have, and wish that we could use it again in our family intimacies. In Whittier, the only person who ever said *thee* to me was a tall good-looking widow, highly respected because her own mother had been a minister. She was called Mrs. Osmun. Once she invited me to drive clear to San Gabriel with her and her friend, in a surrey, the only one left in town. I think I was five. Mother let me go.

There was a man along, but I do not remember him except that he took care of the horse. It was a long hot ride, with an occasional automobile whipping past us. The two ladies were swathed in dust-colored clothes and veils, like Mother's when she went riding in our Ford. Almost as often as I would have liked, little boxes and baskets were pulled from under the seats (I rode backwards, as befitted my stature and age and so on), and we ate tepid but delicious dainties. We forded a wide shallow river, perhaps the Rio Hondo. Once in San Gabriel, we could look only from the outside at the old mission and its outbuildings, in spite of the signs begging for visitors, for they were *Catholic*. Then we turned around and headed for home again, and it is interesting that when I finally returned to San Gabriel as a free and much older heathen I felt that I had really been there before, even so tentatively.

The important thing about this first visit—somewhat peculiar if one considers what energy it took to get four people and a horse there and then back again—is that I was called "thee" and "thou" as naturally as leaves floating down a little stream, by the beautiful old Mrs. Osmun. I was a child to her (even if our church was not a *real* one!). It made me feel fine. It sounded right, and this feeling had nothing to do with either religion or semantics.

(Once an older cousin of ours was accepted, as a paying lodger of course, into Mrs. Osmun's large empty house. He stayed there while he worked as a reporter on the *News*, between two somewhat more active sojourns in Greenwich Village, the modish place for all young men from Iowa to go. He has told me that he heard his landlady talking quietly on the telephone with her sister about some proposed purchases in Los Angeles. Mrs. Osmun said firmly, "Well, Susan, thee

can bee-ee-tee I wouldn't pay any such price for a footstool!"
He said it was as if the Deity were a not-very-bright child;
but as a longer resident in the town, I believe that a respectable Quaker lady simply did not use loose terms, such *words*,
straight out. . . .)

Nobody ever said "thee" to my parents, of course, although
after a few decades some men began to call my father by his
first name, at least in the right surroundings (Chamber of
Commerce meetings, Rotary, the country club . . .). My
mother, asocial both by training and because she was personally unsure, remained aloof from people after the first
few years of being the loyal young clubwoman wife of the
struggling new editor, but she had quiet and lasting affection
for two or three of the Quaker ladies, and they for her, although of course she was never invited to drink a cup of tea
with them. In fact, the nearest any of us ever came to sharing
food with them was the day she died, when Caroline, the
banker's eldest daughter, brought us a delicious apple pie,
"to help a little, with all the arrangements to make now," as
she said sadly.

My sister Anne and I often went into the Friends' church
for missionary lectures with Grandmother, when we were
little, but I was not invited to "meeting" until I was almost
fifty years old . . . and then by a revolutionary member of the
Society who was fighting to return to the old simplicity, and
do away with things like vested choirs and processionals and
such, which were twisting and bedecking the first patterns of
worship. As my school friends got to the marrying age I was
invited to a few weddings in the big church, and true enough
they had a Romish flavor to them, with an unseemly pomp
which in our own church would not have surprised me.

When I was still young enough to be forced to take piano
lessons, my Quaker teacher was also the organist at her
church, and of course I could never have endured the
privilege of practicing "In a Persian Market Place" if my

family had not been given unwritten approval to employ her, admittedly the only "acceptable" musician in town. After we moved into the country, Mother eased me out of that situation with daring and wiliness, and put me into the much less skilled hands of *our* organist, but her dreams of listening to me ripple through Chopin and Schubert, as she herself had learned to do, were soon broken rudely when the Episcopalian decided, once again, that I was best left thudding through the marketplace.

But how can anyone talk as I do, saying mean things with obvious malice and misinterpretation, about the quiet Quakers, so universally known to be filled with humility, brotherly love, and the general vision of George Fox on the hilltop? In Whittier, perhaps we learned more about that love than was intended, and largely because it never entered into the scheme of things, as such. We were never hurt physically. What is more important, our own culture or lack of it was never questioned or invaded. It was ignored, as long as we behaved ourselves. We, in turn, never thought of trying in any way to "understand" and participate in the religious and social habits of the people we lived with. We were not of their persuasion, which in itself was not exactly friendly but on the other hand was not antagonistic. They in turn had less than no interest in our foreign goings-on in front of our own altars.

The townsmen who very gradually began to call my father Rex, and even to down a nip of his good Scotch after they had played together around the golf course, like good community leaders, were not being Christian, or understanding, or kindly. They simply liked him.

In Whittier we all led our own deliberately separate lives, with mutual respect. The Friends were there first, and if they seemed a little smug it was probably because they still felt, after a few generations, like refugees from a scorned and even persecuted minority group, and what can be more holier-than-thou than a persecuted minority? They had been brave in their flight, and strong and canny in their chosen haven. . . .

There were many good kind generous (well, I do not feel sure about that loosely used word, for Rex always said it was like pulling teeth to get money for some of his projects) . . . there were many good and kind people in the town, I know, as well as a few mean cruel ones, and at one time they had the biggest and richest meeting house in the Quaker world. I went there with Grandmother to the free missionary shows.

She lived with us, or we with her, or anyway all together after her husband died. She was a smallish woman, compared to my parents, and I often leaned against her in wonderment, to see if there was a single soft place on her firmly encased body. Her cheek might have been one, but it never occurred to me to kiss her. She did not believe in enjoyment, much less joy, and was a rigidly disciplined Puritan from her eighth year until her death at a ripe or at least respectably withered eighty-two. She disbelieved in everything pleasurable, that is, except what was directly connected to Christian Life, preeminently as lived by her fellow Campbellites but peripherally by other white non-Catholics. She believed passionately in clothing and then converting nonwhites to her own form of Christianity, except for possible colored Catholics, who would perforce be too damned to succor. That is how and why I went occasionally with her to the grand building where the Friends worshipped, to a missionary show: it would be about bringing faith to the heathen, and therefore it was a duty (never a pleasure) to attend.

Once there were Swiss bell ringers, for some reason, along with a preacher from Palestine who illustrated unforgettably the phrase "My cup runneth over." He poured many too many grains of wheat into a basket instead of a goblet, which I thought would have been more fitting, but it was still a good act, and nobody had to bow his head in prayer, which my granddam approved. (It stuck in her throat to think of her own daughter Edith kneeling and perhaps even genuflecting, in the local outpost of Anglican popery and secondhand mouthings of the Scarlet Woman of Rome.) Grandmother would never have made a good Quaker, being too belligerent of nature, but she appreciated and enjoyed what they offered her as a decent Christian woman, and made no attempt to question them, especially since they would not think of doing so to her. Once more, brotherly love may have hung invisibly in the air of the enormous wooden hall, as the missionary roared and capered, and the stolid musicians tinkled their bells, and we sucked hungrily at the free orange of entertainment.

I sometimes wondered why my school friends, the ones in whose church I sat so happily for these shows, were never there. They went to bed correctly, at the proper time, while I caroused. Dramatic performances were not for Quaker children, and were generally frowned upon in those days by their parents. Perhaps they were offered to us, the "others," a little as Caesar gave circuses to the potentially troublesome Romans, to soothe them. Whatever the motive, my introduction to high-camp entertainment began in the old wooden church, and no amount of later compromise, with vested choirs leading the category, can erase the feeling of friendship and excitement it gave me when I was a child.

My music teacher played there. My friends went there to Sunday school. People rang bells and even water glasses right up there in front, the place where in my own church we were never allowed to set foot or even to kneel, until after Confirmation. Later in my life there would be splashy weddings, and the church would be rebuilt, no longer the biggest Friends' meeting house in the world but very luxurious and even elegant, and rich of course. (It was then that a few rebels split off and went quietly and often mutely to a room in the College, where they sat together until the Spirit either moved them or did not, and then as silently went home again. They had no need for organists, hymns, ritual . . . and with the smug and even sanctimonious attitude of all religious refugees, they knew themselves to be One with their fathers.)

No bugler blows "Joy to the World" any more, to the four corners of the town and perhaps the planet. But those were fine Christmas mornings, thanks to the Quakers who let us live in their town in peace. Exactly at seven, from the steeple of the Friends' church, the triumphant blast would come to us, fainter to the north and west and south, and then right into our upstairs sleeping porch, as little Anne and I lay close to Father in the big bed, quivering happily. Soon Mother would be home from singing at Early Service. After breakfast there would be the Tree, even though Grandmother disliked it as a pagan custom, and then we would go up and down the sidewalks of Painter Avenue, and compare dolls and tricycles and wagons with our Quaker peers.

The white children I knew when I was little had no need to be anything but well fed and secure, in the best houses in a town where they belonged to its best families, the ones with the settlers' names . . . Hadley, Bailey, Newlin, Comstock, Maple. Their ancestors, buried in the Whittier cemetery or along the routes to California, had given up other homes just as solid, positions just as secure, to live their own lives as they saw fit, in a place where they could practice their beliefs unscorned. The settlement they named for their American poet would be theirs, and theirs it was when we came to it.

It still remains a firm core in the sprawling suburb of Los Angeles that was once Whittier, and the part where we lived is now called the Old Town, by newcomers of all faiths and races. It is, in its own sedate tree-shaded fashion, just as much a ghetto as was Jim Town down on the river, where most of the Mexicans had to live when I was little. The comfortable old houses like ours have largely been converted into small apartments or doctors' offices. And all around it, in elegant suburbs, and "housing developments" that range from solid to shoddy, and high-rise buildings, live nearly a hundred thousand people. Most of them work in Los Angeles offices or the several great war industries. Freeways make escape quick and easy, and I am told that most people still leave town, as did my own parents, for their frolickings.

Whittier College, which had barely enough young ladies enrolled in it to dance around the Maypole when I first set foot on its campus in 1913 to watch the seemly caperings (another free show!), was definitely worried about overcrowding when I studied there for one semester in 1928, and almost four hundred students bulged out the few buildings on its neat campus. By now it is, in its own contained way, as sprawling as the town, with more than two thousand young people seething discreetly, so far, at its consistent conservatism. It even has an enrollment of fifty or so black students, which one report says is nearly the entire Negro community of the town.

Arithmetically that is surprising, to put it in a correctly gentle and quiet way. It seems to come out as a percentage of one-fortieth of the college student body, and around one two-hundredth of the town's head count. Surely my figures cannot be right, as my fourth-grade teacher at Penn Street would agree from her grave if she could. I do know, though, that our family harbored for a time, too short, the only Negro in Whittier, big Cynthia, who finally left us with mutual hot tears because she was lonely, except for us. She was, in fact, dying, pining, except for us. She was not welcome anywhere, even in the stores. Especially there was no place open for her to worship. The people did not seem to *see* her. . . .

Most of those I grew up with in Whittier are gone,

either up or down. If some of them still live, they may have forgotten me, as I have many of them. More clearly do I remember their composed remote mothers, always seen from a polite distance, and their quiet fathers, the men who looked over my own sire for several years and then almost smiled at him, as they met in passing on the corner of Greenleaf and Philadelphia. They went to a different church, and never bothered to doubt why. They ate and even dressed differently, because of their conditionings. They recognized good souls and bad, mostly within their own walls. It is probable that they taught all of us more about brotherly love than they realized.

I hope I learned enough about that, in all its forms, while I was a child there in the quiet enclave, to keep me learning more. Some of those forms would not be recognized as love itself, by many of my known and unknown teachers. But every lesson, every lecture listened to, must be interpreted into a personal dialect of the human language, and that is what I keep trying to do. . . .

Part I

The Family

1

Then Begin Again

Most minds have someplace in them a scrappy collection of
phrases that are *there*, caught like gnats in the honey of
memory . . . flies in the amber. Seldom does one know how
long they have been there. When did I first read, ". . . the
ever-returning roses of the dawn"? Why do I still chant now
and then, even aloud, "She moves, she breathes, / She seems
to feel / A thrill of life along her keel!"? And there is, "Begin,
and cease, and then begin again. . . ."

I began in Albion, Michigan, and was born there on July
3, 1908, in a heat wave. I leapt forth only a few minutes
before midnight, in a supreme effort from my mother, whose
husband had assured her that I would be named Inde-
pendencia if I arrived on the 4th.

Father was not only editor and co-owner of the *Recorder*,
with his brother Walter, but was a stalwart member of the
volunteer fire brigade, and through his cohorts was able to
keep our wooden house sprayed occasionally with a few good
jets of hose water, to cool the air for Mother and me. This
cost him a manly spree of ice cream and beer, later, in the
back room of the firehouse. (People drank a lot of beer then

in Albion. It was cheap and good, fetched from small neighboring breweries, as we were later to get it in Whittier, from the little German town of Anaheim.)

It has been told to me that an old woman from across the street visited the lying-in room, upstairs, took one look at me with my long hands spread out on my bellyband of flannel, and said flatly, "She won't last out the week. Healthy babies always clench their fists." This must have been interesting news to my mother, who knew that I was as strong as a horse but in a slightly dazed condition. So was she, of course.

She felt more amused when the biddy said, upon hearing that I was called Mary, for my maternal grandmother, "My land! I thought, being so religious and all, you'd call her something from the Bible!" This made my mother feel quite cheerful, and she defied all local protocol by getting up from her bed before the prescribed two weeks, and taking me for a ride in the only automobile in that part of the country, owned by the town's richest bachelor. I do not remember it, of course, but feel sure, for some reason, that it was a Reo.

It is a coincidence that the next car I rode in, after we moved to Whittier early in 1912, was driven by a fellow Episcopalian who noticed me sitting with fists clenched, this time, and said teasingly to my mother, "I can see your little girl is very selfish and stingy! Look at the way she has her thumbs inside her fingers! Generous people always clench their fists with their thumbs outside. . . ." This worried me, for even when I was three-plus, I *felt* generous. I later became very fond of the blunt nice woman, but her first comment about me still sticks in my fainter thoughts.

I know a few apocryphal things about my parents' life in Albion, some of them obviously worth having been retold to me, but the only actual memories I have of my own two-plus years there are vivid although secondhand: the name of Phil Church, who ran the back room of the *Recorder*, and that of Doc Hafford, who delivered me and then my sister Anne.

I often heard Phil Church mentioned as I grew up, and quite a bit later in life I had a fine experience with his widow, and she confirmed many of the legends and made them no less real but perhaps somewhat more accurate.

She came to see us at the Ranch when I was about forty-five years old, I think. I was living there after my mother's death, to try to keep the house going and the *News* more or less the way my father thought it had been. (Until his death, he believed that he was running a small-town daily, in a community that was heading for the hundred-thousand mark!)

Mrs. Church had called from someplace like Pasadena, to say she was visiting California and would like to stop for lunch. I asked her to stay overnight, because I had heard of her at times during my life. She turned out to be the Lady Who Came to Dinner, as well as the Madwoman of Chaillot, and seldom have I met a better person. I think I am safe in saying that she was, at that late stage, quite batty. By the time we met, I had already piled up an imposing list of such people, so we fitted together like a well-shaped hand into a well-made glove.

After Mrs. Church had been there about a week, my father asked me over our late-afternoon drink how long she planned to stay. I looked out across the wide screened porch to watch her walk through long shadows onto the green lawn, my little daughters clinging to her either hand, and I heard their three voices, all very much alike, singing some private song, and I said to Rex, "Would it much matter?" That seems like an ambiguous reply, but he understood me and grinned a little. He had revered her husband.

Mrs. Church showed me several things about my newly wed parents, which were the other side of the coin of what I already knew from them about themselves, and from Uncle Walter and Aunt Tim Kennedy who had not only shared the *Recorder* but also the house where Anne and their first daughter and I were born. I picked up the piece of money gratefully, now that it had two sides, and put it in my mental bank.

According to Mrs. Church, the most dramatic thing about the arrival of the new young editor in Albion, fresh from his honeymoon in Iowa, was that within a few hours after he got into town he fell writhing to the floor of the pressroom with a burst appendix. Apparently Mother had been quietly weeping ever since her wedding night, at least now and then, and this dreadful emergency precipitated a heavier flood of tears, which annoyed everybody but in some way comforted the spoiled, tired, horrified young woman and perhaps, by osmosis, her new mate. She stood around on the edges of things, mopping at her face. Her nose always swelled when she cried, and she undoubtedly looked a sight.

In spite of that, she was a lovely willowy girl, according to her pictures and to her new brother-in-law Walter, who had a true eye for beautiful females. She wore clothes well, and according to *him* she looked like a foreign princess in the elegant trousseau she had bought in Dresden, where her family had cloistered her in hopes of her forgetting forever the gawky young journalist she was determined to marry. And there she was, sniveling in a strange small town, in a strange refuge. She told me, once I was safely married for the first time, that she did indeed cry a little in Albion when Rex exploded in agony as he was inspecting his new domain, but that her tears were largely from an ashamed relief, to have him lying alone in bed for a while, unable to continue his prolonged and enthusiastic honeymooning. (I did not betray this confidence to Mrs. Church.)

Phil-of-the-Back-Room's wife was a trained nurse. She called Doc Hafford, when Rex went down like a poled ox somewhere between the press and the linotype machines, and it was decided at once to sterilize the Churches' dining room table and get Rex onto it. He was in grave danger. Sheets were spread on the table, once it was padded with newsprint. Like all dining rooms in small towns in those days, an electric light dangled above, on a long cord, and Mrs. Church filled a kerosene reflector lamp for Walter to hold for the close work, and went about boiling the instruments Doc pulled from his bag.

It makes a good clear picture for me now, full of chiaroscuro: Mother weeping as quietly as possible in the far shadows, sketched in by a cross between Aubrey Beardsley and Charles Dana Gibson; strong stocky Walter holding up the lamp and trying not to faint dead away, as he later told me; Doc Hafford hacking and probing and cleaning, and that little fine Mrs. Church doing everything he could not mortally take care of with two hands, while she dripped chloroform onto the gauze laid over a medium-sized kitchen strainer. . . .

Obviously Rex survived, as so did they all for many years, and the only one I cannot envisage now is the doctor. Was he portly? Men often were, in 1904. Did he have a beard, as was then common in his profession? Was he tall, short? The only positive thing I know about him, except that he was a good obstetrician for myself and several people dear to me, is that I have never heard anything but an unusual tone of affection whenever anyone says the three syllables Doc-*Haff*-ord . . . which of course nobody I know can do, any more. Was he married, with children of his own? He saved my future father's life, and undoubtedly salved many of Edith's wounds over the next seven years. . . .

I have a battered copy of *The Miriam Cook Book*, A Collection of Tested Receipts; Published by the Miriam Circle–Ladies Aid Society of the M. E. Church, Albion, Michigan. I use the word "battered" wisely, for the loose-bound ugly booklet is a mess of stains, spots, torn pages, scribbles, and general desuetude. It has no publication date that I can find anywhere. It must have been printed by the *Recorder*'s job press after Rex's arrival, though, for in the margin of one of the front pages (unnumbered of course!) of paid advertising is a correction in his bold pointy writing: "Sig cut at top . . .

Reset Mat. Use same style Type if Possible." Plainly this was
a reject copy he took home to his bride, to prove what both he
and the Ladies Aiders were up to.

There were a few doctors in Albion who seemed glad to
advertise discreetly, to help a new editor as well as their
Methodist patients, and it is this ad I like the best, a half-
page at the front of the book, in genteel type:

Dr. Geo. C. Hafford
Comstock Block, S. Superior St.

HOURS: 1:30 to 5 p.m.; 7 to 8 p.m.
SUNDAYS: 12 to 1   PHONE 112—*2 rings*

I tie all this together, whenever I think of the beginnings of
my new life. Especially it was Mrs. Phil Church, *La Folle
d'Albion* as we came to refer to her, who made it seem real,
in her one dreamlike timeless stay at the Whittier Ranch.
After she left, none of us could remember when she had
come. Suddenly she went out to a waiting car, through the
back door which we all used for every entrance and exit except funerals and to bring in wood for the fireplace, and her
zany voice was gone. Her lost eyes in her shrunken face had
smiled at me, and she had kissed me, and felt like a cobweb
in my arms and on my cheek. . . .

After she left, I found myself holding a little packet of
Christian Science pamphlets she had put in my hand. I went
to comfort my children, who stayed pale and reticent for a
couple of days, and when Father came home from the *News*
I showed the printed stuff to him. "Oh, sure," he said. "She's
always been hipped on that."

She had never once hinted it to me, although we talked a
lot about his dramatic operation and then many other almost
equally wild times, when her dining room table was the only
place for surgery in Albion. I wondered how she could have

spent her life in this direct contact with human illness and pain, and yet remain a believer in the tenets of her church. And she was, and still is, the only Christian Scientist I ever met who never once mentioned that fact to me; neither did she wear the sweet fixed smile I unfortunately associate with my many devout acquaintances. Her face was remote and small, the kind Dürer would draw. She had a nice slow way of talking, with some few gestures of the hands, and while she made me feel that she enjoyed me, she was most at ease with my young girls. And they were mysteriously drawn to her.

In fact, the whole adventure of her coming to the Ranch when I was a far-grown woman has stuck in my mind. How did she decide to do this? She seemed almost never to talk with Rex, partly because he was turning deaf and could not follow half she said, in her soft wandering voice. He was plainly puzzled about her being there, but not impatient, even though I think he may have wondered at times if she had simply come to the Ranch to end her days. If so, I honestly do not think it would have bothered him. Often I wish now that she had stayed (or that I had had the sense, the courage, to beg her to), for she made all of us feel good. I don't know where she did die, or when. When I think of this, I long to run after her, my hand full of her quietly bestowed pamphlets, and ask her please to turn back, to live with us some more . . . or even forever. It would be to begin again.

2

A Footnote on the Scabrous Possibilities of the Most Innocent of Publications, Such as "The Miriam Cook Book"

It was strangely titillating to me to discover, not long ago in a delayed and largely professional look at the church cookbook my father's job press turned out in the back room of the Albion *Recorder* in about 1905, that the third recipe was donated by Addie Gale Butt. Therefore, and this is what still occupies my gentler thoughts, he had been in the little Michigan town for more than a year, since his marriage and then his dramatic introduction to Albion high life on Mrs. Phil Church's dining room table, where his burst appendix was removed. And plainly Mrs. Butt was in town too, between that date and my arrival in 1908. . . .

She may still be living. If so, I salute her. I met her a few times when I was a preadolescent, beginning to be stand-offish, and she was peddling a line of indestructible three-piece knitted suits to old friends and former acquaintances like my mother. Edith, by then approaching the monumental in size, had decided that the clothes were more adaptable to her lathelike budding daughters than to her own silhouette, and Mrs. Butt came several times to the Ranch to measure and "fit" us.

She had, it seems, known my parents in Albion, through both her good local standing and her occupation of selling undergarments tastefully to the Best People. She must have been a dashing figure then, for even a fat decade later she was quite handsome for a crone of at least forty-five, tall and well laced into her clothes, usually a knitted suit provided by her current employers. She maintained a resolutely jolly manner with us, and in spite of my innate loathing for her wares I was fascinated by her visits because my mother had managed to make it quite clear that she was an old flame of my father's.

The time sense of naïve young girls is, or was when I qualified as such, very odd. I smiled a little pityingly at Mother's intimation that anyone would ever have looked desirously at an old man, like my father at thirty, especially a withered woman even more ancient, and I enjoyed with budding sexual awareness the slightly catty tone Edith permitted herself on our fitting days.

She managed to turn the name of our brisk and cheery visitor into a small female joke, so that when she rolled it out melodramatically to Grandmother or the cook or Anne and me we would go into titters, and then promise never to do so when the lady next appeared with her tape measure. I would look keenly at her when she did turn up, and wonder how it could feel to be a former girl friend of my father's, and have to depend upon his wife's orders for her dreadful knitted suits. But it never occurred to me that there had actually been any shenanigans between my noble godlike sire and this comparatively ordinary woman. Certainly they would not happen after he married Edith! I assumed that people got over any such foolishness *before* they became married, and then parents of people like me.

That unquestioning assumption on my part, at least about Father and Mother as such, lasted until not long ago, and its innocence is the reason that I felt really startled, even though well past the age of blushing for anyone but myself, to find that Addie (!) *Gale* (!!) *BUTT* (!!!), as my mother called her with delicate vicious mockery, was probably rolling her eyes in Rex's direction when he was a serious young husband and perhaps even a father! There was the proof, suddenly, in the *Miriam*, as it was always referred to at home when the cook would bring it to Edith for interpretation (interchanged with the *Settlement* and less often the *Boston*, our other culinary stand-bys).

I wished, as I put two and two together, that I had discovered this damningly suspicious fact while I still had to submit to Mrs. Butt's yearly blackmail, which is what those dreadful suits suddenly became in my eyes. Mother, the once helplessly outraged wife, had let this bumptious creature con her into buying her wares . . . and Mother had let her, because it made her feel powerful, triumphant, to be more prosperous than her old rival, as well as obviously enjoying the continued presence of the man the quondam peddler of ladies' personally fitted corsets and knitted cement-and-iron suits had once sparkled for and at. Suddenly, removed by more than half a century from those artless days, I felt aware of a muted Michigan Peyton Place, another Hecate County, at least a Winesburg pushed slightly westward, unfolding behind my eyes as I read Mrs. Butt's recipe for what was bluntly called "Waffles," right there in a place of honor in my own father's printing job. . . .

I remembered how my mother would sigh and say, the morning of another session of pins and measuring tapes, "I suppose we should urge her to stay to lunch again. Your *father* would no doubt like that. Old times. She eats like a horse. But she has had a very hard life. I believe her husband left her. She has sold things from door to door! Anything to keep her head up. She is really a very admirable woman, and you girls must try to remember that. And those suits will look all right, I promise you, once you have worn them for a while.

They'll soften, or something. . . ." Then Mother would *always* add, "We'll have waffles! Your father loves them!" She would laugh a little.

The suits never did soften. They probably lasted forever, although Anne and I managed to grow out of them fast, to send along to less fortunate young ladies in the Mission Fields. Mother, basically a generous sentimentalist, permitted her beneficence to grow less acid as time went on, toward the strong cheerful saleslady whose rolling name had always roused cruel Irish mockery in her.

By now the two women and the man are long past caring, and I can forgive Mrs. Butt for everything she did to my first dreams of *la haute couture,* and indeed for everything except her recipe in the *Miriam,* which must have made waffles of about the same tenderness as my first, second, and third "sensible yet stylish knits for girls":

> Three scant cups milk; two eggs; three scant cups sifted flour; one heaping tablespoon butter, melted; one-half teaspoon salt; 1 tablespoon sugar.
>
> Bake in waffle irons.

Is this the food of love?

3

The Predilection for
Lame Ducks

Time makes it easier to trace hereditary influences than it
does environmental, I am almost certain, although I do not
want to be. It is fortunate that much that we grow aware of
in our later years was a fine mystery to us for a period of bliss.
I, for instance, was supposed to have many of my father's
points of behavior, although I was a girl. When I was intelligent, generous, nicely behaved, I was told that I was just like
him. When I was impatient, rude, bitter-tongued, I was just
like him too. There was plainly some resemblance, tempera-
mentally and of course genetically, since it was unthinkable
even to this child who would like to be a foundling princess
left on the doorstep that she was anything but the result of
lawful mating of Edith and Rex Kennedy.

One thing I began to hope for at an early age was that I
would inherit my father's nose. It was a noble racy beak,
touched with divinity by a football break which grew left-
ward when nobody was around to set it, and divinely sizable
in proportion to his very tall body. I cannot know what it
would have looked like on a soft female face, for it never
happened, to my knowledge, and certainly not to me. I got,

through the genes again, a nondescript thing called retroussé by the merciful or coy, and snub or turned-up otherwise. Rex let me down in other ways too, and I turned out to be the midget of the family, a bare five feet eight to this day. I scuttled around underfoot, always looking upupup.

One thing I did get from my father, though, and loud and clear: his predilection for Lame Ducks. I still claim it jauntily.

Charles Somerville, a withdrawn, gentle man from Edinburgh, our best tramp of them all, was proof positive of Rex Kennedy's need for such drifters. There were others: Little Ears, Chucka-da-Noos, Buck the Rough Rider, mostly men but now and then a female waif. He was drawn like a moth to their flickering flames: the torch of the alcoholic, the phosphorescence of an evil refugee, the glitter of a broken gambler.

In the early teens of the century there were thousands of men roaming this enormous country. They drifted in unpredictable patterns, so that for a time there would be two or three a day at our back door, asking for food or perhaps a little work, and then there would be none for a week. They were called bums, mostly, or hobos. My Anglomaniac mother called them tramps, so we did too. The ones I remember were very old, which to a child means anywhere over the age of being able to shave, probably. I did not wonder about them, for they were part of the way life was for me then.

Only once did I face their oldness: for some reason I was alone at the back of the house, and a man came to the door and asked for something to do so that he could eat. I was about six, I think. Instead of calling the cook as I'd been told to, I decided for myself that since our own tramp Charles was with us there would be nothing for this man to do, and I never opened the icebox unless told to, so I quickly gave him a couple of big fat pears ripening on the window ledge, and he went off. I felt a new twinge in my stomach, at the way he was so sad and quiet. I told what I had done at lunch, and Mother said that I must always call the cook even if she was upstairs, and that I must not give away things without asking. Then she added, "And those pears are still as bitter as gall. Poor devil!"

I felt mixed about all this. There was no denying that Charles was with us, and supposed to cope with all the things like kindling and paths and weeds that the other roamers suggested doing . . . but to give a hungry man bad food!

The way Charles Somerville came to us was through a project Father started with the minister of our Episcopal mission and some friends who were fellow vestrymen there, Peter MacLaren, whom we called Uncle Mac, and Matty Matteson, and probably others. They rented an old building down near the railroad tracks where the tramps rolled off the freight trains. Under the bridge, they had a couple of "jungles," wretched mucky pits during the spring rains, and always hazardous in the tinderbox times between them. Word was spread; from all over town came cots, clean blankets, help to install showers and washtubs and a big cookstove. And I was carefully taught to tell all the men who came to our back door to go down to the hostel, on South Greenleaf, I think. They could sleep and get clean and eat there, and not have to pray for it first, or at all.

Charles Somerville, I think, first lived at the shelter, which was down at the other end of town. Then next thing we knew, he was living in our garage. But before that I must, as a woman who loved him, tell how he looked. (As I think on it, I believe he came like all the others to our back door, and then came again from the shelter, and we were so aware of him that we asked him to stay. . . .)

He was a frail thin man, with delicate bones, but still tall. He had a fine face under silky white hair which was long but not straggly, and was always clean-shaven, which may be one good reason Edith accepted him . . . she had a neurotic dislike of hair on faces, male or female. He had blue eyes, and I know they were large and steady and far back under his brows. His voice was low, and he spoke with the soft accent of a man from Edinburgh, well bred and well taught but always a Scot. (One of the first things he told me in his little room was how to pronounce the name of his town, and not to put a hard *g* on its end, as Americans did with Pittsburgh. . . .) I think he brought in wood for our big fireplace, and tidied the back yard and mowed the meaningless front, and swept the paths. But I never saw him sit down in either kitchen or front rooms, and I doubt that my mother ever set foot in his small hole that Father managed to carve out of the side of the garage, once he knew (probably from the first encounter) that Charles should stop roaming and stay with us.

The room had been meant for tools, I assume. It was big enough for a cot, which was always tidy, and an old Morris chair, and a decrepit office desk. The walls were part of the garage, with newspaper darkening on them to keep out the drafts. There was a small round kerosene stove, the kind we sometimes used in our Laguna summer place, with a murky glow through its window and a good warm smell. There was a soft light from an overhead bulb. There was a shelf of books, but what they were I never knew. From the roof beams hung slowly twirling bundles of half-cured tobacco leaves, which Charles got through some strange dealings from Kentucky. He dried them, and every night ground their most brittle leaves into a pipe mixture in the palm of his hand. He would reach up, snap off a leaf, and then sit back in his old chair and talk to us, my sister Anne and the new one Norah and me, until it was time to puff out more delicious fumes.

I still cannot imagine where Charles washed himself, or defecated. Both he and Rex were healthy decent men, and I am sure some provision had been made for continuance of such attributes, but where and how I do not know. To us children he always smelled wonderful. . . .

In the same way, I cannot remember where he cooked. There must have been a gas plate in the room? At first he ate at the shelter . . . really was it called a Mission? . . . but I never remember any smells of cooking in his room, and I spent at least an hour a day there for several fine years, after he came home from his work as janitor at the *News*. Probably, once he started regular work, he went to one of the few dismal hash houses in the town.

Soon after he came, he told Father that at one point in his wanderings he had been a master candymaker, and would like to make something for the little girls. Mother had a compulsive and almost suicidal love for sweets, and while Grandmother frowned on exotics like chocolate-covered cherries, which might have a foreign liquor in them, she admitted to keeping an occasional small bag of salt-water taffy in her desk drawer. Could this new tenant, this latest example of Rex's misguided quixotism, possibly prove his origins by making a batch of real butterscotch? He could, and did, and it was pronounced flawless.

This must have been when Anne was about four and I six, for I remember clearly the whole sequence of our sessions in the kitchen. Anne sat on the high stool, near enough the stove to watch, but out of the paths between it and the sink and the table. I stood nearer, on my little dictionary stool. Charles left his hat on the back porch as he came in, and the dangling kitchen light shone on his white hair as he bent over the pot and moved about in the late afternoon shadows. He talked along as he worked, telling us what he was doing and what would happen. The smells were beautiful.

At exactly the right moment he tipped out the pale brown syrup onto buttered cookie sheets, to let it spread evenly, magically, like glass, and he cut a knife across it to make little squares. Then we had to wait, and his voice went on softly, with his Scottish accent so like Uncle Mac's and yet different. Finally it was time for him to crack off a sliver of the glass, and if it was set enough he would break more for Anne and me to sample. Deftly he picked up the panes of colored crystal, and broke them into neat patties along the knife marks, and placed them in fancy pyramids on two or three plates, for Mother to put away as she saw fit. Just as deftly he washed off every sign that we had spent a good afternoon in the kitchen, and he went out the back door.

Once there was a slight hitch in the satisfaction from the front of the house, when he changed our private pattern a little and told Anne and me that we were going to make lollipops. Sure enough, he had perhaps fifty proper sticks for them in a little bag, and that day he made only half of the butterscotch into squares for Mother and Grandmother, and with the rest he created dozens of what we called all-day suckers at school. It seems to me now that they were shaped like stars, like strawberries, like sunbursts, but I think they may have been plain blobs. They were artfully done, though: the sticks never fell out too soon from the last licks, which to any connoisseur of such sweetmeats is a proof of superior workmanship, and very rewarding. I think Charles was as pleased and excited as we were by the beautiful gleaming things, and he arranged them in an elaborate whorl on a platter, and as he disappeared told us to show them first to Mrs. Kennedy, before the regular candies.

The trouble came when Mother, as admiring as we, asked where he could have bought the sticks in Whittier. I told her proudly, for it was one more proof of his general wizardry, that he had found them all himself, and had picked up every one of them around the Bailey Street School grounds on his way home from work. It took him a long time. They were of different sizes, but all as good as new.

We were allowed to eat that whole batch of supernacular lollipops, after Mother talked with Father and he talked with Charles, who assured him that he had boiled the sticks in water for a long time (. . . so he *must* have had a gas burner in his room!). But he never made them again for us, and when we begged him to, he said that nobody seemed to throw sticks into the weeds any more. . . .

The dim delicious afternoons, with the three of us alone in the kitchen, peaceably murmuring and tasting, stopped forever not long after that. By now I cannot know which of us children innocently blasted them, so I shall share the honors with Anne. It was after dinner, and for a treat all of us there got a little patty of the beautiful tawny-clear butterscotch we had watched Charles create that afternoon. (It must have been on Sundays that we collaborated, because he was not at the *News* and the cook was never around. . . .) Before we left the table, we tucked a sweet into our cheeks, and Mother said, "How does that old man do it? The best I ever ate, *ever!* And always the same! How can he possibly know, I wonder, just when to take it off the stove?"

As I remember, Anne and I were so proud of Charles that we almost burst to tell of his artistry and his incredible courage, and we talked together:

She: He puts his hand right into the boiling candy . . .

I: He puts his thumb and finger right down into the candy, and pulls them out and . . .

She: . . . he snaps them together, just once very fast, and if they sound right . . .

I: He just snaps them once, and if they come apart right, it is time, and he never gets burned.

She: And it never even hurts him. It would hurt us, he says.

I: Oh, Charles says we must never try it. You have to know how. It is a special . . .

She: . . . trick, a secret.

I: It's a secret. But he told it to us.

And of course when we were gently prodded into disclosing it, we did, probably in unison: All you need is a whole lot of real spit on your thumb and your finger, plenty of it. Then if you do it fast, you won't get burned.

Mother and Grandmother were plainly if quietly upset, disgusted, repelled, put out. Father said that the high temperature of the boiling candy no doubt changed the . . . uh . . . saliva in many ways, but admitted on further complaints that the casual introduction of cast-off sucker sticks was . . . uh . . . perhaps part of the picture of shiftless and wanton irresponsibility of a confirmed vagabond. Mr. Somerville *spoke* like a gentleman, the ladies also admitted fairly, but hygienically he was not up to American standards. Granted, he made the best butterscotch ever tasted. But he never made it again for us.

Every afternoon on the way home from his job he passed the bakery, and picked up a leftover bun or doughnut. Anne and I always got a good piece of whatever he had scavenged or been given (he was a distinguished man, and sensitive people were proud to know him . . .). And after Norah began to walk, while Mother was readying herself for David, he splurged and bought or otherwise acquired so many dreadful sweet rolls and cream puffs and suchlike that finally a halt was called. Anne and I, and our darling little sister, would stagger up the back steps when the cook called us in for supper, so sated that we could hardly lift our eyelids. Edith talked to Rex, and Rex talked to his friend Mr. Somerville, and from then on the three of us got one tobacco-flavored sliver of chocolate-frosted greasy doughnut, and no more, and because Charles was a gentleman he never murmured sly destructive comments to us about our thinning rations and their reasons.

He changed and grew warmer than at first, after Norah started trotting down the back stairs to his room. Mother knew that the little girl was safe there, and concentrated on other matters, and the cook was glad because Norah was out from under, and Anne and I were glad because we knew we would find the new sister there, safe in the grey-blue stench of Charles's castle, a princess in his loving gaze.

Charles did honestly love her. He taught us a new way to be gentle and as if awestruck by her innocent beauty. Anne and I would sit on his cot, and the little golden-colored girl would perch like a plump bird on his bony old knees, and slowly he would divide one leftover bran muffin or a withered doughnut into four even pieces with his tobacco-blacked pocketknife, and we would commune.

After David was born and well established, Mother became aware that her three older children were invisible from the time Old Charles came home from the *News* until they were called for supper, which we ate together, but often hurriedly because Father almost always had to get to a meeting by 7:30 and it was too complicated to arrange otherwise about table settings, what with the Help one could get. . . .

Charles was an unknown (certainly to Mother). He was the Hired Man . . . or at least a temporary lodger of mysterious origin (here he qualified as the first of my father's endless string of what we later came to call Rex's Lame Ducks . . .), who smoked too much vile tobacco. Anne and I were getting too old to sit in a man's bedroom. What was worst, he probably filled little Norah *secretly* with cheap bakery pastry, on which she seemed to thrive (Charles *never* cheated!).

Mother put her foot down, and Norah was kept indoors at the one time of day when she wanted to head for the Garage and Mr. Somerville's gas chamber, and Anne gradually tapered off too, and finally I was the only Faithful to the 5:15 call to arms, complete with slow tobacco mixing and courtesy bite of a sweet roll. I know that Rex sometimes went out to the Garage after dinner, and I suspect that he took along a little flask of Scotch. I hope so. But not long after Charles was made out of bounds (Norah would head down the back stairs right on the dot, and the cook would pull her back and say gently, "Not tonight, honey . . .") he moved upstairs in the new *News* Building on North Greenleaf.

Until then Father had been running the whole daily operation in one big store building, with no more than a low fence separating Business from Editorial, and the presses right there at the back, with the two linotype machines a nervous barricade against their mighty whopping sound. Now there was our own building! On the ground floor, back of Business and Editorial (where Rex had his own office with walls made half of cloudy glass and half of plyboard, very impressive), were the linotypes and the presses, a small room with a special smell where paper was kept for the job work, a big garage-type door on the alley where classmates of mine rolled papers for their delivery routes. . . . It was a palace of a place! And upstairs was a room, like the Captain's Quarters on a tight little freighter, that belonged to Charles Somerville.

My heart swelled with pride and happiness for him. He had everything there from his room at home, but more space for books, which I still do not remember: the bed, two chairs now, the old desk, and of course the tobacco twirling slowly in bunches from the rafters.

Then he broke his leg, and when he came back from the hospital everybody at the *News* gave some money for a party for him and there was a noble armchair as the present, the kind that tips and revolves. It was colored a good blue, too, like his fading eyes. I went after the formal "office" presentation to see it, and he seemed quite shaken, so we did not stay. Later Mother told me he had cried at the party, in front of everybody, which of course we had all been taught not to do.

The way he broke his leg was that he fell off the Electric, on his way to a dinner party.

There was a lanky attractive freight agent in town, a friend of Rex's of course, whom Mother did not "know": he was not a Quaker, which made him unimportant professionally, and he was not an Episcopalian, which excluded him from our inner circle. He and his wife "adopted" Charles Somerville, as my poor mother never failed to put it icily when the relationship was mentioned. She would ask Anne and me if Charles was getting into his party clothes when we last saw him, to go to be spoiled and flattered by people who thought they *appreciated* him . . . that sort of thing. It was really an odd antagonism for such a nice woman to feel. But I think Mother always resented the Lame Ducks. There was jealousy there. . . . Why did not her husband, the simple Iowa newspaper reporter she had given her hand to, know the bankers, the lawyers? Why did he pick up people like Charles?

She was at an impasse, of course, in Whittier: bankers and lawyers in that tight fortress of brotherly love had no need for Rex or for her, except as he could run their advertisements, and would play some of their political games. The *News* was a public commodity, and the people running it were part of the machine. This isolation may be one reason why my father became more and more prone to Lame Ducks, and my mother to her couch and the English Novel. . . .

It is probable that the people Charles was going to visit the night he slipped off the Electric and landed with a broken leg were unusually nice people. They had the same recognition of a fine man that we did. It is too bad that we were not friends, drawn together by him. And they invited him often to their house, for meals at their own table, and he went there for Christmases.

On that holiday, while he lived with us, Anne and then Norah and I would always take out to his room, when he sat alone in the garage under his twirling bundles of tobacco by his kerosene stove, a pipe and some tobacco and a sweater or a muffler. If Norah was there he would put her on his knee in a close gentle embrace. But he never came into our house, festival or not, after the Butterscotch Period.

This seems *impossible,* too painful, as I remember it. Why

was it this way? Why did Father not change things more? Was he a weak man really? Why was Mother so detached from any lives but those sharing her own blood? Why was I so stupid and docile, not to kick like a sick fawn at the ice forming? Perhaps Father was right, to rescue tramps and even to bring them to the edge of his own campfire, and then to let them stay there if they wanted to, but never come in any further. Was that because he was afraid of his own inner need to join them? Did I have to join *him*?

The nearest I got to this possible explanation of Charles and many other people was one day when I was almost twelve, and Rex was taking a carload of his own and neighbor children to something or other, along what used to be called Whittier Boulevard. There was one house I always looked out for, because it had a gazing globe in a little square of lawn edged by box hedge and gravel. At first I had thought this stylish, but soon it became only a visual tease to me. As we neared it, and I peered for the concave flash of it, there was a hobo walking against the thin traffic, with his bindle. I said something trite about being sorry for him, for there were not as many as in my earlier life and I was more aware of their dusty search. Rex said, in a quiet way, something that still rocks me, and that day left me hanging on a thin silver wire of puzzlement, twirling like Charles Somerville's tobacco high above a room that I thought was there forever but had almost disappeared. He said, "I envy him." It may have been the first time that I asked why to him, and he said, "He has nothing. He is a free man."

Now, I do not think Father was being bitter. Perhaps he was desperate, with a carful of sprats, but he was not a man to feel sorry for himself, at least consciously. He gave me an honest answer, and I said something about the hobo's probably having a toothbrush anyway, and Rex snorted and the talk ended. But I wondered how a man like my father, with Mother and a newspaper and us four children and a ranch with the beans growing between the rows of orange trees, could think a poor lurching dusty hobo was free. The more I wondered, the more I came to conclusions about not only freedom but Father. Mother. Myself. Charles.

Charles hopped around the *News* for several years. People liked him deeply, and the girls from the Front Room gave him little parties with homemade cookies, and the Back Room kept him fairly well supplied with a gentleman's ration of potables, and sometimes we did walk up to his room and have a rather formal shy meeting with him. After his accident he used a cane, and finally, for better or worse, a crutch. Then he could not get in and out of the fine blue swivel chair. The tobacco fell from his hand.

Father and the freight agent got him into the County Farm. Mother remained apart from all this, as far as I know. It was as if a leaf had drifted across her path and then on into the forest. Two times at least I went with Rex to the impressive hospital, but by now I do not remember Charles there at all. It did not worry me much. He was part of my life, and I was just beginning. . . .

Other wanderers came from far lands, speaking other tongues, and I came to understand without question that this was like honey to Rex, or perhaps more like a spiritual physicking to his pot-bound restlessness. They had known lives forbidden to him, lives of waste and recklessness and derring-do, and his own nature plainly drew some vicarious satisfaction from being able to talk with them and feed them and then, more often than not, send them stumbling along again on the paths he secretly dreamed of treading.

That is surely one reason, perhaps unsuspected, why he dove with all his heart into that quixotic "mission." Nobody interfered, as far as I know. Mother condoned it because it was tacitly sponsored by the St. Matthias Church: what other attitude was there, with the minister and two vestrymen acting like schoolboys over it? The businessmen in Whittier remained aloof, for the most part, unless they were religious mavericks. The Quakers had their own quiet charities, and this was a dangerous kind of sport, a variation from their normal and established procedures in rescuing men's souls from their bodies.

And business was good, at the hostel. Those were lean years, before and during the First World War, and most of the men who drifted back and forth across the American continent like lemmings with no place to head for death rode the rails, so the little mission next to the tracks and an overhead bridge was a good location. I like to think that it was Rex who chose it. As a latent frustrated bindle stiff he would know. . . .

It would be easy to trace the development of the place into the present Salvation Army branch in Whittier, but better people have done it, and I prefer to leave it lay where Jesus has flang it, in the convolutions of my wishful memory. It is enough that slowly it became important to everyone with what is called a Civic Mind, and that while this was happening (small-town people, especially if they are temperate judicious members of the Society of Friends, move without undue or overemotional haste), my father spent a lot of his vigorous hungry nature on the Lame Ducks who fluttered in and out of his unwitting blind.

He needed them. Part of his nature was fiery and impatient. The larger part was timid, at least to the point of believing in predestination as outlined to him by the people he respected and loved, including his wife and her family. He had been *meant,* they told him, to be taller, stronger, better equipped to stay respectable and honored, than many people he knew secretly to be much braver and more privileged than himself. His absorbing interest in hungry broken transients was proof positive of this inner doubt and quarrel, I think.

My mother accepted Rex's compulsive brotherliness, but with scoffing tosses of her head, and a fairly successful withdrawal from any direct involvement with the steady parade of his pets, both male and female, through our lives. Actually she liked only people related to her; they were her reality, and the rest of her inner landscape was filled but dimly by "the others." Members of the Episcopal Church were less shadowy, but seldom did she part the veils and let them into her warm loving presence. As an Anglomaniac, she was helplessly swayed by any scoundrel with an upper-class English accent, but fortunately the only people in Whittier who spoke that way were members of St. Matthias, which made life simpler for her, socially.

When Father might mention, which he did rarely, an interesting fellow who had come into the office that morning, Mother would shrug scornfully and say, "Of course he *wanted* something! You're too soft, Rex. You're an easy mark . . . you and Mac too!" Rex would agree quietly, and say, "He seemed like a decent enough fellow. Has a wife and some children in South Dakota, and . . ."

"Naturally," Edith would interrupt, tapping her right foot vibrato under the table. "South Dakota! Who would live there? No wonder he's a tramp! *Escape!* And please don't send him around here. Four men this morning, all saying you'd told them there might be something to do. Not a slice of bread left in the house. . . ."

This firm and continued antagonism from Mother finally forced Father underground. Gradually, little was said, in front of Anne and me anyway, about my father's increasingly sub rosa friends, transient and otherwise. Granted, Charles Somerville was a fine man and had once been a gentleman. As for the rest, they were not Episcopalians nor were they good solid respectable Friends. They were not businessmen, and therefore not advertisers in the *News* and therefore not to be patronized for meats and toothpaste and such. . . . They were not of Edith's chosen and circumvented world, and Rex learned how to see that they remained so.

He consorted enjoyably, and for many years, with people like the Catholic priest, the secretly radical high school principal, a renegade Mormon who ran a garage for a time, a two-bit orange rancher with a French wife who pickled olives with garlic, very good with his home-pressed red ink. . . . None of these people ever set foot in our house, any more than we did in the "nice" Quaker homes in Whittier, but they were indefinably within our awareness of the lives we all led in our own ways, and not Edith's.

One man we always stopped to salute, as we left Laguna after a weekend there, was a short Dutchman who got out a weekly sheet when he felt like it. Rex saw at once that he was a peculiar character, and was drawn helplessly to the smell of ink in the little building, and to the sound of the foreigner's talk. Here was another newspaperman . . . and here was one who had come from a great town in Holland to sit quietly waiting to die in a deserted wintry Pacific village redolent of rain and eucalyptus buds.

I think the man was named Harry Hansen. He was short and white-haired, and I can see him standing thick and solid against the light in his dingy little building, waving to us like a priest and bowing silently to Mother in the front seat of the Ford. She never got out. He seldom came to greet her.

When we slowed down on the late Sunday afternoons in front of the newspaper office she would sigh and say nothing. Then when Rex jumped back into the car she would sigh again, and ask him if he had the last issue of the Laguna paper. She liked it, but could not help being sarcastic about a typo ("He sets it all himself," Rex would say as we tore along through the Canyon at a good thirty-mile clip . . .), or a lapse in syntax ("He speaks five languages," Rex would say, and she would add, "Four of them better than English, let us hope"). All this went on nicely, with no bickering: Rex was in love with the *idea* of a man's leaving his own land and starting a new life in a far country, alone; Edith was resigned to her husband's need for this strange un-Holbrook hunger in him, and protested almost dutifully.

Somehow Rex told us of the picture on the shabby desk in Laguna, of a beautiful woman and several smiling children: they had all died in the fire that burned the best newspaper in Holland. "Why didn't you tell me?" Mother cried out with true anguish, but there was no answer, for it was something between men, beyond female compassion.

This removal from the woman's sphere was a part of Rex's whole Lame Duck Syndrome, of course. The reasons for his adoption of misfits and underdogs and human rats and crippled gentlemen were separate from his wife's own ways, and it was a good thing for everyone concerned that for the most part she seemed willing to confine herself to her family, her Church, and the British Empire as represented in fiction. He went right on rubbing himself in the dust of other men's spiritual shoes, much as another man would keep a mistress or two, or study Swahili.

The difficulty of keeping a mistress has too often been considered, as it relates to living in a small American town in the early twentieth century. It was done, of course, but not by a cautious and aspiring young newspaper editor with a highly respectable wife and a growing family. Fortunately I was able to discuss this peculiarly Yankee dilemma at length with my father, long after there was any immediate need to remedy the situation. It was a sad-but-true picture he sketched for me. . . . As for studying Swahili, he settled for Spanish, an unheard-of whim in Whittier then among the white citizens. This enabled him to travel occasionally to Mexico, where perhaps he found answers to other questions.

Only once did Edith permit herself to lend a hand with one of her husband's continuing involvements with the seamier side of Whittier society, and it was, as she well knew from the start, a great mistake.

We began to acquire some pieces of beautiful ancient

Spanish brass: flat shaving bowls like Don Quixote's helmet, an exquisite ewer which could well have been Greek. Mother loved brass. It was everywhere at home (the first test of a new Hired Man was how well he handled the polishing kit), and it is probable that Rex used the fine foreign pieces deliberately as bribes or foils, in what turned out to be one of the wildest of his crusades.

It seems that there was, flying through our staid town like an exotic tropical bird, a family straight from South America, Peru, I think. There were several little children, a nurse, a couple of maids, the invisible lady of the house. The father spoke excellent English. He was a very nice fellow, Rex gradually reported, a mining engineer down on his luck, looking hard for work with one of the California oil companies. They were crowded into a miserable little house (this detail was ignored blandly by Edith, as he surely knew it would be, for in spite of the first desirable gifts of Spanish brass, she could see that her husband was helplessly involved with another Lame Duck . . .), and we never met any of them, except Anita.

Gradually we acquired several more really lovely objects, which are still part of the family holdings: a big Talavera jar, a rare embroidery made of beads, two rugs from the tent of a sheik, things like that.

And gradually the rare bird of passage collected enough of Father's money to fly on, hopefully to a richer jungle. He left one last thing for us, the only gift Father did not pay him for, at least directly: Anita. He would send soon for her, he promised Rex, who was by then completely hypnotized: such adventure, such exciting glamorous strangers, such noble courage. . . .

Anita was a tiny woman, a bag of bones with fuzzy black hair, a face snow white with powder but dark in the wrinkles, and a shocking use of make-up around her sunken beady eyes. She would learn English with us, and Father would study Spanish with her on the rare nights he had no meetings. She would help in the house . . . cook, sew, anything.

The first thing we learned, by a kind of Esperanto, I suppose, was that she had never been a *servant*. She had lived all her life with the unseen señora's family, as a kind of maid-duenna-nanny. This meant that she was incapable of admitting any familiarity with things like carpet sweepers, mops, garbage pails, beds, wastebaskets. . . . She and Mother were oddly alike in this great talent of ignoring anything too dull or unpleasant to admit recognition. Anita simply did not *see* what she preferred not to do, and early in her stay with us Mother took to her bed, her own answer to every dismay, her solution to any problem. (Grandmother was on a lengthy series of visits to her Eastern relatives, and by the time she got back everything was in order, except perhaps for a sore but hidden spot in Father's ego.)

The second thing we found out about Anita was that she could not cook. She loved to tell Anne and me, in growing detail as we got used to hearing real Spanish instead of our border-Mex, that she had once taken a course of lessons from the former chef of the King of Spain, and it is true that she could make two dishes superbly: a vanilla flan, and an elegant version of chicken enchiladas. That was all. She did not even know how to make toast!

It was easier with Mother out of the way, and Anne and I got Anita so that she would present decent coffee and eggs for Father's breakfast, and apparently none of us starved. And at least twice a week she would spend most of the day crashing around in the kitchen ("How can any human being make that much noise?" Mother would ask irritably from her chaise longue upstairs . . .), baking her famous flan. It was a perfect *crème renversée*, made always in the big Custard Dish reserved for special feastings, and then turned out at the last, with never a crack in it, never a flaw, and the brown subtle liquid running at just the proper speed over its flat surface and down its impeccably sloping sides. On flan nights Mother always dined with us.

It was when we ate the chicken enchiladas that she stayed immured for the two or three days it took to assemble them. Her basic resentment of the whole business was that it not only involved Anne and me in precise demanding assistance in the kitchen, but it actually got Rex to leave his desk and drive clear in to Los Angeles to a tortilla factory, a special one near the Plaza, and to an herb shop on the edge of the Chinese quarter, and to a ranch on the way home where Anita felt the best possible chickens were to be found (for twice what they cost in Whittier, Mother would manage to add sarcastically . . .).

My little sister Anne soon tired of all the skillful mashings and choppings and so on, but I stayed as much as I could in the kitchen with the weird bird of a woman, working contentedly to her directions and listening to her chirps and twitters. She measured as precisely as if she were filling a dangerous pharmaceutical prescription. She let some things stand for three hours, some for overnight. She cooked this and that, and set little dishes aside. Always she checked and rechecked her pages of lacy Spanish-convent writing. When it was the normal time for us to eat during this pageant, nothing would be ready for a plain American meal, and I would scramble eggs, or invent a hash of sorts. . . .

Anita's chicken enchiladas were like nothing I have ever tasted. Except that they were made of superfine tortillas instead of crêpes, they perhaps most resembled the elegant cannelloni served on an Italian luxury liner at the captain's request, to a prime minister traveling incognito, two international movie stars, and the Prince and Princess Sostenuto Klein-Ragazzi. They were not Mexican, although they did have the herbs from the little "native" shop in them. They were not bland, but neither were they like the enchiladas we knew in Southern California, crudely heady with peppers and tomatoes. The lightly stewed chicken was pulled off the breastbones (usually by me) in long tender pieces, and laid precisely on the warm tortillas before they were rolled. The sauce was smooth and yellow-creamy, but it had authority. The dish was a masterpiece . . . and like the flan, it was infallibly so.

It would have been a strange sight, there in the Whittier dining room, to see the Kennedys eating slowly, in a kind of rapture, a dish so foreign to everything they had been raised to consider good food. Father and Mother talked softly between their bites, and she forgot her real antagonism toward the strange woman hovering in the kitchen door to watch her accustomed triumph. Edith, like any true gourmande, sensed always that she must live for the moment, and told Rex firmly that she would like some dry sherry. He was a little shocked, the first time: sherry was for when the minister came, and to be drunk before a meal. It was the perfect wine for that dish, of course, as I taste it now on my mind's tongue. Anne and I found that cool fresh milk was the right tipple for our own palates. We ate and sipped happily, and it was not until the next day that poor Mother returned to her toe-tapping on the chaise longue upstairs.

"I suppose our Spanish *Lady* is exhausted today?" she would ask me in a mildly furious way, looking up from a new novel from the Public Library as I set a tray across her knees. "Three days on nothing but that one dish! And this time your father drove *twice* to town, because our Spanish *Lady* decided the tortillas should be fresh the day she put the whole concoction together! And I don't like to have the *cook* open the kitchen door and watch me eat."

I soon realized that my poor mother was uncomfortable. That was why she stayed in bed more than usual, and had her meals in her room. She was basically ill at ease, with people saying things all around her that she could not even guess at. Perhaps she felt they might be mocking her? She was a shy woman, strangely insecure behind her regal manner. She was superbly Nordic as Caucasians go, even with her large brown eyes and dark hair, and maybe small wiry people, especially females, made her feel tall and heavy and clumsy. (I surmise this because I myself, as an adult, often feel like a great pink Anglo-Saxon cow when I am with Japanese women. . . .) Yes, it may have been the contrasting sizes of the two females that made the real trouble.

I am not sure about Anita. It seems strange now that her probable loneliness, abandoned in a foreign country, did not affect me in any way. I did not like her. Her affectations, her little gesturings and twitterings, her strange smell of rice powder like a stale marshmallow: all this bored me. But I loved to help her work on the enchiladas, and watch her whisk eggs for the flan and tip the melting sugar in the Custard Dish. She did not matter to me as a human being, nor apparently to any of us except perhaps Father.

The clue, as I now see it, to Mother's resentment of this strange jungle bird's insolent and unprecedented perching on our sacrosanct fruit tree was a realization of what happened when one night Rex said casually at the table that he was going to work a little later on his Spanish, with Anita Patita. There was a bad silence. Then Mother asked whom he meant, with that crazy name, and when he said he meant Anita, she asked casually something like Ah, the cook? and then said something like What does the new name Patita mean? Perhaps Patata?

It was just about the coldest I had ever seen my mother, at dinner or anywhere. Anne and I sat in a kind of daze, knowing something mean was going from the smiling woman at one end of the table to the casually unsmiling man at the other.

He said, "I think it is funny: Anita Patita. It sounds

funny, that's all. And there is the French word *petite,* but of course it doesn't rhyme in Spanish, and anyway it doesn't mean anything either. In Spanish, that is."

"And what do you imagine it means in French?" Mother's nonchalant smiling voice made it clear that *she* knew what it meant, having traveled in France, but that Father, a backwoods semiliterate journalist, could not possibly understand any foreign words except perhaps a few in lower-class Mexican. Her right-foot toes were vibrating like a snake's tongue at the end of her long leg. She pushed back her soft dark hair from her forehead, to show her admirable forearm, very white and silky. (All this is straight fantasy, of course, but from my memory of my own shock I think it was about thus. . . .)

"That's it," Father said easily. "*Petite* means tiny, little, in French. And Anita is tiny, and so I call her Anita Patita to rhyme."

He seemed pleased, and Anne and I thought it was a nice little joke and laughed one relieved laugh with him. But Mother backed out her chair roughly from the table and swept to the stairs to her room. Her eyes were flashing with tears and an outraged dignity, and she looked about ten feet tall instead of only six.

I don't remember anything more. Perhaps the jobless engineer sent for Anita to live with his family again and see to the First Communion dresses of his numerous little daughters. Probably Father gently paid her to rejoin her own people . . . and the faster the better. Things took on a jauntier look after she left, anyway. There *had* been something spidery about her . . . and the house was hung with the real cobwebs she never saw, and the dust Anne and I never quite stayed ahead of. We got a new maid-of-all-work, of course, the kind who cleaned cheerfully, put three hearty meals a day on the table, and did not come home too drunk from her Thursdays off.

Gradually Mother began to insinuate the term Anita-Patita into our family vocabulary, and if Father winced a little at first, he came to understand it to mean something indefinably meaningless, silly, laughable . . . not *personal* at all. "Well! Anita-Patita!" we would say, for the next fifty-odd years, and then go off into cryptic titters if someone took to bed to avoid a domestic crisis, or on the other hand spent hours making an exquisite soufflé when some quick plain scrambled eggs were indicated. . . .

As far as I can remember, Father was the only one who never said his own pretty little words again, even teasingly, and I think there was a wound in him about them. He did not mind at all being gently twitted about all the other Lame Ducks on his list, but that tropical bird left fluttering in his hand, on his hands, was different in ways we need not ponder. She was a woman, although too wee and skinny to count as such in my young eyes, accustomed as they were to giant goddesses like Mother and Aunt Gwen. She was alone in a strange land, and that was incomprehensible to me, who had not yet wandered. She had been entrusted to my father, and whether the reasons for that had been dishonest or not, he was not one to forswear his obligations. Yes, it must have left a wound. I am sorry, and I wonder if my mother ever was.

Meanwhile I wish I had the two recipes from the King of Spain's cook and that tiny woman, whose name, right now, I have no wish to say again . . . or for a while at least. I resemble Rex Kennedy more than is comfortable, in some ways.

4

The Bodies and Otherwise

The people I knew when I was little were all-beautiful. That
is not the same as saying that all people I knew then were,
but either sentence might do, for probably most of them
have died or changed from their first state of grace, and it is
my memory of them that is good. I even liked my Grandmother Holbrook, in spite of the rigid encasement of her
short firm body by unimaginable Victorian lacings and
bonings.

Often my little sister Anne and I, while Father shaved,
bathed in the extra-big tub he had brought with untoward
extravagance from Michigan. We loved these steamy sessions, and sang softly so that it would not disturb Mother:
"Waltz Me Around Again, Willy" and "Camptown Race-
track" and "Onward, Christian Soldiers" . . . things like that,
lifetime favorites of us all, even at five or six.

The tub was six feet long. This was fair enough, for Rex
was much longer than that, and as far as I know he never
bothered to justify keeping it handy at any cost. Anne and I
floated around in it like happy tadpoles, and Father hummed
and occasionally scrubbed at us, and played tricks on the

best mornings with his lather. All of us were of course stark rosy naked, and it was a special treat when he would casually put a dollop of the foam on his handsome and unbothered penis, and then dab us on our shoulders or noses or little pink breast-buttons. It was part of the satisfaction. We were nice well-made healthy children, and he was a manly fine man, and it was a good way to see the beauties of our bodies.

A few doors up from us lived two other little girls for a while, with an ailing mother who ate chalk. One time we must have been talking about how men are made, but I cannot remember why, and they said that they had peeked at their father, an action that had never occurred to us, and he had *two* things he could put lather on if he wanted to. We were sure Rex had only one main one, sufficient as it might be. We felt embarrassed to think anybody had more of anything at all than he had, and went at once to Mother to ask her about it.

She assured us that he was made as all men were made except perhaps better, and that she believed our little friends were mistaken about their father's attributes, owing to their hasty view. Then, it seems plain to me now, she and Father must have decided to give us a final demonstration and call a halt to further neighborly exchanges on the subject.

Rex stood up in the lovely steam one more time to shave himself while Anne and I bathed, and he dabbed a little foam here and there on all three of us, and after that he wore his BVDs in the bathroom when we were there. It is too bad. Perhaps it was another of the breaks between innocence and evil. I never really loved those little girls anyway, although I still dream occasionally of one of them.

My mother had a fine body too, and it was never hidden from us, nor was it ever flaunted. When it was the time for her to be dressed, half-dressed, naked, that is what she was, like her husband except for the baggy white underwear they apparently decided he should wear while we bathed. She was growing fat, but she was tall and well boned, and her skin from the first time I remember touching it until the day she died was an exquisite pearly white. She never turned mottled or bruised or more than delicately blue-veined. She had large ripe breasts like melons, and was so naïvely voluptuous that she loved to let Anne and me squeeze spongefuls of water over her back in the big tub, and then dry her long legs, heavy but shapely, as she stood like an odalisque on the bathmat. How sad that we could minister to her when Rex did not, could not! She would have looked beautiful with shaving foam here and there. . . .

In other words, we grew used to the quiet beauties of nakedness without knowing it, and without any peeking and simpering, which is a fortune few people possess.

When Mother got pregnant, I often hovered over her in the first mornings as she lay hiccuping and gagging on the big bed. She always managed to put this off until Father had gone downstairs for breakfast, for he did not like such female weaknesses. When she had got over the spasms, I knew how to put some 4711 on a handkerchief and lay it in her slack hand, and then go away. I would feel joyful, for it meant another baby in the family.

Once she was near death: some kind of growth inside her which threatened the new child's life and hers too. I was eight years old. The day she was thought to be dying, relatives of our current cook took Anne and me home, and at lunch we ate, for the only time in my whole life, raisin pie. It was delicious. I heard two of the cook's sisters murmuring that Anne and I did not know about "it," and I was amused, because I did. Perhaps Anne did too, but I never remembered to ask her in the next decades.

Mother did not die, but was moved up to the top of Painter Avenue to a big old house that had been turned into a kind of hospital. I cannot now understand how she was taken there: there was no ambulance for many miles. Was it in the one hearse in town, stripped of some of its draperies? Rex and Uncle Mac and Matty Matteson and almost anyone else who might have helped carry her down our narrow turning staircase were big enough to handle such a big woman. And anyway she was supposed to be dying. Perhaps that was the solution: no matter to *her* if she sat in an armchair or lay flat on a stretcher, or even got dropped.

I learned later that Grandmother urged her and Rex to get rid of the fetus along with whatever else was killing her, but Edith refused, and it was one more reason for mostly silent dislike between the two women. The older one had borne nine children as her bounden duty, and had made no bones about the fact that the last one, the afterthought called Edith, had been the most unwelcome. It is no wonder that my mother, in deep revolt against all this, longed as deeply to have babies. She loved the whole animal procedure, although she found the miracles of conception and birthing and lactation revolting when a cow or a mouse did the same things. Of course Rex wanted a son "to carry on the name," as he sometimes explained it, but he never seemed to find anything but real pleasure in fathering girls, at the moment and forever. He and Mother finally produced David, but there was no change in the comfortable feeling Anne and Norah and I had about being there.

When I was allowed to see Mother, that time she almost died, she was lying in a dim enormous room, looking very young and like the princess in the sleeping forest. I knew that I had to give her a special offering. It would have been impossible to discuss this with Father, of course: he seemed preoccupied. He was mostly at the *News* and the hospital, and when we ate together there was little conversation. Grandmother was even less accessible for counsel, and I know now that she was doubly rigid with disapproval of the whole folly of her daughter's stubborn decision.

I needed money. It was early in Lent, and I had a Mite Box made of folded stiff paper into which I had obediently put all three of my allowances of five cents a week, to be sent after Easter to missions or aborigines or something. Plainly I must break into it, and this I did, in a botchy way but with one nickel slipping out of the tear in the horrid cardboard.

I was by that moment so deep in unaccustomed skulduggery that I sneaked downtown without a tremor, and bought a scratch pad, and wrote on every page of its yellowish lined paper. It had a strange smell, rather powdery. My pencils hardly showed on it. I wrote some original verses, drew a lot of pictures, and quoted from *Hiawatha,* my current literary excitement. I worked hard, and nobody seemed to notice.

The day before Mother was brought home, to stay in Grandmother's first-floor apartment because she could not possibly climb stairs until after the new baby would be born, I gave her my book. She kissed me gently, and I can see the big dim room of that converted mansion, smelling of strange troubles, and the high hospital bed in which Mother lay. Father came in from the hall, and she showed him the book and they both told me it was a fine present. Praise as such was rare from them, and I walked down Painter to our house feeling noble and even exalted about it. The crime was behind me, and I had forgotten about punishment in the glow of creative recognition.

I cannot say how much later it was that things took their ordained course and Mother, sitting up in a chair in Grandmother's room, asked me about how I had bought the notebook. I think I tried to fib a little, but then she showed me the wretchedly mutilated Mite Box, and I told her. It would be like a Russian novella if I could say that she made me destroy the notebook before her eyes, but this was in Whittier in about 1916 and all she did was destroy my pride in having made it for her. Somewhere along in there Rex added to my sorrows by saying that he thought I was *mistaken,* to have cheated and stolen and lied and all that.

I wish they had never mentioned the Mite Box, nor the notebook filled with my verses and pictures. I do not think I would have, if I were a parent or rather the parent of myself at that moment, but since I am one now, I know that such can happen. Father and Mother were products of their upbringings, and could not possibly have known such nice people as they were. They did what they believed they must do.

When they asked me why I had not told Rex I needed an extra nickel, I was incapable of explaining to them that I could not bear to impinge upon his own anguish at Mother's state. When they reminded me of the starving children somewhere who needed my five cents a week and of how devious I had been, I had no possible answers. Certainly it was no time to correct Father's statement that I had lied, which in my own eyes I had not done.

I kept right on making peculiar smudgy smelly volumes for great occasions in our family, but I believe that I never stole again. I suppose it was another loss of innocence, the way it was when Father nevermore shaved without putting on his BVDs, if we were with him. It is good to be able to say that the *bad* book was never referred to again, and that Anne and I bathed Mother's pearly back for many more years.

5

Love Blemished
But Abiding

Soon after we moved to Whittier, in 1912, Anne and I climbed
onto the high back seat of the Model T, on a fine summer
evening, and drove with Father and Mother down Philadelphia, past the place where Greenleaf intersected it, and on
toward the State School for bad boys. We turned to the left,
farther down a street I forget the name of, although I could
still go to it, and finally stopped in front of a shabby small
house under old eucalyptus trees. There were no sidewalks,
but lush bushes of oleander grew taller than a man, and I
know now that all the houses there were ones built hastily by
the less privileged camp followers of the first Quaker settlers,
in a kind of slum. The air was probably sweet and cool.

Out from the cottage and then down to us in the car came
a tall fine young woman, and it seems to me now that my
heart opened at that first view of her, as did my sister Anne's.
It was our Aunt Gwen, related by love alone.

My parents *were*, the way the sky is, or a great tree. My
trust in them was unquestioning, I never thought about
things like love or hatred or insecurity. I was almost eleven

before I said a flat and very unsuccessful *No* to them. I was much older, perhaps into the comparative senility of seventeen or so, before I heard them have a real row. They were young and beautiful and intelligent when I first knew them, and I accepted them as my father and mother without the slightest need to question their being so.

I early knew some of their moods, as when Mother felt a little nervous during the Sunday afternoon "drives" Rex would take us on, to let Grandmother have a quiet house for her weekly letters to Pittsburgh and Ireland. Edith would turn her face from the cliff edge we were skirting jauntily in Turnbull Canyon, Father's favorite place to practice high curves, and press a fine handkerchief to her lips, and I would feel my breathing chopped off in sympathy, although the wild road really did not scare me at all. Sometimes in downtown Whittier when we were allowed to sit in the back seat while Father drove Edith here and there, I am sure proudly, she would push her foot frantically against the floorboard when he nudged the back of a farm wagon or another car, and I remember hearing him ask sarcastically, "If you can't drive, why use the brake?"

That was as near to bickering as they got, as far as I know. There was one argument, about how to pronounce "allies" (this was in 1917 when the word was suddenly important . . .): Grandmother won it as usual by sending me to the dictionary stand in the corner of the dining room. Now and then Edith would weep, but never as much as she would have enjoyed doing, when Rex was sharp-tongued . . . "Your father is like his mother, very quick-tempered," she would say. "But have you noticed that his eyes turn absolutely *black* when he is a little put out? *So* handsome!" (He had the kind of eyes that were normally grey-green, and I do too, but I no more inherited this flashing change of coloration than I did his big bony nose, to my lifelong regret.)

So I lived wrapped in the unquestioned love of those two people. They *were*, and I was their pup, taking everything they gave me because it was mine.

Aunt Gwen was a different matter. She flowed through my life, all our lives, like a gusty river bringing food and excitement and adventure. She was strong. She was loving, but no nonsense there . . . strictly stiff-upper-lip, with strong doses of *Uncle Remus* and *Stalky and Company* . . . and of course *The Jungle Books:* "Go down without a whimper. Never be a tattletale. Protect the weak. Do what you are asked to do and a bit more. Be polite. Don't lie, or cheat at parcheesi. Don't grouse." All this sounds awful, but it was not, for she accepted the rules she taught us as part of herself, and we wanted only to be part of her too.

My mother leaned upon her, and surely gave her courage and strength in return. Edith needed security, above all except perhaps love, it now seems clear to me, and Aunt Gwen was even taller than she, and more firmly if not as heavily built. She possessed an enormous energy in her strong body, and gave of it eagerly to anyone who would accept it: her dog Pat, her parents and brothers, the St. Matthias choir and refreshment committees, *us*. For a long time *we* were the lake into which most of her flowed, from all her generous springs and sources. It was an awesome gift, and we accepted it as our due, much as dry ground accepts fresh water. We *used* her.

She spoke always with a weirdly British accent, thanks to her missionary beginnings in the New Zealand bush and then the most isolated northern islands of Japan, and finally adolescence in a kind of asylum-orphanage run by the Church of England for its more hapless dependents, somewhere near Brighton, I think. Mother, always so Anglomanic, would put up with any reasonable facsimile of British linguistics, which to her automatically meant noble-cultured-educated-charming as long as all the aitches were in place. It is only by the Grace of God that the few people in Whittier who said "cahn't" and pronounced "aunt" as if it were not an insect were perforce members of the Episcopal Church and therefore available to us as friends . . . people like Uncle Mac and his tiny quiet wife Barnie, their girl Isobel, Gwendolyn Nettleship. If Aunt Gwen had been a Quaker, we would never have known her, an impossible thought. . . .

Her accent in Whittier was firmly enunciated, unchanging, and almost unintelligible to many of our displaced Midwesterners, and I think the greatest tribute to it is that while I still slip now and then and say Bean instead of Bin, and even Agayn for Agen, and occasionally Tomahto instead of Tomayto, I listened for years to her when she read Uncle Remus' tall tales and never once laughed at her peculiar interpretation of that equally strange dialect spelled out by Joel Chandler Harris. It all seemed right to me, and I can still smile when I think of Aunt Gwen repeating Br'er Fox's insistence that "it *is* Sparrygrahs. . . ." Ah, yes: "*looks* lahk sparrygrahs, *tase* lahk sparrygrahs . . . ," and off I go chuckling. Much later, when I got to live with Negroes who were supposed to talk that way, it never occurred to me that there was any connection between them and Uncle Remus, and indeed there could not possibly have been.

Fortunately she never forgot the jungle ways of her first days: when she was not a week old she had been slung in a hammock and trotted through the bush, ahead of her mother, in a long line of aborigines carrying the woman doctor to a sick village. During the years I myself trotted alongside her, with Anne only a step or two behind, she taught us a thousand things too intangible to report, as well as how to roast kelp leaves, steam mussels, tease a rattlesnake away from a frightened saddle horse, skin an eel after sundown, stay quiet while a night-blooming cereus unfolds . . . things like that.

I never wondered or asked how Aunt Gwen came to the

same place we did, and at the same time. Perhaps it was because her father knew a great deal about bugs and such, and had some kind of job in the laboratories of the local Citrus Association? Her mother was often far away, or else invisibly at home, a frail beautiful woman who was said to write for newspapers Down Under and "at home," which meant England of course. Then there were three younger brothers, all handsome and, like their parents and many other English people who lived in America in those days, aloof and seemingly disdainful of everyone. The two older boys soon fled the nest for marriage and like adventures, and Raymond, our favorite, stayed within our worshipping reach until he had graduated from high school and enlisted, in 1917 or so.

And not long after the Nettleships all moved to the little cottage in Whittier, Aunt Gwen married. This rocked the Episcopalian enclave almost as violently as it must have her own family: she seemed cut out to be the spine, the provider, the classical Devoted Daughter, and not the flighty victim of a quick romance. (I was of course unaware of all this at the time, but lived in its widening ripples for many years. . . .) And that daughter, dutiful and devoted, may really have been what she was meant to be, for the wedding lasted only one night.

Lieutenant Shaw was, according to a picture I vaguely remember, a delicate young man about half or a third the size of his bride ("She would have made three of him," my mother said almost maliciously), a lonely Englishman who had shyly presented a letter of introduction to Mr. Nettleship . . . something about a common interest in fruit flies. A week or so later there was a hasty marriage ceremony, and he and Aunt Gwen spent one night in a moderately priced hotel in Los Angeles and then she saw him off at the station and went back to Whittier on the Electric, in time for her job at the packing house, where she wrapped oranges. Her husband went straight to France, where he was killed immediately. How sad that they did not make a child! It might have robbed me of much of my own full happiness, but I love Aunt Gwen enough to wish it for her.

Not long after that, she moved bag and baggage and complete with her parents and her brothers to a shabby house on the corner of Painter and Philadelphia. I think there must have been some arranging and discussing between her and my father and mother, and perhaps between them and her own parents. But any such finaglings were never mentioned in the next decades.

The house, although plainly falling apart, was better than the wreck of a cottage the Nettleships had been living in. It was probably an old farmhouse, and there was the remnant of a fruit orchard on its big lot . . . peaches, no-good apples, a wonderful apricot tree. Our house came next, at the southmost edge of the "nice" Quaker area.

Edith was a few years older than Gwen, and more polished and experienced as a female, and in spite of her naïve respect for anything remotely connected with the Anglo-Saxon persuasion she dominated the strange couple they made. She had a natural but imperious daintiness about her, in spite of her increasing bulk, and of course she did indeed need help and comfort as she dawdled through her dangerous pregnancies; she was largely ignored by both Rex, who disliked ailing women, and Grandmother, who found every aspect of reproduction distasteful, in spite of her own Victorian brood of nine. Aunt Gwen seemed to love Edith without cavil, especially after Mrs. Nettleship died, and Mr. Nettleship remarried, and even Raymond flew off. More and more Mother handed over large pieces of her whole matronly existence to the big red-faced Englishwoman, and devoted herself to herself, and of course to the next child. And more and more Anne and I came to recognize Aunt Gwen as the core of our lives.

Part of Mother's voluptuous acceptance of all of Aunt Gwen's devotion and energy (I am sure Edith believed unquestioningly that she was rescuing her friend from a drab existence, being nothing but kind and supremely generous to her . . .) was based on the convenient fact that while she lay waiting for parturition her husband was healthily active in correct chaste pastures, which indeed he was. Rex soon began to feel, in his male way, a little like my sister and me about our large loving goddess. With lesser people this could have turned into the classical sex game, but Rex seemed simply to enjoy the way she was always ready to fry a mess of fresh sea bass, or swim out with him to Mussel Rock at dangerous low tide and help him pry off a couple of bucketfuls of the delicious shellfish, or make a powerful if heavyfooted fourth at tennis. She played a passable card hand, and she laughed well. Mother never seemed to question the real enjoyment Rex showed in doing things with Aunt Gwen that she herself neither could nor would attempt, and, in spite of her real affection, it was partly because she could not have got along without the other woman, so quickly and fully had she and all of us come to depend on her. How fortunate this was! I really think that if Aunt Gwen had been forced to leave us when I was between four and about ten years old, I might have pined and withered into death . . . and Anne too.

After we moved to the Ranch, in the second decade of life in Whittier, my mother no longer needed Aunt Gwen, and there was a strong cooling, at least on Edith's part. It is too painful for me to discuss with myself, but one thing I remember Edith's telling me, in a gabby moment, which showed that *all the time* there had been a latent resentment of the other woman, not in the children's lives, apparently, but in Father's. Mother said that before Norah was born, when she was supposed to be dying, she discussed with her husband what he should do without her, and asked him to marry Aunt Gwen, to take care of the children. And there was a small vicious smile on her sweet mouth when she said he had recoiled, yes *recoiled* from the thought. "But she's not a woman to me," he had protested. Mother went on about how foolish and blind even the best of men can be, but I wished she would smile differently and talk about something else. . . .

Her open love for everything English did not quite cover the rest of the Nettleship family, and as far as I know there was no kind of friendship between my parents and Aunt Gwen's. I think Mrs. Nettleship may have upstaged Edith a little, with her obvious refinement and her fluty voice, so different from her worshipping daughter in every way. Like many displaced English ladies she hated America, and made no attempt to change her views. And while she was alive, Anne and I never went upstairs in the old farmhouse, where she had her "study," and we tiptoed when she might be writing or resting.

Her three sons resembled her in their fine bones and their aloofness, and contrary to Aunt Gwen were almost pretty. They were like the father in their womanizing, and there was usually a little quiet buzz going on at home about their escapades, to which Anne and I paid no attention. All three were in the Army during The War, and I can remember some shocked astonishment when Raymond, the youngest, brought home a German wife called Hanni, indecently soon after the Armistice . . . strange behavior in a good American doughboy! And Aunt Gwen was the only person in Whittier, or at least the only one we knew, who could have three blue stars, and a gold one for the dead husband, on the red-bordered cotton flag hanging in her window. This dubious honor was only one more proof to us of her grandeur, and Anne and I looked proudly up at it as we passed her house toward school.

Raymond was a nice fellow, a kindly faun. When he was

finishing high school he wanted to go right away into the Army, which he managed with some chronological connivance with the Draft Board, and to prove his virile aptness he grew a little golden moustache. It made my heart quicken, for he had the kind of skin that turns very brown in the summer, and it was almost too beautiful to see that crinkly badge on it, even though it meant that he was no longer a boy we could punch and hug and try new riddles on.

In the summers, until he went into the Army, he earned money by collecting rattlesnake venom in the Laguna hills. He wore high leather boots that laced tightly up his legs, and Anne and I loved to have him show us little scars on them where the snakes had struck at him. He killed them by jumping on them, mostly, just three or four inches back of the head, and once he missed and all the color came off his boot where the poison had sprayed into it as the snake struck. My father was strangely angered by this story, and called Raymond a damned cub, but Aunt Gwen laughed proudly with us.

Mr. Nettleship was largely invisible. My mother could not stand him, a courteous handsome man, because he wore a short grizzled beard which Anne and I found quite lovely. (This was our first intimation that Mother was almost unhinged by the sight of a beard. She was the youngest in a family with several older teasing brothers who grew them as soon as possible and cultivated them foppishly, and her dearly loved father was of course bearded all his life. Her favorite of them all was her brother Evans, who, to his chagrin, could never grow more than one dollar-sized spot of silky whisker on his smooth pink face. And when the one living boy in our own family, David, planned to come home for Christmas with fine curly whiskers he had grown at art school in Colorado, my mother bit back fierce sobs

and refused flatly to see him unless he shaved first. He was
the pride of her life, but she so clearly meant what she said
that young David bowed to her, one more time a child and
not a man.)

Mother saw Mrs. Nettleship now and then in the tiny
parlor of the farmhouse, and reported somewhat maliciously
to Grandmother that Aunt Gwen waited on the lady hand
and foot, and kept her as dainty as a princess. A few times
Father and Mr. Nettleship went deep-sea fishing with a
group of local heathens like Sam Jackson, foreman of the
Back Room at the *News,* but that ended when the old
Englishman got very sick and lost both his upper and lower
teeth overboard. At Christmas Anne and I dutifully took
him a small tin of his favorite pipe tobacco, and a necktie
for Raymond. But never, as far as I can remember, did any
of that family but Aunt Gwen ever come into our house.
It seems impossible to me that such a warm good place
could have stayed cold when Mother wanted it that way,
but such was the case.

Not long after the Nettleships moved next door, perhaps
in a couple of years, the mother vanished even more permanently than before. I knew nothing about it until I came
home from school and told Mother that on Aunt Gwen's
front door there was a lavender silk scarf of Grandmother's,
tied in a big bow. Mother said that Mrs. Nettleship had
died, and that we would not see Aunt Gwen for a day or two
and that we should not bother her if she sometimes cried.
She said that Aunt Gwen had loved Mrs. Nettleship very
much. This all seemed natural, and Anne and I probably
thought nothing more about it. I cannot remember ever
mentioning it again, although I do know that Grandmother
sometimes wore the lavender scarf. And soon after Mrs.
Nettleship's death the widower married a tall thin spinster
named something like Hutzenpiller, or Seegmiller, the

town's librarian, and was summarily dismissed by my mother, although I cannot see from what, as a nasty old rake.

Perhaps my sister and I were a little more loving than usual with our goddess after her bereavement, but I can remember no difference in her straightforward no-nonsense stiff-upper-lip wholeness to us. She went on doing odd jobs in the community, always admitted to the best non-Quaker homes, because she had what sounded like an English accent to the Americans. And she sang contralto in the Episcopal choir. Sly people of today might have hinted it was more a low baritone, to match her rather whiskery face as she settled into an apparent spinsterdom, and it is true that she and Uncle Peter MacLaren did a very good male-trio arrangement of "On the Road to Mandalay," about once a year on a good picnic in Laguna, because he could sing both tenor and bass.

One time, before Christmas, Aunt Gwen spent days nailing layers of old newspaper to the inside of a little shed behind the Nettleship house, where tools had been stored when a small farm stood there, and she installed a borrowed sewing machine and started a little studio, as she called it. She made really dreadful things, like cotton flannel nightgowns. But they hung against the walls, which she had pasted with magazine covers over the newspapers, on dainty wooden hangers covered with puckered satin ribbon, and usually they had a little bow somewhere around the neck. They looked nice, to us. There were also potholders made from scraps of bright material she had got from the ladies of St. Matthias: she sewed them together zigzag, and I was allowed to stitch a bone ring on one corner of each. Little Anne, probably, got the more infantile privilege of picking up pins and thread. The tiny room was warm and bright and stuffy, with a wonderful smell of newsprint and burning kerosene from the stove and cheap fuzzy flannelette and ribbon, and Aunt Gwen hummed along loudly at the sewing machine, which ran with a foot pumper like the church organ. Mother was a bit scoffing of the venture, but saw to it that all her acquaintances helped deplete the jaunty supplies by Christmas, and as I recall it, Aunt Gwen felt successful: although no richer, she was hardly much poorer, and it had been fun. . . .

Mainly, though, as time went on, she devoted herself to *us*. I assume she was "helped" with this, financially, but have never known. I do know that once during the War, when sugar was scarce, rather a fuss was made at home about Father's giving her a hundred pounds of it. Or perhaps it was a barrel. There was Conversation about such foolish generosity, and what is left from it makes me feel that the sugar was more or less black market, of inferior quality, relatively cheap, and that Aunt Gwen would do some of our summer canning anyway, so who was being generous? This sounds niggling, and perhaps it was. Meanwhile Anne and I spent more time every day in the wretched old farmhouse with Aunt Gwen, and liked nothing better than to be asked to stay to supper, although Mr. Nettleship was not too friendly about that. It became much easier, however, as he began to court the town librarian and then moved to her house on the west side of town.

I have no idea of how all six of the Nettleships fitted into the house when they were together, in the first year or months of it. I would be willing to wager that it was Aunt Gwen who slept on the living room couch, or even on the floor. . . . Downstairs, as one entered, there was a tiny parlor with a silk-covered love seat in it, and I think a little marble fireplace, neither ever used. Next to it down a dark narrow hall with a peculiar smell which I now recognize from English novels, there was a little room where Raymond slept and studied, never entered by Anne and me of course, and then a primitive bathroom. And on the right side as one entered, there was a dingy living room, dark and comfortable, where Mr. Nettleship sat and read and smoked his pipe, and then an even darker kitchen where I spent many fine hours of gluttony and general escape.

Upstairs in the narrow rickety house the best room, the only one with light and air, looked east to the hills and south into a tall tree, perhaps a magnolia. There were probably two other little rooms, but that is the one I remember. It belonged to Mrs. Nettleship. I suppose her husband slept in one of the two beds, but there was no sign of anyone there but the tall frail lady. There were pretty white curtains billowing gently in front of the four windows, and the wallpaper was striped with wide bands of blue and ivory, different from any we had seen. (Mother went in for very British cretonnes, and lots of sprigs of things on the wallpaper . . . impossible flowers and leaves. . . .)

And there was a dainty dressing table made of pale bamboo bent and fixed into lacy patterns. It was unforgettable. Aunt Gwen let us look at it now and then, and told us that it had gone everywhere in the world with her mother, from long ago in Japan. It was a symbol of regal femininity to me, and later when I knew all the queens and princesses in and around the Wonderful Land of Oz, I always saw such an elegantly fastidious piece of furniture in their most intimate closets, in the palaces made of emerald, of ruby. . . .

In the kitchen there was a big black stove with a trash burner, so I suppose it used wood. Certainly it was much more interesting than the one at home. In the middle of the shabby room a generous table was covered with oilcloth, which I still have a weakness for, and on a long shelf covered with the same bright stuff there was a beautiful set of china freckled with small pink carnations, which Aunt Gwen had collected gradually by using a canned milk that gave prizes.

From such drab cheap china, those bowls and cups and plates still as clear to my mind's eye as any Wedgwood or

Sèvres I have seen, I ate happily and whenever I could, for several years. I ate things we never had at home, and of course a few we did, but not with the pungency and savor they had in that farmhouse kitchen, and at Laguna when Aunt Gwen and Anne and I were down there.

And we were down there as much as we could be, on bright chilly Sundays in winter and all summer long. In winter Rex drove us from Whittier at a reckless speed, and we ate a shivering picnic and watched the angry waves from clifftops, full of anticipation for summer. In summer we were *there,* Anne and I, because we were alone with Aunt Gwen except for the family Sundays, always a pleasurable invasion but basically something to be tolerated until we could be alone again.

We walked a lot, because Aunt Gwen had almost literally been born on her feet, like any self-respecting English-woman. And we never went anywhere, along the cliffs or up into the hills, without a hefty fried-egg sandwich or two in our pockets . . . and time for the fruit when we got home again. There and in her Whittier kitchen we knew that if the moon and stars were right, we would have deep rich floating puddles of hot cocoa for supper, with buttered toast sogging deliciously in them. . . .

I do not think my mother ever knew of our gastronomical treats: she was deliberately bland about "what went on," secure in the knowledge that we were safe while she carried on with other duties like reproduction.

In Whittier we walked too, everywhere, because it was the way Aunt Gwen moved best from place to place, and always for an exciting reason. We walked in the rain, and in the scorching heat, to Bailey Park, to the hills behind the College, best of all to the hills back of the town reservoir, where occasionally a motor would start coughing in the little shed and make us laugh. There was a big wooden cover over the round pool of water, and we could look through the fence and see black glints and now and then hear a rippling sound, as if perhaps a mouse had jumped in. We would walk through eucalyptus groves and in the springtime pick wild flowers, and then settle our backs against a fallen tree and look down upon the rooftops of our town, and across brown plains to the occasional shimmer of the ocean, many miles away. On fine days we learned to study the horizon and find the long blue line of Catalina Island. This always pleased Aunt Gwen, to agree with us that indeed it was that far place, where I finally went when I was eleven.

Aunt Gwen was a wonder with flowers. I learned how to put them in a "garden bunch" as if they were growing, not head against head but at different levels. She taught me how to take care of them, once in the house and the vase. (She called a vase a vahz, which always irked Mother when we did too.) She also taught us respect for growing things, so that we never pulled up the tiny garlicky buds of the *Brodiaea*, which grew in sweeps of blue in the springtime, or broke stems with our feet unless we had to. And she knew resounding names, always with a reason, like Indian Paintbrush which is indeed dipped in color, and Monkey Face which makes a monkey face, especially when it is pinched gently in the right place, which she always knew too.

Aunt Gwen never lived with us. Often after her mother died, Anne and I stayed with her overnight, and of course we were together for several long heavenly-beautiful summers in Laguna, and for the miserable-but-marvelous-and-merry months of May–June in 1917, when we both had thoroughgoing measles and Mother had Norah. After the first miseries it was exciting to be in the defunct Mrs. Nettleship's own room, with her elegant fluty dressing table. Father came to stand in the doorway every day, to tell us a poem he had composed for us, and one night Raymond, the only one of Aunt Gwen's brothers still at home, appeared there to show himself to us, dressed as Monsieur Beaucaire for the

high school Senior Play. We could have swooned at his silken
beauty, had we not been prone, and as I remember the ugly
smell of measles, and the pathetic *sick* look of little children
who are in its clutches, I wonder at Raymond's real gallantry.
However, perhaps sometime in his life he understood that
never again would two females let out that same moan of
delight at the sight of him. . . .

We looked at Norah through the front screen door of our
house, in the nurse's arms, while we were getting onto our
pins again after this bout, and although the prospect of living with a third sibling in the family was vaguely delightful,
we would have chosen, I am quite sure, to stay forever at
Aunt Gwen's if it had been left to us.

As far as I can remember, nobody ever marveled at her
cheerful acceptance of us for that month when she was so
fully occupied with helping Mother bear the baby, helping
Father run the house, helping Raymond into his pink satin
costume, helping us go to the toilet and all that. But we
loved her, and she loved us.

Although we never really lived in the Nettleship house
after that blissful accident in Time, we often ate there in the
big dark smelly kitchen, thank God. It seems never to have
been when Raymond was home from school, or Mr. Nettleship's new wife was visiting her relatives and he needed a
cook. Aunt Gwen made large meals for the men, and served
them deftly . . . and I doubt that she often sat down while they
ate. But when the coast was clear, Anne and I would set
three places on the glamorous checked oilcloth, and help
carry the cups and bowls and plates that Aunt Gwen would
fill before she joined us. Occasionally she said Grace, as
much to teach us how to behave when Grandmother's missionaries were at our table at home as from any religious
effort. We always ate nicely if with unconcealed heartiness,
and talked a lot, and then washed the dishes together.

By now I wonder a lot about the inner life of this goddess,

the one we never were aware of. I feel sure that she was happy for several years, to have us love her so much, but it is painful to know, now in my own life, that she was a young vital woman cut off firmly from things she must have longed for: a world of her own, children of her own, a good man. I sigh and stretch with sadness for her position in her own family *and then ours:* the kind cheerful drudge, adoring her fragile princess of a mother so totally unlike her, and serving her autocratic father and spoiled handsome brothers *and then us,* like a big ruddy Cinderella, day and night for too many years. Yes, how did it happen?

It is dangerously easy for me to think that my parents, and especially Edith, kept Aunt Gwen under their thumbs as long as they really needed her: that is, while Mother was busy with the second batch of children. This is not quite fair to any of them. The truth is that some time after the War, Rex and Edith both did everything in their power to encourage Gwendolyn to become a trained nurse, and they used all the pull they had in Bishop Johnson's hierarchy to brush aside a few rules and encourage her to enter training at Good Samaritan in Los Angeles.

Aunt Gwen was too old for the requirements, and thanks to her Church "education" in England she was abysmally ignorant of almost every subject on the list of the precurriculum. But she had proved to be a brilliant student in the Red Cross classes given in Whittier at the last of the War, and everybody in the little Episcopalian colony rallied loudly enough to be heard, and she was accepted at the hospital for several years of what must have been straight Hell. She had to work four times as hard as any of the slim young students who brushed past her big thick middle-aging body, girls who knew secrets about mathematics and chemistry she had never dreamed of, girls who went out with boys. . . .

Gradually there was less of her in our lives, perforce. She

stayed friends with Isobel MacLaren, Uncle Mac's daughter, and formed a strong and lasting relationship with—perhaps not too oddly in that town where the circles outside of Quakerdom were so restricted—the spinster-companion of the town librarian, who had taken Mrs. Nettleship's place in her widower's heart, if never her daughter's.

Mother disdained this new friendship as unworthy, although I am not sure of what, since the two women understood and liked each other, and even indulged in a few ladylike capers such as starting a small flower-and-gift shop which soon went broke, and taking little trips together which must have made Edith Kennedy's subconscious grit its teeth in frustrated rage. I think the reasoning, if such it could be called, was that if Aunt Gwen was to know any real happiness it should be with us, not with "other people," even though there was obviously no room for her in our own home. Still, Edith corresponded once a year or so until Aunt Gwen died, and I don't know when that was, now . . . sometime after World War II.

They wrote letters twenty pages long to each other. I have no idea what the sick lonely woman in California said to the big eccentric woman on Molokai, where she was running a hospital for everybody but the lepers, but Aunt Gwen's letters are somewhere in my boxes of family detritus, and although Edith read parts of them aloud to us with less than her usual mockery, I prefer not to dig them up again for myself.

But I did find out from my mother once, after I had written two or three books on the pains and pleasures of our basic need to eat in order to live, that Aunt Gwen had expressed a sad note about me in one of her annual screeds. It was uncharacteristic. Her reports were usually factual and vivid, but dealt little with her own or other people's emotional involvements. She still believed in a stiff upper lip and no whimpering and all that, just as she had decades earlier when she was my goddess-mentor-pillar. She never hid troubles, but she considered it poor taste perhaps, or boring, to talk much about them.

For instance, when my sister Anne found herself at twenty-five or so a spoiled beautiful brat with a little son to raise alone, she reverted instinctively to the ruler of her infancy and childhood, and wrote often and fully to Aunt Gwen about becoming a nurse. It might have been salvation for her, but Aunt Gwen apparently advised her against it, or at least made clear to her the quarrels such a profession would cause in Anne's nature. Anne said nothing to Mother about this deep correspondence with the Islands, perhaps feeling it might hurt Edith Kennedy to have advice asked from anyone else. But Aunt Gwen wrote to Mother something as simple as, "Our Annie seems to be in a bit of a pickle, doesn't she? But everything will straighten out. She is a fine brave girl, and will land on her feet. You are all made of good stout stuff, you know. . . ." This implied tactfully that Edith knew about Anne's questing, which I doubt that she ever did, probably with secret relief.

When I heard that Aunt Gwen had let down her guard, and written sadly about me, I was shocked, and although much time has passed since then, I often feel a stabbing, poignant regret that I hurt her by never once mentioning her, in whatever I had written about "the gastronomical me," while she was still alive. She had read my books with great pleasure, she told my mother, but she wondered why I did not remember some of the good things we ate together when I was little. . . . (It pains me even to write about this now, but I think I should.)

I tried to explain to my mother that I was not mature enough, that my focus was not yet right, that Aunt Gwen and the things she cooked for us and taught me to make were still either too immediate or too removed from whatever life I was then leading. Someday I would do it, I said. "Don't wait too long," she said. But I did. I was not yet enough of a *person* to write straight to Molokai and say, "I am not ready. . . ."

All I could now say about Aunt Gwen will never be said, but it is sure that much of my enjoyment of the art of living, as well as of eating, comes from her . . . as well as my certainty that the two are, or can be, synonymous.

After she moved her whole Nettleship family to the old farmhouse on the corner next to us I began to learn the nuances of cooking in relation to the him/her who does it, and why. We always had a cook at home, indifferent, bad to terrible, and occasionally good. We ate almost everything that was set before us, and mostly without much more than animal satisfaction, which we had been taught to keep unobtrusive. On Saturdays, or for Father's birthday, Mother might produce a handsome cake, and it tasted different from anything the cook ever made, because it was done for a personal reason, to please us and to make Edith feel generous and skilled, not just a kitchen drab working for pay. Increasingly I myself would cook for much the same reasons. But Aunt Gwen's every dish had a special savor to it, beyond routine and far beyond any need for praise.

Her repertory was small, and I doubt that she ever looked at a cookbook in her life. But she had a kind of casual deftness about her, combined with excitement, that I cannot forget. Perhaps the meals she managed to produce in the thinnest of the thin days for her family were compounded from desperation, but I am firmly sure they were presented with dash, and consumed with healthy if discreet British gusto.

Her kitchen was dark in the corners, and warm and deliciously smelly. The one dangling bulb above the big table shone on its glamorous oilcloth cover. The big stove with its trash burner sent out small crashing sounds of whatever was inside it, like coal or driftwood, or tightly rolled newspapers. On a high long shelf and on the table gleamed the beautiful bowls and plates and cups speckled with pink carnations.

On the table: a list of what came and went on that shiny checkered altar would follow the seasons, and always be simple, and perhaps it is where I came to enjoy a meal of only one or two things to eat, instead of a forced pattern of courses with their proper dishes. Aunt Gwen's ideas of cooking were circumscribed in many ways by her late-Victorian girlhood in an English "institution," but were saved by her earlier years in jungles and on desolate islands. She knew leaves and even flowers that were good to eat. She wasted nothing. She would slice ripe tomatoes in the morning, for instance, and season them lightly and cover them until suppertime. Then, instead of pouring their juices down the drain, as any of our cooks would surely do, she would pour them into three little glasses for our supper, or into a pot of soup. . . .

I think the only liquid she ever threw away was the juice of sliced cucumbers, after they had sat all day, heavily salted and with a weight pressing them down. This water, she told us, was "the poison." The rest was delicious, very limp but still a little crisp. By now I do not often use or approve of this method, but the results of hers were always fine. She would douse them with a little vinegar and perhaps some olive oil. (She was a great believer in vinegar. We even ate it on fish, which I've since done in Cornwall, over a paper twist full of Fish-and-Chips . . . and of course in the public fish market in Marseilles . . . and always a lot of it on spinach, both at Aunt Gwen's and at home. It was a sign of progress in Growing Up, to be allowed to use the vinegar cruet without help.)

I think that I have found a printed method for Aunt Gwen's cucumbers, from an English cookbook which ascribes their potential gastric mayhem to their juices, in the face of many people who blame it all on the seeds . . . in refutation of theories that cucumbers should always be eaten with plenty of bread and butter, that they should never be eaten with any starchy food, that they should always be accompanied by alcohol strong or weak, that they must never be eaten with even a pale wine. This formula comes from a book printed in London in 1957 (*Delightful Food*, Salter and Whitney, Ditchling Press), which could as well and in every way have been compiled a century before:

To Make Cucumbers Digestible

> Peel the cucumber and cut in very thin slices. Put these in a soup plate and sprinkle the slices with a great deal of salt. Leave it to rest for one-half an hour. Then drain it well and squeeze it in a cloth, so as to remove all the water, which is the indigestible part of the cucumber. Put the cucumber in a small serving dish and season it with wine vinegar and freshly ground pepper.

Summer and winter, Aunt Gwen made stewed tomatoes, pungent and seedy and with spices in them, not the watery pink stuff we were served in little vegetable dishes beside our dinner plates at home. Aunt Gwen's never had bread in them, and could be eaten with a spoon for a treat. They were lumpy and fresh-tasting, even from a can, after she had shaken them around in a saucepan with fresh onion and butter.

She also made a marmalade from tomatoes. It was thick and delicious on hot toast. Anne and I asked Mother to make it too, but it was not in her own "closet" of strawberry-peach-apricot-cherry, and there could be no true marmalade but orange, for her. And thus we enjoyed the best of two worlds....

We ate a lot of fruit at Aunt Gwen's, picked from the twisted old trees between her house and ours, or brought from the packing houses where she often worked. At home fruit was usually stewed, in deference to Grandmother's Nervous Stomach and the general tone of an Iowa cuisine, but at the other house there was always a bowl of fresh fruit on the table for dessert, lightly washed or not in those days before insecticides. We learned how to peel an orange or a peach nicely, eat cherries like little ladies, even tackle an unskinned banana with knife and fork in a way that many years later helped me save face at European dinner tables. Gone were the familiar dishes of soupy and oversweetened compotes! Onto our blossom-sprinkled plates went pits and skins and seeds, always correctly but painlessly, and with a kind of enthusiasm that still flickers in me, so long after. . . .

There was one trick Aunt Gwen played with ripe bananas which I have never seen anywhere, except now in my own homes. Anne and I loved it, and so did the next batch of us, Norah and David, and then so did my own two daughters. But I have tried it on all their peers, and it has sometimes been a gastronomical flop, perhaps because it is not a pretty color. Myself, I still think it is a good way to eat fruit and bread, neither of which much interests me by now.

The method is to mash a ripe banana for each piece of toast, and sweeten it with dark brown sugar beaten in and, if wished, a little nutmeg. The hot fresh toast is buttered generously and then spread the same way, or almost heaped, with the mashed fruit. For small people smaller wedges are cut. If eaten quickly, and when one is very hungry, this can be a crisp fruity delight. I state this firmly, recollecting it in tranquillity.

I cannot remember any other vegetables than tomatoes and cucumbers at Aunt Gwen's (if indeed they are not fruits), except onions and beets. I suppose they were among the cheapest to be bought. At home we occasionally ate sliced beets in the little vegetable dishes, but they tasted like nothing, not even *red*, which of course has several definite flavors. We never had pickled beets, which the Nettleships seemed to eat the way we were supposed to enjoy mashed potatoes, almost every day. Aunt Gwen boiled a great kettle of them, in a way she taught me and that I saw later in the poorest houses in France: the skin would slip off and the beets be as ruddy and almost as sweet and crisp as in life. Then she would slice them warm into a big bowl, season and douse them with her vinegar, and let them stand.

Raymond would come home from high school and eat a big snack from them. The bowl would be put on the table for whoever ate the next meal in the kitchen. It was a kind of salad, mildly sharp and snappy. I often play with the general theme in my own kitchen, but the nearest I come to it is to eat it in a third-rate honest café-restaurant in a small French town, from November to February. It is part or even all of a first course, a "poor man's hors d'oeuvre." . . .

She knew how to treat onions, too, and often there were thin rings of them, raw, with the pickled beets. They turned an impossible pink, and made a fine pattern on a slice of buttered bread. One of the best things I ever ate in my whole life, though, was the way she fried them. As far as I remember, we never touched that vegetable at home, except for the ritual dish of creamed onions at noon on Christmas. I think Mother disliked their odor spreading from the kitchen, and felt from her steady reading of English novels that they were meant for the lower classes. And of course they may have disagreed with Grandmother's gastric activities. . . .

Aunt Gwen never fried onions except in Laguna, and even then only a few times. I think she would have done it oftener if Father and Anne and I had not been too naïvely enthusiastic in reporting our bliss to Mother, for I do not put it past her sense of honor to believe that she managed to turn off many such enjoyments, if she felt her own scene was in any danger of being dimmed in our eyes. (I do not blame her for this self-protection. It did, however, lead to a tacit and increasing silence on our parts, about many things we sensed might be better left undescribed at home. And it is too bad that the fried onions had to be sacrificed to this education.)

Aunt Gwen's onions were as delicate and light and apparently as digestible as gossamer might prove to be. They seemed to float onto our fingers and down our throats. Father and Anne and I sat like hypnotized chickens at the round table in the Laguna house, waiting for her to bring them to us in a delicious pile on a hot platter. We were allowed to pluck them one by one from it, and eat them with our fingers, while she prepared another batch in the little kitchen, in a precise formality that was basically Japanese. With the last and biggest platter, she herself sat down with us, and while she tucked in, we nibbled in a sated way, and sipped at our beer or milk according to our ages.

The rings were always perfect, always crisp and of a delicate gold color. The onion was not stiff, but it was still definitely fresh to the teeth. The thin coating held it in shape, and although we did not let any rings get cold, I doubt that they would have wilted as do the ones I order in restaurants. (I became an addict during that one short happy summer when Father would come down from Whittier with supplies, while Anne and I were living there with Aunt Gwen and before we betrayed our gastronomical bliss to Mother. Afterward, when we would beg our goddess to make them, she would say they were too much trouble, and we understood, without more words. But I still order "French fried onion rings" now and then, compulsively, and even buy them in cans, or frozen. They are a sad facsimile.)

I have read many recipes, especially in the Victorian cookbooks which probably influenced Aunt Gwen's kitchen methods, but none of them has what I think was her own trick. She sliced the onions about a quarter-inch thick, and then let them chill in a generous bowl of fresh milk for several hours. Then she separated any rings that still stayed together, and let them all drain on a folded tea towel, so that they were almost dry when she shook them a few at a time in a paper bag with seasoned flour in it. In this way, there was hardly more than an even dusting of the starch on them.

Still a few at a time, she put them into deep fat, and hooked them out with a long wooden chopstick when they were golden, and served them at once. It was a slow and finicky job, and certainly not one for a harried cook with a full dinner to present.

At least it happened a few times in my life, and I am fortunate, no matter if frustrated, to have a yardstick. The nearest thing to them, for lightness and delicacy, is the fried parsley one is served occasionally in a fine French restaurant. There is a kind of tiny *explosion* in the mouth. . . .

And the mussels! They too happened only in Laguna. It never occurred to any of us, ever, to take them back to Whittier. They had to be a rare now-and-then feast in the lamplight of the beach house dining room, with salt-steam still rising from the back yard where they had cooked, and the sound of high tide crashing over the rock where they had lived only two or three hours before. (Perhaps what I mean is that Aunt Gwen had to be there . . . we with her?)

I cannot even remember ever hearing about "seasons" in those unpolluted times, but probably we ate them in the summer, because Aunt Gwen and Anne and I were in Laguna then, and it took Father to make the whole trick work, when he tore down through the Canyon from Whittier to bring us things, and to report on the progress of the newest baby and all that.

One person had to swim out at low tide to the biggest rock off our shore, right in front of our house. It was not an easy paddle: there were riptides now and then, and always currents swirling around the smaller rocks between the one we called Tide and the surf. Whoever made it to Tide Rock had to carry a piece of the springs of a dismantled Ford, and his end of rope to make a two-way pulley to shore. Once up on Tide, meanly encrusted with big breathing mussels, he would shout back for the bucket, which the person on shore would send out to him. Then came the job of filling it, prying the shellfish off their huge colony with the old piece of metal.

And then, if the surf was kindly and the hunting was good, Rex on the rock would signal to Aunt Gwen on shore, and swim back, guiding the bucket along the ropes. Sometimes he would lose his whole catch, and we on the sand would groan and roll dramatically into the waves and out again. The next trip, if things had not been too rough, would be Aunt Gwen's, for she and Rex were equally powerful swimmers, and almost of the same weight and height.

And usually before we had enough, whatever that was, it was time to call a halt, because the tide would be coming in fast, and we had to climb up the cliff and walk back to our house, carrying gunnysack and bucket full of loot, the car-prize, the rope, another bucket full of sea grass in its water.

It was, in other words, an operation, a project. Everything had to be right: the tides and their timings, the surf, most of all the people.

The only way we ever cooked mussels was outdoors, in one or two carefully scrubbed ten-gallon kerosene cans, with artful vents cut into them, perhaps four inches from the bottom and on all four sides. Thick hot coals would be glowing between some old bricks and rocks, in back of the house. We would pack six or eight inches of wet sea grass, sometimes with kelp, into the bottom of the cans, fill them with mussels which had been rinsed and scrubbed in plenty of water, and then cover them with two or three folded clean flour sacks. I cannot know how long they steamed over the coals . . . perhaps ten minutes? They all had to be open. . . . They would send out fine salty smells, which in the pure air always perfumed with eucalyptus made a pillar of incense.

At precisely whatever the right time was, for anybody knows that a mussel must not be overcooked, the fire would be doused and we would line up with bowls, for Rex to fill with a trowel from the steaming can. We would run into the house again (why is it that we never simply squatted on the ground and ate like primitives?), and on the dining room table would be another smaller bowl at each place, and a pitcher of melted butter with lemon juice in it.

From then on, each one used his own technique, the way natives of San Francisco do when confronted with a fresh cracked crab. Some of us might collect a few of the beautiful orange lumps and eat them slowly, all buttery, with a spoon. Some ate them one at a time, each tidbit pulled off its shell with a fork or spoon and dipped in the bowl of butter. Father usually looked intently at every mussel as he ran a teaspoon around the shell to loosen the "rubber band," and then scooped a little butter onto it and tipped it neatly into his mouth. Aunt Gwen liked extra lemon on hers, and squeezed a few drops over each one before she went on, sometimes, with Rex's pattern. We ate until we did not want any more, even with bread and butter to refresh us, and if any of the fish were left, Aunt Gwen pulled them out of their shells while they were still warm, and covered them with a strong vinaigrette, for a chilled salad the next day.

Needless to say, this peculiar feast was a messy slurpy one, not to be indulged in when Mother was there, and although we never made a real secret of it, and felt that she was *almost* perfectly happy to be excluded, it was part of a special Laguna solidarity, shared mostly by the quartet but with Isobel and Uncle Mac sometimes there, while he and Father gradually made a sizable house out of a small shack.

As for the *taste* of our mussels, it is impossible to say more than that it was the first, for me, and by far the best, in a long life of mussel tasting. Ours were the freshest, the simplest. Probably they were eaten in their own right "season," for Rex and Aunt Gwen were great respecters of the laws of nature, but certainly they came from unpolluted water. They were crisp in the mouth, delicately briny, plump and often bearded. They were above all beautiful, of an ineffably soft but vivid orange color in their nacreous purple and blue-black shells. Rarely there would be a tiny whole mussel inside the bigger one. Often, I suppose, there would be some sand, but it never seemed to bother us.

All of the cooking at Laguna was more robust, less mannered, than in Whittier, and of course I was more happily involved in it, with Aunt Gwen instead of some hired slavey in command. The Laguna kitchen was small and light, the opposite of ours and hers at home. There was a sink with cold running water, which when it ran at all was potable on the good days. On the bad days it was for several years dark brown and stinking of sulfur, and we still drank it. We had a two-burner kerosene stove for a long time, which Mother when she was there found almost impossible to use, conveniently, but which Aunt Gwen soon taught me how to light and attend to. On its top there was usually a big battered aluminum teakettle, for boiling water for Aunt Gwen's floods of strong black tea and the dishes, the first of which I never indulged in and the second I accepted as a boring part of rosy wonderful Life.

We had a small tin oven to be set on one of the burners, and in it we made delicious heavy edibles: biscuits as big as pie plates, one at a time of course, and stuffed with raisins in what our refugee from a British seminary felt was truly Old Country style. We also baked, in old bread pans, cakes like pure lead, which we sliced thin for sandwiches made preferably with peanut butter, best for bringing out the subtleties of more raisins, leftover prunes, a dash of beer or bourbon left from the last weekend picnic. . . .

Since for at least five days of each blissful week there was nobody in the house but us three, Aunt Gwen was slovenly in admirable ways she would not permit herself in Whittier, and we not only left scraped dishes neatly piled in the sink until we had enough to justify lighting the stove for a kettle of hot water, but we kept a big black skillet "going," just swabbed out with a wad of good clean newspaper now and then, unless of course we had fried fish in it. I liked this slaphappy way of adapting our energies to our social demands, and it has probably annoyed and shocked many good people in my own behavior since those days.

We also fried a great many things, most of them unlisted in cookbooks. Aunt Gwen really liked this way of cooking, and could do it squatting by a fire between three rocks as well as she could standing nonchalantly in front of the little kerosene stove in Laguna, and her own big black woodburner in Whittier. She liked fried eggs, fried bananas (Oh, delicious!), fried rice, fried fish, and especially fried sandwiches. I think she liked these last the best because they were so eminently shaped to carry in a sweater pocket on a short walk (which to her meant anything under five miles) . . . and I confess that every two or three years, even now, I make a fried cheese and/or bacon sandwich for myself. After I have eaten about half of it, I feel stupefied, and discard the rest regretfully.

In the good Laguna days, though, it was an exciting promise, to warm up the pan, ready the ingredients, and make fried-egg sandwiches. Aunt Gwen insisted that we have at least two pockets somewhere on us, one for shells, stones, small fish, or lizards, and one big enough to hold these greasily wrapped, limp, steamy monsters. Then we would race the sunset to a high hill. The sandwiches stayed warm against our bodies, and when we panted to a stop, and fell against a good rock or an old eucalyptus trunk, the packets sent out damp insistent invitations.

We each had two sandwiches. The first we gnashed at like fairly well-mannered puppies. The second was for contemplation, as we watched all of the quiet empty slopes down to the cliff edge, and the great ocean with the sun sliding into it. We sang right through *Pinafore* and the Episcopal Hymnal, with a little Harry Lauder for the plunge down the hills again before dark fell . . . : "Rrrrroamin'-/In the gloamin' . . . ," and Aunt Gwen keeping a sharp eye out and her stick ready, in

case we met a self-indulgent rattler roaming for his own picnic in the cool of the day. (We did, several times, in the first
years. There were fewer of them as people began to settle
near the village. ....)

I wrote a tentative recipe for our favorite sunset feast, and
it was published too late for Aunt Gwen to read it, in 1948.
At the risk of having to sue myself for plagiarism, this is it,
from *An Alphabet for Gourmets:*

Aunt Gwen's Fried-Egg Sandwiches

INGREDIENTS *(Physical)*
1/2 to one cup drippings
6 large fresh eggs
12 slices bread
waxed paper

The drippings are very English, the kind poured
off an unidentified succession of beef, mutton, and
bacon pans, melted gradually into one dark puddle
of thick unappetizing grease, which immediately
upon being dabbed into a thick hot iron skillet
sends out rendingly appetizing smells.

The eggs must be fresh, preferably brown ones,
best of all freckled brown ones.

The bread must be good bread, no puffy, blanched,
uniform blotters from a paper cocoon.

The waxed paper must be of honest quality,
since at the corners where it will leak a little, some
of it will stick to the sandwich and in a way merge
with it and be eaten.

INGREDIENTS *(Spiritual)*
These have been amply indicated in the text,
and their prime requisites—Aunt Gwen herself
would be the first to cry no to any further exposi-
tion of them. Suffice it that they were equal parts
of hunger and happiness.

METHOD

Heat the drippings in a wide flat-bottomed skillet until they spit and smoke. Break in the eggs, which will immediately bubble around the edges, making them crisp and indigestible, and break their yolks with a fork and swirl them around, so that they are scattered fairly evenly through the whites. This will cook very quickly, and the eggs should be tough as leather.

Either push them to one side of the pan or remove them, and fry bread in the drippings for each sandwich, two slices to an egg. It too will send off a blue smoke. Fry it on one side only, so that when the sandwiches are slapped together their insides will turn soggy at once. Add to this sogginess by pressing them firmly together. Wrap them well in the waxed paper, where they will steam comfortably.

These sandwiches, if properly made and wrapped, are guaranteed, if properly carried in sweater or pinafore pockets, to make large oily stains around them.

Seasoning depends on the state of the drippings. As I remember Aunt Gwen's, they were such a "fruity" blend of last week's roast, last month's gammon, that salt and pepper would have been an insult to their fine flavor.

PRESCRIPTION

To be eaten on top of a hill at sunset, between trios of "A Wandering Minstrel, I" and "Onward, Christian Soldiers," preferably before adolescence and its priggish queasiness set in.

I cannot remember anything about meat at Aunt Gwen's, either in Whittier or in Laguna, except for one thing she never served to Anne and me but made often for her father and Raymond. It was called, succinctly, a Cold Shape, and although I know where I can find printed methods for making

one, as in Mrs. Beeton's *Household Management,* I prefer not
to repeat them. I might like a Cold Shape now, on a hot day,
although I doubt it, and when I was little I was glad that the
jellied mold of dubious butchered titbits was meant for
grownups and not me. It is the only dish in Aunt Gwen's
cookery that I withdrew from . . . although on second or third
thought I had some reservations, once my hunger had been
satisfied, about a dessert she called Steamed Spotted Dog. The
saving grace in this heavy bland lump was its spots, made of
big flat raisins that had real seeds in them, not the tidier kind
we used at home.

One of the best things in the Gwendolynian repertory, I
believe, was Cocoa Toast. We usually ate/drank it on Sunday
nights and birthdays, and always when Aunt Gwen's shabby
kitchen or the Laguna cottage were ours, all the people gone,
nobody but us in the soft light of her one hanging bulb or the
kerosene lamp at the beach:

> good toast, hot and buttered
> rich dark cocoa
>
> Cut the toast into one-inch squares and put into hot
> soup plates, about ten to a plate. Cover them care-
> fully with hot cocoa until they are swimming. Eat
> with soup spoons.
> For a special treat add two or three good marsh-
> mallows to the pieces of toast, and let them melt in
> the hot liquid.

That is a fine recipe, a part of Anne's and my tacitly un-
mentioned and private life, and one I have no wish ever to
try to duplicate. I could say that the bread and the milk and
the butter are mediocre now, and the marshmallows and the
powdered chocolate too. I could say that there could be no
kitchens like the dark one in Whittier, the lean-to in Laguna,
and no plates like the ones Aunt Gwen had won with can tops

from the Carnation Milk Company. The truth is that there can never be, at least for several civilizations, the three of us there together, so completely trusting: my little sister and I, and the mysterious goddess, sure as a great river or mighty as a ship's prow, and as beautiful, cutting through our lives. I hope she could know and enjoy more than any of us gave her, of real and quiet bliss. I doubt it, though. I doubt that she ever had any physical lovers, for her femaleness was powerful and perhaps frightening, except to the child in all of us. She died full of honors. Perhaps she should have become some kind of nun or saint and been done with it.

She and my father were fine together, in what I think was as near a sexless way as a normally constructed man and woman can be, and I doubt that it was deliberate in its impersonality. She was a never-failing companion and help to him, and I think he may have wondered at times, with Professor Higgins, why more women could not be like that.

As for my mother, she loved Aunt Gwen to the day of her death, and I regret now that I could not ask her why for a time she tried to betray the wonderful woman to Anne and me. I regret that I did not ask Anne too about this, for betrayal it was for a time, and for a time it worked. And as I have already confessed, it is too painful to get far into. The best thing is to think of the woman as I first saw her, and then for the wonderful years after. She came out of the little cottage, so unlike our own big ugly shingled house on a "right" street in a "right" part of town while this was plainly "wrong," with not even a sidewalk in front of it, and she strode to our car like the wingèd Nike of Samothrace, with her full torso thrust forward and her flimsy dress flowing back from her strong long legs. She had big pink cheeks, dark thick hair springing back from her coarse-skinned face, and fine teeth in her smile. The die had been cast.

Anne and I loved her, and from that day on there was on this one sacred subject never a shadow of envy or jealousy in either of us, about how much we loved Aunt Gwen and she us.

We avoided any mention, later in our lives, of the Bad Years. Indeed, we seldom talked about her. There was no need to, and it would have seemed piddling to compare notes about our feelings, for they would have been so shaped by our different natures that we might try to argue: she wore her hair this way, not that . . . she smelled like a poppy petal and not lavender cologne . . . she made the toast first and did *not* butter it when we had it with hot cocoa. . . .

But there could be no argument about our devotion, and perhaps that is why I never wrote of it, or much of her. Silence can be a song too. She would hear it, sooner or later, for we were related by love.

6

The First
and Best Batties

The meaning of the word "batty" is perfectly clear to me, although I cannot find it in any lexicon at hand. A person who is batty is a harmless gentle madman. I feel fortunate that I have known several. We have been in many ways kindred spirits, and I understand them and am not shy or scared with them. Once a man urged me to spend a winter in an almost legendary hotel in Coney Island where all the upper-class freaks from the sideshows went during the cold slack months. He assured me, without any malice, that I would feel completely at home with the sword swallower, the fat lady, the midgets and hermaphrodites and monkey-men. I liked his suggestion, and still savor it as a compliment, in the same way I like to remember how happy I have been with the true Batties I have known.

The first one was very soon in my life, when I was perhaps going on five. She spent a winter with us, because her sister was my grandmother's rich sister-in-law and a kind woman as well. I cannot remember her name, although we called her Cousin Something, and her shape is hazy, smokelike, but pleasing. She had a sweet vague face and an almost steady smile, and I think rather tumbled drifty hair, and was a middle-aged spinster tacitly considered "not herself" by her kind relatives. She seemed to like having me with her, which of course gave my mother more time to spend on my somewhat sickly little sister Anne. Grandmother did not approve of the unfortunate soul at all, because she plainly filled my head with pagan nonsense.

Once we spent a whole exciting day making paper chairs and beds, perhaps three inches high, which we placed nicely on the ledge of the front porch for fairies to enjoy during the night. In the morning we found that the wind had blown them off into the bushes, but my friend told me that was because the fairies *had* used them, and were permitted only one night with them . . . a strong law in their country. This outraged Grandmother—heathenish prattle! Another time I made the mistake of dashing into the house and crying out that a fairy was caught in the rosebush in the back yard. It was a cobweb with dew on it, the old lady said in a cold way, but the younger one took my hand and begged me to show it to her at once and we hurried outside, leaving a hollow of stern Christian disapproval behind us.

I liked the way she read poetry to me, in a very lilting voice which could set my teeth on edge today, and apparently affected all the grownups that way, so long ago. It was probably a gentle request from my mother (everyone was very nice to this visitor, because she was not quite right in the head) that made us choose to go to the Park with a book, rather than whinny happily at each other in the sun parlor where Grandmother read her Bible, or in the living room where Mother read English novels on her couch.

And when Cousin Whatzit felt like it, she went on in a cozy way about fairies. She knew a great deal: their eating habits (dew, the drop of sweet water at the end of a honeysuckle blossom, occasionally one or two beads from a ripe blackberry . . .); their means of signaling by certain movements of their wings; even the sound of their usually inaudible conversations, which she had often managed to catch. All this was because she knew they were there, without question or quibble. I have no idea if she had ever been considered well enough to see a performance of *Peter Pan*, but all of her own faith is in the plea the ageless boy makes to us to *believe*, and I suspect she told me many things which perhaps were in violation of the fairy laws of secrecy, but which I never betrayed.

She was a great one for quoting, more or less appropriately. She was well read but very shy about talking, at the dinner table for instance, and probably it made her feel less apart from normal people if she could fill in a possible gap with a few lines from Tennyson or Kipling. Mother might say something down the table toward Rex about the next meeting of the St. Matthias Guild, and our visitor would laugh musically and say in her lilting way, "Ah, me, 'twill e'er be thus, as Howells wrote!" This got heavily on the family nerves, except for mine, and once impelled Father to forget his training in good taste and Grandmother to use that as an excuse to storm in a regal way from the dining room.

I remember it clearly. Rex had said something about the current crop of Valencias in the region, or perhaps what the weather might be like tomorrow, and Cousin Whozit gave her merry little laugh, and everyone waited while she went into her "Ah, yes," and then

> *"The days of Old,*
> *The days of Gold,*
> *When knights abroad did ride . . ."*

and my father put down his carving knife instead of using it on her and continued firmly,

> *"They dropped their load*
> *In the middle of the road,*
> *And went on satisfied."*

There was a gasp of shocked amusement from Mother. Grandmother rose coldly, said to my father, "You surprise me. At the *table!*" and left. I forget what the rest of the meal was like, but much later Mother told me that Rex had indeed forgotten his manners, and that from then on he was especially nice to the poor bewildered guest, but that he had simply been driven out of his mind for a minute because she was so damned *batty*.

The next real Batty I remember in our family with especial clearness, although I am sure several of Grandmother's visiting missionaries may have qualified, and certainly the old lady who spent a week every Spring and Fall with us to make school dresses and let down hems and such was mighty peculiar. The brightest light in my private collection was and still is Cousin Lizzie Beatty.

She was an Irish relative of Grandmother's, who had spent perhaps fifty years in China and was stopping off with us on her way to her death, a few months after she left us (in a "home" where Mother had placed her after Rex and Grandmother agreed with her that it was "*too much*" . . .). I was about eight then, I think, and already adept at malingering, just enough to stay home from school but still feel well enough to spend the whole day roaming in the hills with Cousin Lizzie.

At first Mother was a little worried about where we went and what we did, but it was plain that the old lady loved me and was able to recognize things like danger. As it seems to me now, there were no cars on the quiet roads, no fences across the rolling hills, no mean dogs, no rampsing cows. The only accident in that whole lovely Spring and Summer was that once I stepped on a long nail in a board hidden by thick mustard weeds. I was horrified and scared, but I resolved not to mention it in any way, and enjoyed every melodramatic minute of our long walk homeward, for I could feel blood welling up in my high-laced shoe, and wondered hopefully if

I might possibly faint or something and be carried limp and white onto the living room couch, where my brave secret would be discovered. It was bitter to find, when I carefully took off my shoe in the bathroom, so that all the blood would not stain the rug in my room, that there was only a little reddish bruise where the nail had gone onto my skin. I never mentioned either the mark or the hole in the shoe leather, not caring to feel foolish in public.

Cousin Lizzie was a favorite with Rex, who was fascinated by her accent and her innate bravery. She was from an upper-middle-class family in County Tyrone, and was the first woman ever to go to the College of Surgeons or Medicine or whatever it might be, at the University of Dublin. It was told to me with shock at man's brutishness that she was actually stoned on the streets by the other students, so much did they resent her invasion of their prerogatives. (I have a book about her, but prefer to leave my souvenirs blurry and mine own. . . .) She fled Ireland, pursued by the ghosts of her family's increasing alcoholism, a common demon in those days and circles. She went to China as a medical missionary, and was honored by the Dowager Queen for her courage during several waves of the Plague (Smallpox? Typhoid?). She was allowed to wear the imperial shade of yellow, and to treat the old ruler for various female weaknesses unseemly to discuss with the court physicians. She spoke many dialects. She was good-looking as well as famous, and once at a ball at the British Embassy, wherever that could have been in those far-away days, her dancing partner laughed so hard at a remark she made that he dislocated his jaw. At that the trained doctor replaced the Irish lady, and she hauled off and gave him one expert socko that restored him to his rightful shape but needed plenty of explanation to the other genteel prancers. I like this apocryphal vignette of high life in Hong Kong or wherever it was, and so did my father. . . .

When Cousin Lizzie could no longer function as a good

medical consultant, much less operate on everybody from a royal eunuch to a village elder, innumerable enormous bundles and boxes were packed with belongings, and they and she were shipped to her closest relative of space if not consanguinity, in her case my maternal grandmother. This must have caused more than the usual ripple in our house, but we were used to lengthy visits from both kith and kin, and we welcomed first Cousin Lizzie, temporarily very tired and permanently in a near-senile state, and gradually all her trunks and bundles.

These were of constant fascination, although they never could match the spell she herself cast at once on me. They were intricately wrapped, and had a completely Chinese smell about them, like the back of F. Suie One's store on the Los Angeles Plaza, or the inside of a dusty ginger jar. Father would greet them with the real gleam of a frustrated adventurer in his eye, and would spend too much time for comfort, mine anyway, trying to work the thousands of knots loose so as not to cut into the exotic ropings. We kept all the strange cloth that was used instead of paper, and for years had lengths of it for curtains and bedspreads. A lot of it was dyed a deep true blue, and that color still makes me feel some of the old excitement of Cousin Lizzie's bundle days.

Inside, packed in all kinds of dubious waste, were jars, bottles, pieces of amber and jade, pipes, daggers in carved ivory sheaths. And in the big clumsy trunks, really boxes with hinged lids, were lengths and more lengths of silk cloth, brocaded, plain, mostly of the imperial yellow. There were fur-lined boots. There was a big carriage robe of sable, full of moths. There were tall caps of fur, and many kinds of slippers, and long robes heavy with embroidered ribbons. Everything smelled, of incense, and perhaps of camel dung, and certainly of decay.

I am not sure about what happened to this strange loot, but through Mother and Grandmother it was disposed of, to give

Cousin Lizzie more than enough to live on for the months before she died. And one day after she and I had eaten four hard-boiled eggs, a great treat for me, and then taken a short snooze in a meadow high on a hill back of Whittier, she put on my finger a thick silver ring with a rectangle of bright blue enamel on it and a silver symbol of friendship. It would grow with me, she said, for it had wings that could be unfolded at the back as my finger thickened with age. I have never worn such a thing with the same astonished pleasure, and I have no idea what became of it.

This ring made my sister Anne very unhappy. She did not like Cousin Lizzie, and was the kind of fully developed female from birth onward who could make such reactions very plain. Cousin Lizzie, by that time perhaps the same age as Anne in her return to infantile behavior, was as overt as the other child, and it is possible that the ring hastened Mother's decision to have Cousin Lizzie taken care of in another place. (Later I learned that she did need to be helped to bathe, or rather reminded that she *should* bathe, change underclothes, all that.)

My mother wept a little, once when I was perhaps fifteen and we were talking about the whole business: she plainly felt regret and some guilt, but she was pregnant during that Oriental invasion, and Grandmother was exceptionally disapproving and unbending with her dotty relative, and even with Father's obvious enjoyment of the old lady it was a steady strain to have her there all the time, so childlike and garrulous ... especially since she never knew whether she was speaking a Chinese dialect or her own half-forgotten Irish-English. (I never knew either, and I seemed to understand all the stories she told me in several tongues during our long rambles. My grandmother flatly said I was lying about this, until I repeated to her some of the North Chinese legends I had heard, and Cousin Lizzie nodded in complete agreement, although neither of us remembered how I had learned them.)

Mother told me, that tearful afternoon, that once Cousin Lizzie was ironing something in the kitchen, and rattling on in her disconnected and often meaningless way, when suddenly she stopped and looked deeply at Edith, who stood nearby to see that neither the old doctor nor the ironing board got burned, and then began to cry quietly. "Oh, my child," she said, "you can have no idea of how dreadful it is to know that I am as I am."

Mother burst into the generous sobs that came naturally to her, and put her arms around the frail woman, and they stood there in the dim room clinging to each other, until smoke billowed about them from the ironing board. A few minutes later, with the damage cleared away, Cousin Lizzie seemed quite unconscious that she had wracked my tender mother with a cosmic sorrow, but it haunted Edith forever, and made her fear a batty end for herself, which I am happy for her sake that she did not have.

When Cousin Lizzie was in a good state she could be very funny, and I have seldom heard better laughing at table while Grandmother was still alive. Usually we spoke politely and with some constraint, especially at dinner (and of course Anne and I not unless we were spoken to). But there could be a good relaxed feeling with the mad old woman there, which I don't otherwise remember except when my grandmother was away at a religious convention.

And the reason I learned the word for the frail harmless zany who arrived in my life and then left it was that once my father with a straight face introduced her to somebody as Dr. Elizabeth Batty, when by then he well knew that her name was pronounced Batey. She did not hear him, but Edith did, and could not help using the word from then on. We would describe someone, and still do in what is left of the family, as "a real Batty" more than we'd make it correctly into an adjective, and it is so much a part of our language that I find it hard to believe that I cannot find it in good dictionaries. Does it come from the expression, "bats in the belfry," for someone who is otherwise known as "nuts" or "crackers" or "loony" or or or? Did Rex let it happen, a predestined and mischievous pun?

All I am sure of is that the homeless bewildered old lady was the best Batty in my life, and gave me a taste for her kind that has helped me through many an otherwise empty moment. I am grateful to the lilting Cousin Something for preparing me for Lizzie, whose voice, singsong of Irish and Mandarin, is forever in my head. I can understand what she was telling me, still feel the silver ring on my finger, and the invisible blood of courage in my shoe.

7

Our "Girls"
and a Few Ladies

Perhaps the most unusual, peculiar, or plain extraordinary person who watched over my siblings and me was Miss Marrow. But she came late in my life, when I was almost thirteen, and therefore cannot qualify for description here. Suffice it that she was in the same class with my mother's choice of companion for her prolonged stay in Europe, mostly Dresden, where she had been sent to forget forever the lanky uncouth newspaperman who later became my father.

Mother spent what must have been strange, peculiar, and plain extraordinary months with a former and beloved teacher from her finishing school, who was dreamily attentive and articulate when vertical, because she was stiff with drugs. She was limp and horizontal most of the time, in her own nirvana, which allowed the younger woman to absorb floods of hot thick chocolate, read the scores of Wagner's *Ring,* and dream of her lover so many thousand miles away.

Miss Marrow fills the bill, in retrospect: she lived mostly in her own dream, skillfully self-administered. But she had assisted at my birth, which was proof enough to my parents that she must still be estimable, so long after . . . a worthy guardian of their brood for several weeks. . . .

There were lesser confrontations with the soft and seamy sides of life, while my little sister Anne and I were growing up in Whittier. When my parents felt their periodic and compulsive restlessness in the small Quaker enclave and went away, for a long drive, a dinner in Los Angeles, an occasional weekend, people of course took care of us innocents. They were an interesting crew, drawn equally from teen-agers in the St. Matthias Church and the purest ranks of retired Campbellite missionaries, according to how long they would have to stay. The first were what are now called baby-sitters: high school students doing their homework in the living room while Anne and I, upstairs, whispered discreetly from bed to bed, or sat in our clothes closet with the light on and the door shut . . . all of it forbidden, of course. The other guardians were elderly women being protected and helped by Grandmother Holbrook, the pillar of the local Christian Church and therefore of the Mission Field.

And all through this decorous pattern wove, often literally, our fantastic kitchen hirelings. A few of them were eminently respectable women, found by word of mouth, like the McLure Sisters, but most of them were sent to us from an employment agency, perhaps the only one in Los Angeles at that time that could provide maids-of-all-work desperate enough to accept a job in as dull a place as Whittier. They would arrive on the Electric and be met by Father, or he would drive to the Los Angeles depot for them. They might last a few weeks, and then disappear. I forget them, except for a lingering shadow of human misery, very quiet.

I know now that at the beginning of this century they led a wretched life, with long hours, small pay, and revolting living quarters . . . yes, even in our house where we were clean and assumed that we were kind. Our "girls" slept in a tiny room off the back porch, with one door and one window, a narrow cot and a bureau, a light bulb dangling from the ceiling. Another door on the back porch gave into a tiny toilet, for Her and the hired man (and for Anne and me: we preferred it for long shared ruminations, during which I made up a continued verbal novel that lasted for several years and helped pass the time until our duties had been accomplished . . .). The cook ate in the kitchen, and apparently bathed in the sink there.

It seems impossible to me now, but that is the way it was, and my mother was always called a nice woman to work for. She told us that her father, the Iowa banker, believed strongly that domestic servants should be unionized, like all other workers, in self-protection. But she was unaware of why this was true, I think.

So drabs moved in and out of our kitchen, mixed with a few fine incorruptible human beings. The first of these last whom I remember was the tall heavy black woman named Cynthia. She came to us in faith, and left in sorrow, all of it mutual.

She, and a Negro couple who were very important in all our lives after we moved down Painter to the Ranch, were servants because that was about all that their race was permitted to be, early in this century. Father believed in predestination or something like it, and felt that it was his ordained duty to protect people less strong and educated than he. I am not aware that he did much to help them get out of their obviously inferior ranking, but he was honest and earnest in his lifelong efforts to make their lot better, on the levels it had apparently been appointed to remain. He did not seem to feel that Negroes were inferior to Whites, any more than Mexicans were. It was simply their destiny to work for people like himself, who worked for them. I do not recall *racism*, as such, in our family.

Cynthia slept upstairs, to be near Anne and me, then very

small. There was only one bathroom in the whole big house, until Rex added one to Grandmother's apartment downstairs, and it made things complicated: he had to be shaving when the big cook had to be readying for breakfast, and so on. Also, he had fixed ideas about masters and servants, employers and the people who were paid to work for them: their private lives should be kept separate from their professional. And probably he had never hopped into his own extra-length tub just after a female to whom he was not married had climbed out of it, leaving the bathroom steamy with splashings of scent that smelled more like vanilla essence than Mother's discreet dabs of Indian Hay. . . .

So Cynthia moved downstairs. Anne and I missed her very much, especially after all the lights were out and she had made room for us in her narrow bed for a whispered prayer or two. But we reestablished a good pattern with her in her crowded dark room, her wee toilet.

On Sunday afternoons she would ride in the back seat of the topless Model T with us, and Mother swathed in dust veils and Rex wearing goggles and gloves up front. Cynthia had one costume I loved, mostly of blue satin, with a big wrapped turban. In Whittier, 1912, we were probably a sight to remember.

I think that there was some comment on the Rialto about this weekly jaunt, unseemly in the sedate village where most people had never seen a black. We stopped taking her with us. Perhaps Father was tacitly, gently told to by the City Fathers? Perhaps Father was weak?

After perhaps six months with us, Cynthia left. She was pining with loneliness. There was no church for her, no meeting place. She told my parents that she would like to stay forever with us, if they would move away from Whittier. Anne and I cried at night for her, for a week or so and then lifetimes.

The next person clear in my mind is Amimoto, the Japanese, a slender homesick student at the College. He was the first male servant Mother had ever hired, and she was uneasy and abashed. He was also the first Oriental she had ever met, except perhaps some of Grandmother's missionaries during her girlhood, and she found herself talking much too loudly to him, to make him understand. She was truly unable to communicate with him, and he soon left us for a more comprehending household.

Meanwhile Anne and I loved him and he us: we were almost of the same age in many ways, and he was desperate perhaps for little faraway siblings. We understood everything he told us, as he peeled vegetables Iowa-style and tried vainly to make Grandmother's White Sauce, and we discussed his lessons with him as he studied them under the one light in the big ugly kitchen.

It is possible that Mother expressed her own puzzlement by deciding that we little girls were much too close to him, a grown boy. For two or three years after he left, or was fired, he sent us a long tube of delicate tea wafers, at Christmas. "I don't think he should do *that*," she would say disapprovingly, but Anne and I savored them slowly, still torn with regret for him. (He became a famous admiral, much later, and probably would have liked to bomb hell out of Whittier and other local points during the war, but I know that once he loved us as much as we did him.)

There was another bright flash through our kitchen firmament, a silent austere woman. She and her mother lived in a tent on the west side of town, near the *News*, I think. She was by far the best cook we ever had, and once I was sent from the table because I let out a low moan, very un-Anglo-Saxon and sensual, when she put before Father a long platter of beef hash, which I knew would be superb, decorated with fleurons of crisp pastry and further garnished with tiny twigs of parsley and watercress....

This grey remote woman had no interest in children, but

I knew that she was past mistress in the arts of cutting, chopping, carving, all with her French Knife, as it came to be known. She sharpened it herself, and took it with her on her days off, and on one of them she first cut her mother's throat, then slashed their tent into ribbons, and then did herself in, very expertly. It is a short story with a bloody ending, but it was good while it lasted.

Once I learned a bit of semantical foot play when I thought I was alone in the house except for the current slavey, and answered a knock on the door. Somebody I did not know stood there, and I said, "Just a minute, please. I'll ask the maid." The poor soul in the kitchen heard me, and that night she quit, telling my parents angrily that she'd heard what I'd called her and that she was nobody's *maid:* she was a *hired girl,* and should be referred to as such.

Now and then there was trouble in our steady if staggering procession of kitchen help, when Mother was ill or pregnant and needed a nurse. Those were still the times when trained and licensed women would, and indeed preferred to, stay in a home for weeks or months, ruling their own spheres according to their natures, but not doing any general cooking and cleaning and all that. As I think about it, we were very fortunate. Three or four capable quiet nurses lived for long periods with us, and although I can still hear the crackle of their uniforms and hear their soft steps up and down the stairs, and see one sallow face under its white cap, I do not remember their names. They had nothing to do with Anne and me. But the hired girls determinedly resented them and called them uppity, and occasionally walked out.

There were a few nice daughters of people in the church, who would come to do their homework in our living room while Father and Mother went on a bit of roistering. The favorites were Gladys and Marguerite Matteson, girls with beautiful hair and firm natures. They did nothing to entertain us, nor we them. It was understood that they were serious, and after they checked on things like toothbrushing and clothes-put-away, they went downstairs and we withdrew into our own night world.

I am told that now it is required to leave a stuffed icebox and plenty of Cokes for baby-sitters. Then such gluttonous bribes were unknown, or at least they had never occurred to my parents. There was one dramatic contradiction to this austerity, reported by Mrs. Matteson to my mother: her girls found themselves famished, one night, and rooted around desperately for some possible titbit, and found some little squares of chocolate. They ate them all, to their embarrassment and later misery, for they had downed a whole box of flavored laxative, and were too pot-bound to go to school the next day, even with all their lessons done. From then on Mother left a plate of cookies on the living room table, by the student lamp.

Our mainstays for extended debauches, when the parents would be away for a few days or even a week, were drawn from Grandmother's inexhaustible list of retired missionary relicts or spinsters. She knew hundreds of them. They would come at any time and stay as long as we let them, or *longer*. One of them even decided to live around the corner from us, and for years did odd jobs like mending the socks and letting down hems, and finally died when the "disappearing bed" in her little apartment folded up with her in it. She was found several days later. Nobody had seemed to miss her, one way or another . . . I remember her name, though, and that she was small, with a powdery smell.

A different missionary, this time a rather large pallid woman, added a near-deathless phrase to our mocking repertory, when she innocently told us of how she managed to do herself and her laundry in one tubful of hot water, when eking out her life between such cushy jobs as we sometimes offered her. She would draw the bath, strip down to, but not beyond, her long underwear, and douse. *Then* . . . ,"First I soap myself," she would tell us solemnly, and we could see the big flabby body in its extra skin, rising and sinking in the tub, decreasingly sudsy in the greying water. The result, she assured us with satisfaction at her clever trick, was that she had clean fresh underwear and felt well soaped and then well laved, herself.

But for the next fifty years or so, that would set us off into disgusted giggles: *First I soap myself.* There was no compassion in our laughter, as we teased the world that had turned her stingy, desperate, pinchy. My mother had never lived alone and near-penniless in her life. It is probable that when my young hard-working father had to choose between a meeting with his fellows or a boardinghouse bath, he stayed dirty. And the rest of us? We were callous and unthinkingly cruel fat-cats.

Probably the favorite of our missionaries was the most unsuitable, at least in the Christian sense. At any rate, Anne and I liked her enough to convince Grandmother, on the lady's urging, that she could safely withdraw for a few days from watching over the household while Rex and Edith were away, and breathe the congenial airs of Long Beach, where elderly people from Iowa were flocking like lemmings to the sea. Miss X would watch over us. I do not remember many details about this young woman, younger anyway than all the withered tottering ladies who usually came when Grandmother beckoned, except that she was tall and well formed, with a beautiful reddish topknot, and a fine melodious chant for reading *Hiawatha*, then my favorite work.

Anne and I liked young firm solid women, tall on their feet. Mother was that way, and so was Aunt Gwen. (It is interesting that except for Cynthia, we never hired a cook who was of any size at all . . . *Midgets!*) And here was one of Grandmother's protégées, but still nice to lean against! She had magnificent hair, long and gleaming and supple, which she liked to have us brush down gently as she read to us before we went to bed. And she seemed to understand the intricate beat of Longfellow: BY the SHORES of GIT-chee GU-mee. . . . Anne and I stroked away at her, and then went like sated kittens to our beds.

She would come up for a good-night prayer and a kiss, and then go next door, where her long-time lover was boarding while she protected Mother Holbrook's grandchildren. He was a sailor, much younger than she. She was always on deck for our breakfasts.

I learned about this horrendous betrayal a long time later. It made me laugh: no harm came of it, at least for us, and it seemed fine that at least one of Grandmother's infallibles chose her own path. All the others were very meek nice wrecks. This renegade had some juice left in her veins.

And that was true of the McLure Sisters. There were five of them, but one had got married and had stayed so. The four who were left were, or had been, in and/or out of a few matches, but when we knew them and drew upon them they lived with their father, a retired carpenter, in a nice little house off Painter, toward the hills.

We never knew who would be in the kitchen at breakfast time, because they all slept at home, unless Mother needed someone to stay late at night to listen for our inaudible cries for help. It got to be a mild joke for Anne and Mother and me to wait at the breakfast table for Father to look up from his newspaper, peer again, and then say with the same relief each time, "Ah, good morning, Blanche," . . . or "Margaret" . . . or "Elizabeth" . . . or "Bertha." He would go back to the news, and we would exchange discreet grins with each other and the Sister in charge.

I cannot remember one thing the Sisters cooked for us while they watched over our obvious well-being. I imagine it was much the foodstuff Grandmother and my parents were used to, from the Middle West. All I know is that they were kind and good quiet women. Blanche was the most nervous, and Mother had to caution us not to watch and above all not to laugh when she served tea at lunch, and her hand rattled the cup around like a ping-pong ball on the saucer. But Margaret was the best.

She was the cricket of her family, the old maid. The others were taller and younger, and more obviously desirable or at least once-mated. She had a dry austere offishness about her, but toward Anne and me she was matter-of-fact in a loving way. I doubt that we ever hugged or kissed one another. It would have embarrassed her.

She had a cleft palate, which no doubt set her apart, but my sister and I understood her perfectly, and soon came to know her private patois, and to act as protective translators if anyone looked puzzled.

Anne and I began to talk together in this same language. Mother heard us and asked us to stop, but almost until the day my sister died, some fifty years later, she and I exchanged an occasional private message exactly the way Margaret had unwittingly taught us. I can still do it, but only for myself. It is impossible to write, from so high up in the nose and so near the tip of the tongue. Perhaps it proves that a young person can learn any language by ear. Certainly I carried on long conversations with that little remote woman, as well as many terse communiqués with my sister in real communion. It is too bad that by now I do not know of anyone who would think me anything but out of my mind if I suddenly asked, in the Margaret tongue, "May I please have a piece of bread?"

Margaret had grey-white hair, combed neatly back from a small kind face, with the bright eyes of somebody who must watch carefully. Deaf people look that way, too. There is a faint smile, but not placative and too brave, the way a blind person often does it. Margaret was very strong in her spirit, and perhaps even noisy about it when home from her job in our house. Anne and I went whenever we could to wherever she might be, and if she was not making White Sauce and all that, she would be reading the Bible loudly. It was fine to have her smile at us with her even rows of false teeth, and then start over again in her peculiar whinny. In the beginning was the Word . . . Ihnhh e behhhiinh wuhh e Worgththhh. We joined her, talking in cleft-palate unison and belief, and feeling her skinny old arms warmly, tightly, around our shoulders, as she perched on the kitchen stool.

Margaret was all *right*. She would not cut up her old father, or fall down drunk. She had her own family, and probably her own small congregation of fellow worshippers, somewhere nearby. And if she felt overtired when she trotted down Painter to her father's house, the next morning sister Blanche would be on hand for Father's ritualistic breakfast, clattering the coffee cup hysterically from one side to the other of its saucer. Or Elizabeth would be there, placid and distant, or the other Sister whose name I forget the most easily.

A lot more happened in a sociological or at least domestic way after we moved down Painter to the Ranch. Anne and I discussed several aspects of rape, for instance, with a pretty girl Mother was protecting for a friend. She managed, between changing diapers for her baby and setting a haphazard table, to give us a good simple description of life in the Big City, in her case Omaha. She was only one of our fallen women, and several of them were attractive or at least instructive to talk with.

We had a few toughies, too. The best one was Rose, who had started her active sexual life as a kitchen slob in a remote Alaskan loggers' camp, when she was thirteen. Her language was hair-raising, but we understood and respected her, and she was devoted to Mother.

And there was the tense drama of the time when Edith *ordered* Father to search a departing female's suitcases, which of course he found stuffed with the best Irish silver we owned, and most of Mother's small collection of jewelry. He apologized to her, and told me long afterward that it was one of the most painful things he ever did. She assured him that several of the lady's brooches had been lying right there on the floor as she dusted, so she simply pinned them on her booooozum and forgot them. I forget what she said about the heavy silver. . . .

And of course there was Miss Marrow, on her long trip. . . .

All this made life exciting, but not as innocent as it had been when there were the unexpected kitchen waifs in Painter, the few planets and meteors in our domestic skies, the Sisters tramping loyally in and out. Perhaps the nicest was Margaret, so spare and clean and merry with my little sister and me. Or perhaps it was big dark loving Cynthia . . . or Amimoto far from home.

Certainly Grandmother's missionaries withdrew fast and peaceably into the fogs of Time, except for that big voluptuous woman (how did she happen? Where did she really come from?) who knew how to chant from *Hiawatha*. But Miss Marrow with her needle and her powders . . . the others with their soapings and their knives and their hungers for hidden sweets: they were all women trying to survive among savages.

Part II

The Town

8

Prejudice, Hate,
and the First World War

As I see it now, our non-Quaker family started out in Whittier
with several strikes against us. When I was a child there,
though, I was unaware of almost everything except being
sturdy and happy. I still have no idea of how much and how
often Rex may have been rebuffed and rebuffed as editor of
the *News*, as well as known companion of men who played
poker, drank strong liquor, and even went to Mass. As for my
mother, she took out whatever social desires she may have
had—and they were indeed puny, for by nature and training
she was asocial—in working valiantly for the Woman's Club
and the small mission which later became the Episcopal
church, and in exchanging long cheerful letters with her
Eastern relatives . . . and in running a kind of boardinghouse
for anyone even remotely related to her. As long as she lived,
anyone whose uncle on his mother's side had married a second cousin of Grandmother's sister-in-law could and did
come to stay with us for anything from a week to several
months, although it was a real ordeal for Mother to ask two
"other people" to dinner. Some of the relatives were staid and
stuffy, but there were fortunately a lot of them who could

safely be called eccentric or, now that my candor cannot hurt Edith, downright crazy. They were the leaven in the loaf, and only rarely did my father suggest in a mild way that perhaps it would be nice to have some of his own brothers or nieces around for a few days. I think he knew that his wife's feverish need to open her house to her own clan was a sign that she was, in truth, lonely in her local world of polite but distant Quaker ladies. . . .

Of course Anne and I knew nothing of all this. Painter Avenue was a wonderful street, gummed over with tar which melted deliciously during the first heat waves in May and then settled into a cozy warm ooze which felt good on our feet. And tar meant the steam roller, the most exciting mobile object in my lifetime, until I heard my first and last real calliope in about 1917. Probably the ground was smoothed or scraped a little first. Then, awesomely, the steam roller would rumble into view. We stood almost prayerfully on the front porch and then, as we grew older and bolder, on the sidewalk, and watched it move up and down our block. It was like a gigantic snail, but of course noisier, with a man up in its shell to wave now and then to us. It was faultless in the way it rolled the tar, our tar, into the flattened streetbed. It always went forward, and perhaps did not even have a reverse gear: I am ignorant of anything but its irrevocable progress past our house, a jolly Juggernaut.

We stood as long as we were allowed, probably almost dozing on our feet, hypnotized by its enormous and ruthless behavior, but I am sure that our jaws were not dropped, for we had our backs to the house and were chewing on the tar that had been spread earlier that day, and strictly forbidden by both Grandmother and Edith, a double hazard.

Tar with some dust in it was perhaps even more delicious than dirty chips from the iceman's wagon, largely because if we worked up enough body heat and had the right amount of spit we could keep it melted so that it acted almost like chewing gum, which was forbidden to us as vulgar and bad for the teeth and in general to be shunned. Tar was better than anything ever put out by Wrigley and Beechnut, anyway. It had a high bright taste. It tasted the way it smelled, but better. And it was challenging, for unless we could keep up the heat and the juice and the general muscular involvement, it would flake off and turn our teeth a spotted betraying black . . . black as tar. Dangerous game!

One time after we had flagrantly and plainly cheated, Mother said coolly to me at the dinner table, after we had eaten the first course with propriety and were waiting to see what came next (for Anne and I had been too busy on the sidewalk that afternoon to quiz the kitchen), "Mary Frances, I would like you to show your father your teeth." I steeled myself, and bared my little fangs at him. Things were still as church. Then Rex gave a great good laugh, and said, "*TAR!* Delicious! Best thing I ever chewed! But it looks awful on teeth!"

Later we did discuss the dubious sides of turning our backs, and the knowledge that we were cheating, and all that, but the reaction of my father made it easier for Anne and me to accept our capitulation to Obedience, and within a comfortable time the steam roller stopped its majestic smashing and we had a paved street, which made even ice chips less tasty.

Down on the corner of Philadelphia and Painter, near enough for us to see at night from the sleeping porch which we gradually had to ourselves as our parents started a new batch of children in another part of the upstairs, there was a big light strung over the intersection, and when a man had climbed up to it to clean it, he would drop out a long greyish tube of some kind of clay which made fine chalk. The sidewalks were sketchy in the town then, but we had a lumpy one going along our block, over the bulging roots of pepper and camphor trees. Later I found it hellish to skate on, but for hopscotch and artwork it was very good.

Across the street lived Old Lady Ransome, and her house still stands in its genteel green-and-white remoteness. Now and then my mother would put on a hat and gloves and go across to pay a call, and the two women would come out on the wide cement porch behind the hanging baskets of smilax ferns and perhaps wave to us. Anne and I went there only a few times, to carry Easter eggs or some such trifle, for Mrs. Ransome was crippled, and in pain.

Next door to her lived a series of people we never knew, except that during the influenza epidemic in 1918 Mother made us stay in the back yard while two or three coffins were carried away from it, one of a young woman, perhaps not yet twenty, who had waved now and then to us as she walked downtown to work for a lawyer. We did not feel one way or another about the plague, probably, although it interested us that soon after that Father came home at noon and pulled off the gauze mask requested by the Red Cross and said something like, "*Bushwah!* I can't smoke in it. And my nose is too big."

Next to the sad unknowns across from us, for a magical few years lived the Smiths. He was a lawyer. She had enormous sunken dark eyes, and played the piano very well. I think she was the fairly rich daughter, with what in France would be called a dowry, of the owner of a department store in Kansas City or some such place. Gradually they had two little girls. All four of them were tubercular. The last I heard, at least three of them had died. Mr. Smith's family was very bitter about his having caught the terrible disease from her, and her family felt the same way about him, and Mother worried a lot about their dilemma, but Anne and I simply enjoyed them. We went on wonderful picnics, for one thing. And I remember sitting under Mrs. Smith's beautiful grand piano and holding onto one of its legs while through my body ran the force and delicacy of the music she knew and played well. I think now it was Schubert, Mozart.

On up the street lived the Maples. They were and probably still are important in Whittier, and I remember them as a handsome large family. They were intelligent and well bred, and went to local schools and then away to Western colleges. Mr. Maple was the banker. On the top floor of the large house, into which I never once stepped, lived Mrs. Maple's mother, a small and apparently fearsome woman who looked down all day on the corner of Painter and Hadley from her high windows, but never waved or nodded.

I remember walking to the Bailey Street School when I was about five and a half years old, with the oldest Maple girl, Caroline, who was wearing her first long skirt. This was in about 1913, and it was plainly an important step for her to take. Two or three girls accompanied her enviously, still with skirts flapping above their shoetops, perhaps nine inches from the ground. Much later in our lives I met Caroline a few times and liked her very much, but always felt some of my childhood awe of her having grown up that long before I did.

I was supposed to be a good friend of her little sister Josephine, but it never worked. Both of us tried for years to like each other, because our mothers thought it would be nice for one reason or another; we went to little parties, and had mutual friends, and remained consistently cold and disinterested.

Josephine had blond hair and was solidly built, as a child. She was rather malicious, I think, and I remember that once when I was tagging along shyly behind Red Sutherland, my first and only love in schools until I was well on toward marriage, Josephine in a small gang of my friends spread the word that I had blown a kiss to Red's back or head as he marched on bravely in front of me. This hurt me. I would have liked to blow a kiss to him, but would never have done so. It also insulted me: such a childish gesture, turned into such a lascivious one! I was no dolt, but rather a sensitive proud princess riding behind her knight, whether or not he cared. (He did not.) I felt defiled, no matter how naïvely.

The real thing I still have against Josephine, even now, although by now we well might like each other without cavil, is that once she whispered meanly to a school friend about my mother's looks. This I found, and still find, hard to forgive, and it gave me my first ugly taste of real hate. It must have been in 1918, because Mother was bending over my new sister Norah in her pram at the bottom of the front steps, where the baby lay in the sunshine. Skirts came to the floor or more daringly the ankle then, for a woman of my mother's age and social position, the first of which was about thirty-seven and the second, precarious. She was probably pregnant with my brother David, and her ankles were puffy, and as I watched her tuck the soft white covers about the baby I heard Josephine titter to my other school friend, "Look at her big fat ankles." Ah, there was a flash of rage in me, still felt!

It was the custom for the little girls of one or another neighborhood to meet on the sidewalk in front of their houses and walk to Penn Street School together, in a morning troupe that sometimes held fifteen or so, and I suppose the boys did the same. We never rode bikes, except after school and on Saturdays, and skates were out of the question because of the chancy sidewalks. We walked.

That morning of the slur on my mother's beauty, I knew we would stop for at least eight friends before we got to Penn. For perhaps the first time in my life I was so conscious of being angry that I knew I could not go with them, and especially with the sly secure tittering traitor who had mocked Edith Kennedy's ankles. Mother had suddenly become real and beautiful to me. I wanted to embrace her wildly, which we never did in our family, especially in those early days, and then run out onto the sidewalk and hit Josephine in her blond smug face until all her teeth popped out and her skin turned black and her eyes died.

This would not do, plainly. Instead I gave a bang on the side of the baby's pram, turned away roughly from my mother's tender if preoccupied good-by, and ran around to the back of our house and down the alleys, alone all the way to school. And I was swinging higher than anybody when my own crowd came onto the playground before the bell rang.

Across the street from the Maples, and down a block toward us, so that the house would be only a little north and across from the low brown cottage so full of love and music where the Smiths coughed and rotted, the Fays stayed for several years. Mrs. Fay was very *grande dame*, and always dressed formally for dinner, although they were poor as Job's turkey, according to my mother. When my parents went there, Mrs. Fay simply slung her train over one arm as she carried in the vegetable dishes, I was told later with laughing admiration. They did not even have a Hired Girl, and Mrs. Fay washed her lone child Eleanor's long hair and pressed her middy skirts' countless pleats.

Eleanor was very nice to us, and today might have been called a baby-sitter, on the rare times when Rex and Edith and the Fays would drive into Los Angeles in our Model T for a dinner with wine at Foix's or Marcel's or the Victor Hugo. My sister Anne and I never liked her much, one way or t'other, but I cannot remember why, for she read to us and was not sly or a tattletaler. Later the Fays moved away and she was sent to a fashionable school, and occasionally we heard that she had done things like make a debut (to what, in Southern California?) and get married. Caroline Maple kept in touch with her for a long time, and passed news along to my mother, but it did not seem to move any of us. The Fay we remembered, with varying degrees and reasons, was her father, Charles, always thought of as Charlie.

All I can say now is that he was thin, not as tall as Father, and ineffably distinguished. He wore shabby hunting clothes the way most men dream of doing. He was from Boston, and I loved to hear him talk, although I don't think he ever addressed more than a remote greeting to me. Often he came in for a nip of sherry or beer or a rarer whiskey, before he went on up the street to change into his dinner clothes for the evening ritual of the thin fare he could provide, and I would listen with delight from a nearby room as his elegant high voice hung in the air. My parents were under his spell too, and when he was with them they spoke with more wit, more attention to their own fineness.

He and Rex often went hunting, during several years, and unloaded dead doves or quail from the back of the Ford, late at night. Rex always carried his own weapons, but said that Charlie did the shooting and he was bird dog. Then they stopped going away together, and it was most probably coincidence that about then the Fays left Whittier and never came back, but later I learned that Rex had refused ever to hunt again after a weekend with Charlie in Antelope Valley, where countless sportsmen stoned and clubbed the trusting little fawnlike beasts to death, and then sometimes stripped them of their skins, and mostly left them dead or dying, and went on clubbing and laughing and swigging from their flasks. Before that we had often eaten antelope when Charlie Fay brought us a piece, but from then on we never did, and as far as I can remember, this unwritten taboo covered all game like venison, bear, the occasional wild kid that still turned up in California hills. We did eat birds, but only when people gave them to us, and although my father never shot again, later he liked to go away on fishing trips, mostly for trout, so that he could be with men he enjoyed. (I know he and Charlie parted as friends.)

The only other thing I remember about the Fays, except that he was probably the first man I ever realized was attractive, is that between their small parlor and the dining room hung a curtain made of long strings of eucalyptus buds. I thought this was truly elegant. I think there were colored glass beads now and then on the strings of the scented little nobs, and I would have loved to wrap myself naked in the clicking tinkling spray that hung down with such mystery between the two small crowded ugly rooms.

We never had any such modish fripperies at home, if one overlooks an elaborate edition of *Sesame and Lilies* by Ruskin, and there were a couple of other local status symbols I pined for, but not too strongly, in those days. One was a brass vase, at least two feet tall, in which stalks of pampas grass would stand. This should be placed in a corner of the living room, or perhaps in the entrance hall. If possible, the frothy weird seed pods or whatever they are should be tinted pale lavender and pink and yellow. I have no idea where I got this vision, for we went into almost no homes in Whittier. I can remember only Mrs. Fay's, Miss Brotherton's when I was learning anatomy through inadvertent mathematics, the Smiths', and of course the Thayer Ranch.

There was an old lady who lived out near Jim Town and had an avenue of pampas grass which she sent to a great convention somewhere in America, and Rex interviewed her once, and there was a story about her in the *Saturday Evening Post*. The highway to Los Angeles was lined in those idyllic days with silvery olive trees on her big ranch, and when we drove past the avenue of thick tall grasses that curved away from it we slowed down to look at them, plumy and beautiful and even famous. But a brass vase filled with them? Where did I find this dream?

(And of course it seemed a shame to me, for several years, that we did not have hanging baskets of smilax ferns on our small front porch. Other people did. Nice people did, especially nice old ladies, which probably I thought my mother to be and took for granted that Grandmother was, at least socially. Mother was adamant. She hated, for one thing, to have to remember to water anything. For another, as she confessed to me many years later, she had always considered smilax middle-class and vulgar, especially in hanging baskets, because she had been told that the only way to keep them flourishing was to give them diluted human urine. This haunted her, perhaps with some titillation, for I remember her pointing out especially beautiful fountains of smilax on other people's porches and then laughing scornfully.)

South of the Fay house, one or two doors, lived a tiny ancient Kentucky colonel and first two devoted daughters and then one. Once there was an automobile parade past our house, on Memorial Day, and he rode in an open Pierce Arrow in his Civil War uniform, not seeing anything, but fixed in a regal salute. Sometimes he sat on his front porch in a wheelchair, like Old Lady Ransome and Mrs. Worsham, but we knew enough not to bother him either. I think Mother liked the daughters, but they were still very unhappy about the Civil War and what it had done to them, and Mother was very busy.

Next to the Colonel, in a modest cottage compared to his faded yellow barn of a house, lived two little girls for a time, and they were friends of ours. Their mother had migraine headaches, which one of them later developed, and their father worked on the *News*, I think as a reporter. Helen and Alice the girls were, and Helen was almost too old for Anne and me, and already prone to biliousness and withdrawal. Although they moved away, they continued in the same school as we did, and that was fine, because Alice was a girl one wants to see again.

Between them and us was a big ugly house where for a few years lived the Cutlers. There were several children. The oldest girl, Ethel, occasionally stayed in our living room at night when Mother and Father went out, which was increasingly rare as our family grew bigger and Rex grew busier and Edith grew heavier and more asocial. There was a sister about my age whose name I have conveniently forgotten. She was the first person I saw in Whittier.

All our furniture was being moved from a dray into the house. I stood far to the north of the small front lawn, against a spindly hedge which later fattened. On the other side, in the middle of her own scrap of Bermuda grass, stood a little girl sucking her thumb with one hand and fondling her private parts with the other. We looked at each other several times, for I was interested in what she was doing, but we never spoke, and the process of moving into the house was basically a better show. That night when I was lying in my bed in the new room, a wonderful big screened porch like a bird's nest high at the back of the house, my mother came to kiss me and welcome me there, and she asked me if I had noticed what the little neighbor was doing. I think I had almost forgotten, but I recalled it, and she said that she did not want me ever to bother myself that way, because it would make me nervous. I wondered what that might mean, but did not question it for many years.

The Cutlers took a Sunday paper, and so had Funnies, which Grandmother did not allow in our house, and Anne and I became tricky at an early age in evading the Blue Laws. Ethel would bring them over in the afternoon, and we would meet at the far end of the long pergola of Cecil Brunner roses which led to our garage, Anne and I and a few of Ethel's siblings there, all of us loaded with heavy Bible picture books. We would lie down close together on our stomachs on the grass between the two car tracks of cement, with our five or six heads pointed away from Grandmother's room, and Ethel would read every delicious caption of every page of the Funnies as we kept our Sunday Books open in front of us. We knew, as if in a secret language, the Katzenjammer Kids, Mutt and Jeff, and another saga about a very tall thin willowy character in a prison uniform whose name I now forget. There was also Krazy Kat, which I did not really enjoy for years, except for all those bricks that could close any gap in his conversation.

It seems strange that the Katzenjammers did not suffer from the War, when German Measles were called Liberty, as also were Hamburger Steaks, and when somebody threw half a brick through our side window near the piano.

This was because Mother was playing, and she and Rex and Uncle Evans were singing, some German student songs in variously bad accents, no doubt bolstered by either beer or white wine and a common tenderness for one another. I cannot remember that a curtain was ever pulled in our house anywhere, so there in broad electric light were the editor of the town daily, his wife who had once lived in Germany itself, and her uppity professor-brother from the East, laughing and singing in the enemy's own tongue! Somebody lobbed the brick rather timidly into the subversive group: it went through the glass, all right, but most of the shattered stuff stayed in place, so that the next morning when Anne and I came downstairs after our innocent slumbers, everything was fairly tidy, and by that night a new pane had been installed. I feel certain that Edith cried, for she wept easily and well, although hardly as often as she wished. The German music was put away. Uncle Evans went back to his law classes and Rex to his desk, each mum for his own reasons.

For a while after we went to Whittier there was one bakery

going, run by a German, and usually at Christmas our turkey would be stuffed and taken down to be roasted in his undying oven. I think this happened a few times with large pots of beans, too, which stayed there overnight. The baker left town in 1916, to fight at home, and his brother-in-law took over.

The day before his Grand Opening, he sent home with Rex a great platter of gleaming sweet cakes, called Butter Flies because they made the butter fly, his new ad would say in the paper. We had a special treat that afternoon, and sat around in the dining room and drank pitchers of milk and ate the delicious surprise.

Grandmother tasted one, pronounced it good, and then dismissed it scornfully as a bribe. Edith, who was a helpless gourmande as well as a mild cynic, could not resist eating several cakes, while she murmured coolly to her husband that they could not possibly keep to this standard and would soon be like all other bought stuff, not fit to have in the house. Anne and I devoted ourselves to keeping far enough within the bounds of courtesy not to be noticed, while we got away with more delicacies than we had ever eaten before. It was a fine occasion, on which I think my father drank a beer and sat watching us from behind a cloud of slowly exhaled Bull Durham smoke.

Not long after that, though, the second German baker left town, and this time it was because we had entered the War and it was being said that he had put ground glass in some of his excellent bread. It was a sad thing, and my mother held her hand over her brown eyes, and then withdrew to her darkened room.

There was one other commercial war casualty in our town: our butcher, who had lived there for many years but with a German name, disappeared after several weeks of harassment and gradual bankruptcy, because a little boy, locally famous for his disobedient and ornery ways, had stuck his finger in the sausage slicer. Rumor said that the butcher went right on making and selling sausages from that machine, with the flesh of an AMERICAN CHILD!

There were, most of the time, two Jews who ran the town's variety store. They seemed to change, perhaps all in one family but spending a winter in turn, for their health, from some place like Chicago. They were always small, quiet, and kind, and I loved to go into the store for something like shoelaces or a paper of pins. I think that once a little daughter came to Penn Street School for a few months, but I do not remember seeing her in the store. Jews were simply not *there*, in Whittier. They did not really exist, except within themselves I hope. Their temple must have been long miles away. Nobody spoke to them. I cannot imagine what they did for proper food if they were Orthodox. I prefer not to think of their isolation.

Catholics were a step above Jews, socially, and one or two below the Episcopalians. This was largely because we were all white, instead of having a few Mexican communicants. Rex had one very good friend, a Catholic who ran a garage in Whittier, who finally was frozen out of town (as my father was supposed to have been by 1913 or so). He moved to Santa Ana or Anaheim, or some place like that. He was never recognized as a friend by my mother, who took a consistently dim view of her husband's offbeat intimates.

After the Catholic left town, Rex bowed to pressure and became a Mason, which may or may not be important to his picture. By then he had learned what a small religious community can do to a human being, all in the name of the Lord, and it is probable that in Masonry as in Rotary and the Salvation Army he believed there was enough fairness left to counteract the bigotry all these institutions have been accused of. It is one of the many things we never discussed, later. I do not know if we would have been able to. We were a hot-tongued and articulate family, and by the time Time itself had cooled us, it was too late: we were dead, or physically deaf, or spiritually numb and wary.

There was a small Catholic community in and around Whittier, mostly Mexican and illiterate, and some of my friends in school, therefore, were Catholics, but we never bothered about rituals like going to Sunday school together, or comparing Friday menus. We learned to read and write, at school, and we played wildly and thoroughly, and then parted every twilight, content as calves going to their own barns from a common meadow.

My mother was not used to having people of different-colored skins near her, and was shy about it, but Rex had it heavily on his mind that the living conditions in Jim Town, out around Pio Pico's rotting house on the banks of the Rio Hondo, were not right for man nor beast. He found that the Catholic priest in Whittier was the townsman most in touch with the people there, and they began to work together. I am sorry that I cannot know what they got done, in that Mexican ghetto of so long ago. Certainly it is not the kind of action that would possibly result today from the friendship and concern of two good men, but at least it sufficed for a pair of renegades, and they continued a long life of golf, mild tippling, and zeal, both of them social mavericks but shrugged off, if not actively condoned, by the good Quakers.

Much later, and perhaps as a result of this suspicious activity of the priest and the editor, the Friends installed a small mission in Jim Town, and Rex asked its earnest heavy-breathing pastor to give all of us Spanish lessons. It was doomed to quick failure. Mother gave up at once, and retired to her genteel romance with everything John Galsworthy ever wrote but especially *The Forsyte Saga*. Anne and I were Wild Indians at that period, and could not long tolerate the endless afternoons with Señor Cobos and his fat little daughter Amparo, as we sat politely and drank lemonade and tried to understand the difference between Thee and You (if we had only been Quakers!). Finally Rex went alone to Jim Town and sweated over Spanish verbs, which were suddenly fun for him when he began escaping to Guadalajara, once a year or so. I have often felt sorry about being so stupid with Señor Cobos.

Later I studied Spanish hard and happily in school, and when I was much older I went to tedious night classes in Adult Education to recall some of it, and I can still read and hear it with pleasure. Of course I have never been hurt, except perhaps indirectly, because of another language I love besides my own. Nobody ever threw a piece of brick through a window because I was singing "La Cucaracha" or "Plaisirs d'Amour." But my mother never sang a German song again, after that night in about 1917—nor spoke a word of the language she had learned in several years in Germany, except when one of us would sneeze and wait happily for her *Gesundheit!*

9

Culture and Music
and All That

The Woman's Clubhouse was at the north end of our alley, and I was soon allowed to walk up there, if I held my little sister's hand the whole way. My mother was often there, too, being the good wife to the new editor in town, and I think she was once made president, after some years of proving her mettle. Anne and I liked to stand in the back doorway of the big shingle building, and watch the ladies bustle about the kitchen, preparing for a luncheon or an occasional evening party. As I look back on it, Mother and her friend Mrs. Hersh were the only non-Quakers, but they were nicely treated, because they were *all* nice people; ladies who belonged to the Club *were* "nice," banded together to better conditions or uphold culture or something like that—and of course most of them had children who might have to go to school together . . . willy-nilly.

Outside the low brown building, with its ample kitchen and its big waxed hall, was a row of the most beautiful geraniums I ever saw in my life. They bore enormous salmon-colored blossoms. They were taller than I, thick against the brown wooden walls. The leaves were like green velvet. Anne and I stood close to them, and smelled the subtle sting of the bruised flesh, a perfume which comes out as it does from the same fleeting touch on a tomato plant or a chrysanthemum. By the time I was old enough to go every Saturday to dancing classes in the Hall which seemed to swell into dreamlike proportions, so that waltzing slowly across it, step-slide-together, was like climbing up the inside of a giant soap bubble, the geraniums had been taken out, and soon after that I think the redwood walls had been stuccoed, but I was not as sad then as I feel now, about losing them.

One night I was taken to a Reading given in the Clubhouse by a very old man. I loved it. He intoned some things that made everybody laugh, and then declaimed from Shakespeare and I think Dickens. I was pleased by his wonderful voice, and by the ambiguity of his giving a reading with nothing to read from. Mother and Mrs. Moorhead from across the street took me, but Anne and her first lover, Tolbert Moorhead, stayed home with our maid. This added to my appreciation of the spree, of course. On the way home, down Painter and not through the alley, the two ladies laughed gently about the apparent unsteadiness of the old actor, who was said to be alcoholically unfit for active theater any more. It was a good thing the Woman's Club had a sturdy reading stand to lean on, they said . . . and I thought, *Yes, even with no book on it,* and chuckled at one of my first unspoken jokes.

The memories of the dancing classes are not very good ones, or rather they are unimportant. Once, just after we moved to the Ranch when I was going on eleven and the big Lewis family lived in our house on Painter, Rex and Edith and Anne and I went up there for lunch before the Saturday afternoon session, to which all four of the Lewis kids had to go too. I learned that Ned, the oldest boy, had pleaded off . . . schoolwork or something. This made me furious, for he was only a little older than I, and I knew that he planned to sneak over to the College and watch the football game which all our parents were lightheartedly heading for, while Bill and John and little Hope and my sister Anne and I shuffled clumsily about on the enormous slick floor of the Clubhouse.

I got Mother into a corner by the Victrola cabinet, and whispered to her that I wished I could stay home with Ned, and study or something. She said firmly that I must go, to learn how to dance nicely and to help my sister if she needed me. I whispered back, for the first time in my life, and with a dreadful feeling of burned bridges, rivers crossed, sinking ships, "I won't! No, I won't." Mother looked amazed, and then said very softly, "I am surprised. I will have to speak with you after the class, at home."

That was all. It was a dreadful moment. I got through the class all right, and Ned was smugly back at his desk by the time our rosy parents came home, and all I remember about my meeting with Mother after we got to the Ranch is that she did it fast . . . told Rex what I had said, that is. No blame. No reproaches. He probably expressed his regret and disapproval, and I skulked off. It was quiet, but not painless, like a lot of our family confrontations.

Across from the Woman's Clubhouse was Bailey Street Park . . . and it still is. The Clubhouse is now an elaborate and elegant structure, compared to the old brown hall with its kitchen and presumably its toilets. The Park is still a lovely leafy place. I forget if it has a bandstand, from my quick sight of it a few years ago, but there used to be a good one.

I soon earned permission to take Anne across the street into the park. There were none of the "action" structures now considered necessary for bored children; sand piles and swings and suchlike were confined to the school grounds. But there were fine shady walks, both wide and narrow, green lawns with no prohibiting signs on them, wonderful trash-cans with swinging lids; and of course there was always the tall grand temple of music and culture, I think octagonal, open to all the air and with a sturdy railing around every side but the one the wide stairs mounted to. We never went up into it. I don't think any child in Whittier ever did. It was for musicians, preachers, mayors, and suchlike.

I went with my grandmother to a few revivals in the Park . . . or at least they were preachings, by sturdy but oldish men groomed in the Billy Sunday technique. I enjoyed them, because I was staying up later than my little sister, I was with Grandmother outside a church (the only other place I ever went with her), and the actor was always good for one of my silent chuckles. During the War, I went to some real rantin'-ravin' rallies, probably for the Red Cross, in which I heard with real interest about German atrocities and Belgian infants with their arms torn off at the wrist, the elbow, and the shoulder, beautiful nurses shot at dawn after infamies only slightly hinted at because of the tender hearts and years of many people like me in the audience. As a precocious reader of the Grimm brothers, I appreciated these sadistic details, and returned to my safe kind American home with the untroubled soul of a real innocent.

The music in the Park was not very important, except that it was pure enjoyment for Anne and me. Most of the concerts were given in the afternoon, and people vied for the few benches if they were elderly like Grandmother, or sat on the thick cool grass if they were younger, like my mother or my Aunt Gwen. Mother was fussy about music, after several years in Dresden, and winced audibly, which is a rare but attainable feat, at most of the notes and almost all of the selections. Aunt Gwen was completely undemanding, and rocked voluptuously to the beat of "Barcarolle," was hushed and still during "My Rosary," and almost stood up and gave a Kipling-esque salute when any band went into "On the Road to Mandalay." She was more fun than anybody, in the Park (and elsewhere, for the most part).

On Sunday afternoons, as she became more and more our steady companion, one of our favorite stays would be in the

Park. (The other was by the Reservoir, but that meant a little climbing, and Anne never liked to exert herself if she could walk or remain stationary on one level.) Often, when Aunt Gwen could finish feeding her father and Brother Raymond, she would come early for us, probably so that Edith and Rex might take a long ride in the Model T and later the Maxwell, and we would sit under a chosen bush in Bailey Park and eat bread and butter and gnaw on the drumsticks Father had saved for us from the Sunday chicken. It was fine. Aunt Gwen taught us without ever seeming to: how to leave things tidy, where to hide crumbs for the other animals without being messy, what the names of the birds were, how to be very still for watching them.

When there was to be an afternoon concert, we were neat again and well fed for it, and listened happily to every toot and flourish. As I remember, some old man usually prayed briefly before the music, and Aunt Gwen always said Ah-men, although everyone else said Amen.

Aside from the Sunday afternoon concerts from the band-stand, and the stuff Mother practiced for church or remembered from her past, our music consisted for several years of the regular Sunday afternoon parade of the band from the boys' reformatory on the western edge of town. (We got a Victrola when I was nine.)

Perhaps it was only once a month that the boys were stuffed into their hand-me-down jackets (navy blue with very grimy white edgings, I think). Ridiculously small or large military caps were perched on their heads, and with battered instruments just as ill-fitting, they were marched in a ragged formation up from the institution onto Greenleaf, left to Bailey or Hadley at about Newlin, east to Painter, down past our house, and on down Greenleaf again to the fenced confines of their correctional "home."

They passed our house in early afternoon, always on a Sunday except perhaps on something like the Glorious

Fourth. (The subject is too depressing to warrant any research by me. . . .) I think they were boys aged from fifteen
to about twenty. They kept their eyes straight ahead, or on
the music stuck into little racks in front of their horns and
trumpets. They always played something in our block on
Painter, probably because Father was more than professionally interested in the school and was soon a good and
even dear friend of Fred Nelles, for whom the reformed re-
form school was later named. Anne and I tried waving
timidly, but plainly the boys had their hands full, as they
dragged through things like "Onward, Christian Soldiers." It
is sad to think about now, but then it was an exciting adventure for us in our innocence. (Almost every day, before
Mr. Nelles changed things, the siren would blow for an
escape over the high-wire fence, and the first words Anne
ever said were, "Boy gone!" whenever she heard it. This was
considered amusing—at first.)

With the impact of the War on our little enclave, society
loosened up a bit, and some of the non-Quaker businessmen
like my father were allowed to become energetic and important in the many "drives": Liberty Bonds, Thrift Stamps,
Red Cross, all of them. Rex not only spoke well but was
handsome, and he went around the county giving short pep
talks in movie houses and even church halls. He was called
a Three-Minute Man, and we boasted about him, although
it did not overly impress the other girls, most of whose fathers
were involved in the same hysterical pattern.

Once Mary Pickford, complete with curls, came to Whittier
for one of the fund-raisings, and Rex, *our father*, was told to
get her on stage and in general to see to her. He had nothing
to lose, socially, since he was not a Quaker, and was known
to enjoy a good drink now and then and to have seen plenty
of heathen goings-on as a reporter in places like Chicago. . . .
He liked America's Sweetheart, as did all of us out front, and

later I was puzzled when he said he was sorry for her. He gave no answer, at least to my Why? but Mother undoubtedly quizzed him more fully and seemed smoothed by whatever his reply may have been.

Another time there was a full evening of local musical talent, given in the High School auditorium for the Red Cross . . . or perhaps another issue of Liberty Bonds. Uncle Mac wore or rather was pushed and pounded into a British uniform which his son Fred had worn in Flanders or wherever he was killed in about 1915, and somehow managed to roar his way cheerfully and manfully through all the verses and choruses of "Mandalay." He brought down the house. How proud we were, that he was *our* dear friend! Mother was home, great with child, but Aunt Gwen mopped a few tears from her large pink cheeks as he puffed through the whole thing again for an encore.

That same night a small simpering woman embarrassed Anne and me by pretending she was *young*. (This syndrome starts in early adolescence in most people, and I think we may have been precocious in resenting it that soon. . . .) She fluttered her bony old arms and switched her ruffled skirts and sang in a high affected squeal about "Comin' Through the Rye," with many rollings of her baggy eyes and puckerings of her withered face. My sister and I writhed and wriggled, and finally I let out an embarrassing titter, as unexpected as a sneeze in church. Nobody heard me but Aunt Gwen. She gave me a chilling look. On the way home, up the dark excitement of Philadelphia toward our house so far away in the night, with the overhead streetlights swinging at the intersections, she told me I should never do that again, and then we all began to laugh fairly noisily, considering the late hour, and she agreed that the crone should stay in the rye-field. Uncle Mac, on the other hand, had been heroic. Later Edith was a little mocking, perhaps from jealousy at missing the show, about his getting into Fred's uniform, and then out again, but we had nothing but doting praise for him.

There was a movie house called The Berry Grand, where occasionally we were allowed to go for the Saturday matinees with two or three other female peers, and a lady played the piano there who later, when I was about nine, shifted either up or down a cultural notch and handled the step-together-slide stuff at the Woman's Club. The latter was not half as exciting, at least for me as her devoted listener, but it was probably easier on her. Now and then she would add a nostalgic bass chord or arpeggio to whatever we had just finished trudging through, and I always caught at it gratefully. Edith once told me, casually and somewhat patronizingly, that this lady also was piano for the trio that provided dance music for the occasional nights of respectable debauchery at the Club.

I don't know who went to these routs, besides my parents, Uncle Mac, and a few social renegades and non-believers like the Mattesons and, rarely, the Hershes. Once my parents took Aunt Gwen along, correctly a few months after she had lost her husband of one night, to give her a taste of gaiety. Aunt Gwen's mother was still alive, and spent many days making tiny pink velvet bows to scatter over a tent-sized frock of grey silk. And it must have been a dreadful evening. I heard Mother groaning about the ball-dress, a monstrosity with Aunt Gwen's robust coloring and size. Rex danced with her. So did Uncle Mac and Mr. Matteson. Then they all did it again. Mother muttered to Grandmother for weeks about it, but after that night when Aunt Gwen came in from her house next door and twirled happily if heavily for Anne and me, to show us her beautiful frock, we never saw it again, nor heard any mention of it from her.

And that is all I remember about the Whittier Woman's Club, which I believe is by now more properly called

Women's. I have a copy of its cookbook, compiled by the ladies in 1928-9, but almost identical with the one Father's back room turned out in Michigan in about 1905. The recipes are just as ineptly phrased, and one senses that many of the most prized ones have deliberately cheated on the Secret Ingredient that had made them locally famous. There are many signed by women I knew, whose children I had loved and hated in school. What I like best, though, is an ad for the Worsham Dairy.

By then Mrs. Worsham was dead. I think her faithful daughter Helen had gone away. The Worsham Place was gone too, to make way for the sprawling campus of the College. But the name evokes one of the clearest memories I store in my vaults, willy-nilly, to bring out at unexpected moments like this.

The house was the nearest I ever came to know of a California that was already almost gone when we landed there in 1911 or so. It stood at the farthest end of Philadelphia, after the straight sidewalks ended and the road twisted down through a canyon and then up to the long house in its grove of olives and peppers and eucalyptus. A wide porch ran its length, with some barrels of curing olives at the western end. The air always stirred. There were friendly mongrel dogs, and plenty of tumbling Mexican babies. After my sister and I made our manners to Mrs. Worsham, we went off to get some cool water with the little brown boys and girls, and Mother sat talking quietly in the cool air with the strange old lady.

She was in a wheelchair, monstrously crippled with arthritis. Mother told us not to feel sad or stare, if her hands were lying on her knees, outside her lap-rug, for they were not hands at all any more, but like pieces of a very old grape-root. We did stare a little, perhaps, but were not repelled. The face was wonderful, very brown and serene, with large bright eyes. She could not turn her head, but her eyes in their generous sockets rolled and darted and followed everything. (I tried this in front of several mirrors, but soon gave up.) We walked to her porch now and then, to listen to the sweet voices of the women, with Mother gradually catching her breath after the climb up the two hills. Once I asked Mrs. Worsham about the big barrels, and she told me all I know, even now, about the right way to cure olives. A big dark woman came out from the kitchen (I never went inside the house) and lifted me up, and let me stir a long spoon around in the black juice, to feel the fruit, and then lift some out to share with the other children. I know that we often got jars of them from the barrels, but I don't remember ever eating them at home: they were outlandish for people raised on the plains of Iowa, and it was too bad Mrs. Worsham wasted them on us.

She grew worse, and could not see people at all, but the milk from her dairy, "Guaranteed and Grade 'A' Raw . . . Special for Babies," came every day to our back door. Once Helen Worsham took about ten of us on a long wagon ride to hills where a huge cemetery now lies tidily. She was a nice rounded young woman, patient with such a mob of children, and very generous with delicious sandwiches and fruit, but it is the fine old lady I shall always remember, and her dark eyes, and the shade coming through the floating fronds of the peppers and eucalyptus trees onto the long cool porch.

And a long time later I learned from my mother that it was Mrs. Worsham, sitting so still in her wheelchair, who pulled the wires that made it possible for the wife of the new editor to be accepted so quickly into the Woman's Club, to work up through the Garden Section and the Rules Committee and the Entertainment Committee to be, one crowning day, elected President, even though she was firmly and forever an Episcopalian in the midst of Friends, singing her papish anthems on Sundays and even dancing now and then on Saturday nights, step-slide-together. . . .

10

Lightened Heart
and Quickened Energies

The Whittier school system had a general over-all music teacher in its primary grades, who hopped like an exhausted rabbit from Penn to Bailey and then to a new school in the southwest of town, and from room to room. I think her name was Mrs. Graham. She taught us a surprising lot of tunes and words in her weekly lessons. I don't remember her in the first grade, but from then on I looked forward pleasurably to her "day," and sang loud and clear as I sat with my feet flat on the floor and my hands folded on the desk in front of me, as required of us.

Mrs. Graham always had words on the blackboard behind her, and used a pointer. She taught us to draw the five straight lines for marking clefs, notes, bars, all that. I knew it already: our big hymnal at home, the little ones in church, Mother's music from bound volumes of Chopin and Schumann to sheets of "Zwei Dunkel Augen" and "Aloha Oe." (Perhaps this was my first intoxicating but dangerously destructive taste of being just a little bit ahead of my lessons?)

Mrs. Graham was strong on Stephen Foster and taught us

at least fifteen of his best-known songs by the time I was ready for the fifth grade. Now I could not and would not sing most of the lyrics I bleated out so insensately and happily then, but the music was perfect for its rhythm in our heads. We sang everything at exactly the same speed and with the same complete unawareness of the lyrics, whether it was "Gone Are the Days When My Heart Was Young and Gay," or some jig dance plunked out along the old levee. What was a levee, anyway? We never thought to ask. One-two-three, *one*-two-three, through intimations of slavery, war, sorrow which never reached us: we were innocents, and therefore pure and unquestioning, temporarily anyway.

I was probably the only one in school who had ever seen a real live Negro, and it never occurred to me that Old Black Joe and his Massa, whatever that was, in the cold cold ground, and the cotton fields away, had anything to do with our Cynthia, so long and well regretted. And there was no more reason for Mrs. Graham to explain to us the sweetened laments of homesick slaves in Dixie than there would be for a kindergarten teacher to outline the political implications of the first mocking jingles about Humpty Dumpty, Georgie-Porgie, and even Miss Muffet. We wanted to sing, and that we did, set off by the magical tuning fork, learning the new words from the end of our guide's pointer on the blackboard. It was rousing. It was fun. And on Fridays when we assembled in the six-sided hall in the middle of the building, and Miss Raymer thumped firmly away at the upright piano, we really ripped through not only Stephen Foster but "America the Beautiful," and "Keep the Home Fires Burning (while your hearts are yearning . . . 'til the boys come home . . .)." We sang them all at one steady pace, loudly, gaily. Mrs. Graham beamed at us, and we felt fine, our adrenalin flowing healthily in time to the music, our minds clicking out the unimportant words like well-oiled little time bombs with prudently delayed fuses.

In a songbook published in Chicago in 1888 and called *Day School Gems*, the preface says, in part, and with a sincerity impossible to smile at too broadly:

> Music in school is like sunshine after the shower; music in school will lighten the heart and quicken the ideas and energies of the pupil; music in school is like loving and encouraging words from father, mother, or teacher; it softens the heart and smooths all discord. Music in school, properly directed, would have prevented the great rebellion; teach the children to sing "My Country 'Tis of Thee," "The Star-Spangled Banner," "Nearer My God to Thee," and they will love their country, fight for the stars and stripes, and honor God.
>
> The teachers in our schools are building and shaping the political, moral, and religious destinies of the world. Build for country, home, and God, and the nation will sing your praise on earth, and chant with you in eternity the songs of the Great Builder and Teacher.

It is hard for me to believe that "the great rebellion," or any inner revolution, could have been *prevented* by learning to sing "The Star-Spangled Banner" in school, but it is a comforting certainty that in times of stress we often open our mouths and, with words or without, assert ourselves above and beyond the level of speech. Prisoners, slaves, the condemned: we still sing.

What puzzles me is that few people sing now when they are happy. Perhaps it is that they are not? There are few clubs or societies in America that are created only so that people can meet together and sing. There is one national chain, in which so-called barber-shop harmonizing is done, often beautifully. There are groups of mothers, of fathers, of mothers and fathers. There are small, almost secret, clubs where a few people meet to sing rounds or sea chanteys. But spontaneous music is rare here.

I suppose that if a young man put back his head at two in the morning on a street in Detroit or Santa Ana, and belted out part of an aria from *The Marriage of Figaro*, he would be arrested. But that happened in Aix the last time I was there, just before the Festival of Music opened and the stage-hands were coming home from a final rehearsal. And in French Switzerland, the bread boy who flew past our windows before dawn on his bicycle, with a big basket of hot long loaves on his back, yodeled like a celestial banshee as he shot down toward the lake shore.

Here at home, though, in 1927 or so, college students would drink just enough bootleg rye and then walk to the girls' dorm, and bunch together for a good half hour of sobbing, wailing, howling, lovely near-to-close harmony, under any and all third-floor windows. Nobody stopped them. Behind the dark icy windowpanes we young ladies would feel adored, warm, uplifted. Far below us the happy dogs bayed, hunched together instinctively, a pack of girl-thirsty half-drunk immature examples of what we all were supposed to want to mate with eventually. One of them, I remember, wore the second and better raccoon coat on campus. He was said to be the son of a Chicago bootlegger, and the pusher for whatever booze was available. He was a darling little fellow, what could be seen of him behind all the opulent fur, and he had a voice that soared with the eunuchistic subtleties of a well-trained choirboy into our fairly nubile chambers. He did all the solos, especially extra recitatives and choruses, on things like "Sweetheart of Sigma Chi." The boys who could afford liquor and liked to serenade accepted him. Otherwise he was a loner, and got good grades, and looked right through people like me.

But there was still that corny loud uninhibited *music!* I do not hear it any more, on the streets at least. It is a good sign, a voice from the underblows, that so many young people now are picking, no matter how ineptly and fleetingly, at guitars and banjos and zithers, and sitting cross-legged tootling on recorders.

Meanwhile I whistle and hum, and when lately I was asked *what,* I realized that it is mostly tunes based on what I heard when I was little.

Mother had a nice repertory of the more assailable *lieder* she had warbled in Dresden. She knew things like the score of Handel's *Messiah,* which she scoffed at but sang. She knew lots of church anthems, and of course the Hymnal. We seemed to hear these mostly at St. Matthias, but they were part of the family noise.

Father whistled, but never in the house, and now and then, safely out the back door, would produce a jew's-harp from his yard-pants pocket and twang out something like "Turkey in the Straw." Mother disdained this instrument as a part of yokelry, and when Rex's front teeth began to lose their grip, he stopped his jolly yet sad music. He, and then I, played the harmonica a little, always safely out of Mother's hearing, but we were no good. Father with his big hands could rip out rather dramatic but completely incorrect swipes of sound, which any teacher would have winced at.

Once he decided to take a correspondence course and learn how to play the piano fast right then and there. Mother, and I am sorry about this but understanding, put her foot down. It is too bad, but that is what happened. *She* was the one who had studied in Europe and could still stumble through those bits and pieces of Chopin's Nocturnes. *She* appreciated music. *Ladies* did arpeggios, not men. Father was an American small-town newspaperman, without classical education and therefore insensitive to the finer things of life. His place was in his office, working. Her place was at home, arbiter of culture. (This was a common syndrome at the turn of the present century in America, and of course explains although does not condone, much that has happened since.)

At church, we sang with genteel or at least Episcopalian lustiness. On plain Sundays the effect was one of whuddery well-meaning. The vested choir's aim was to sound as much like Westminster Abbey as possible, with anywhere from three to eight (Easter, Christmas) devout but untrained and rather elderly voices. Mother held firm in mezzo-soprano. If Aunt Gwen was on hand, she and Uncle Mac stayed almost dashingly in the lower ranges. Mrs. Emory, Mrs. Aldrich, Matty Matteson's birdlike wife: they piped along loyally as they swayed up the aisle in their protective vestments (could they possibly have done it in plain street clothes?), behind the crucifix.

It is fortunate that my father, raised as a militant Methodist, seldom went to church. He liked to rock back and forth a little, involving himself in the rhythm if not the statement. He would put back his head and sing out, if a tune came along that was of his persuasion, something gutsy like "Onward, Christian Soldiers." This tendency to break through the thin shell of churchly restraint, as practiced in Whittier by the Episcopalians, embarrassed me when I got to the Difficult Stage, but for many years I enjoyed it and rocked with it. At about twelve I began to find it painful, and was glad that Christmas and Easter came but once a year.

It seems strange, on our shrinking globe, that in the expansive unthinking years when I was a child in Whittier I did not learn anything about the music around me, except in school and church. The only contact I had with Mexican music, which was surely alive in Jim Town anyway, was from *The Mission Play,* in San Gabriel.

That was called a pageant, I believe, and was encouraged by things like Chambers of Commerce wanting to woo people from the Middle West with promises of picturesque native customs, as well as free oranges. It was written by John Steven McGroarty, who while I was still fairly young became a Grand Old Man in Southern California journalism as well as culture. It was housed in a wonderful theatre, part tent, part boardwalk, in the little settlement, mostly Mexican, with its fine mission. It was about the coming of Fra Junípero Serra to San Diego, and then his slow strong walk up the Pacific coast, with a new mission just one day's journey past the last night's rest, and loyal loving captive Indians learning happily how to raise grapes for wine, cattle for leather, all that. There were of course *conquistadores* in clanking armor, beautiful Spanish maidens, noble priests, handsome half-breed villains. *The Mission Play* had, in other words, every-thing but Abraham Lincoln and a pet dog in it, and it ran happily for many years, until about 1927 when it "expanded," just in time to have the Great Crash send it into deserved bankruptcy for building a fat, vulgar, stucco and tile and velvet temple to what it and McGroarty had once been. With radio and talking films, who cared about watching a bunch of amateurs bellowing around on a small-town stage?

The old playhouse was a marvel of inventive desperation, for money was a day-by-day acquisition, from what I have been told. It came in dribs and drabs, now from the Southern Pacific Railroad, now from Pacific Electric, again from St. Bartholomew's College in Monrovia or some place like that. Excursions, special rates, group tours: they fed the kitty. Nice elderly ladies from Pasadena took Eastern visitors to the matinée in their electrics, with a hamper of lunch. People like my sister Anne and me went at least twice a season, of course on paper tickets which Father did not hesitate to use in payment of all his enthusiastic free publicity.

Halfway around the barely sloping floor of the theatre proper was a row of boxes, in a U-shape, and that is where we always sat. They had painted canvas sides, with the crests of all the houses of Spain flamboyantly splashed on them. One time we would be in Aragon; another, Castile. We soon learned how to sit without scraping our camp chairs against the noisy wooden floor.

The intermission was almost as good as the play, and equally familiar. All around the three sides of the rickety hall off the street was a covered arcade, with soft warm sunlight coming through its canvas sides and roof, and there before us, on low tables so that we could see every window, every tile and chimney, were replicas of all the missions Serra had founded. For a few seasons Anne and I would start correctly at the left exit from the hall, and move slowly with all the other gawkers around behind the stage and up the right side, to the last entrancing little carved and painted model. Gradually we got to know the ones we most wanted to look at, without being pushed: San Gabriel, right down the street; San Juan Capistrano, not too far from Laguna where we lived in summers; Santa Barbara which Mother had visited. . . . In the plaster fields Indians planted and harvested. In the patios the Franciscans set long tables with food for travelers descending from a coach outside the Mission, and one brother hurried up the outside chapel stairs to sound the bell. It was a fine dream, and I have often wondered what patient wizards shaped it for us, and where it went.

Inside again, it was usually Aunt Gwen who sat waiting for us in our box, and the orchestra, different every time we were there, would be whipping into some Mexican music, toned down for the American audience of those days, but still real, since everybody who could hold a trombone or a fiddle in the little town was a stand-by in the pit. It was the same on stage, except for the few principals, who were enlisted from the growing ranks in Hollywood of one-time Shakespearean actors. The cast was, in other words, local. There was no need to import Indians, Mexicans, Spaniards, half-breeds, even evil white invaders, for they had been born and raised within shouting distance of the playhouse, and from what I remember they found the annual season of *The Mission Play* a continuing fiesta. I assume they also got some extra change for it, but possibly that did not much matter to the constantly changing crowd of "natives" prancing and yelling and dancing on the ample stage.

By the time we had seen the play a few times, we could have been just as much at home in it as any of the local children who played Indians, wild at first and then happily busy after the Franciscans showed them the Light. I envied them. And it was fun to guess who was whose uncle or mother, in real life, from the way they acted on stage. Once the star of the big fiesta scene gave an impudent young on-looker a good sound slap, and we knew that she was his mother and that he would see her after the show.

She was wonderful, the only character I remember truly, besides the saintlike Serra: a very short fat woman, but solid, with the tiniest most twinkling feet I have ever seen. She had a few parts all through the play, as servant to old Serra and so on, but in the Fiesta she suddenly threw off her shawl and there she was, in a giddy costume of silks and sequins, with little red shoes on the feet that had been shuffling in the dust! Sometimes she danced for half an hour, with everybody on stage part of it, like a good jam session now. She was beautiful, as small and heavy as a fine little heifer, except that she plainly had several offspring playing extras, and was perhaps fifty years old. When she danced, she was just what the music told her to be, and for her the music was beautiful too, inspired.

When the play was over (and it was a sad ending because Serra died, and the sun set behind the painted ocean where earlier a real galleon, tiny but important, had sailed into the view of the frightened cowering savages), the orchestra played as jauntily as it could to cheer us. Adios, adios, it said. And it was the last Mexican music we would hear for many long months, until the paint was freshened on the canvas walls and the little missions were retouched, and the local fiddles and guitars tuned up again for the Yankee tourists.

It would never have occurred to anyone in Whittier to listen to what was being played in Jim Town . . . any more than it would have seemed either interesting or prudent for some of the people down there to come to the annual Quaker concert, drawn from the *Messiah* and given for a small missions fee to the public. During the War there were many "shows" organized in our town to raise money for the Red Cross and to sell Liberty Bonds, but never was there one bit of Mexican singing or dancing in them.

Once, perhaps in 1914, I was taken to a big barbecue Father had helped arrange, to benefit something like the new Elks Club. It was the most authentic I have gone to, I think, in real early-California style, with long board tables under a flapping canvas roof, and a big pit where two whole steers had been roasting all night. It was dusty and exciting, but I was taken home soon, since things got a little rowdy, I was told later. By now it surprises me that it happened inside the city limits, but I know that even outside of town, it would still have been all-white, with only the cooks at pitside the real Mexicans. And where was the music? What good is a real huge old-fashioned barbecue without at least a couple of guitars and maybe a cornet, to sob it up on "La Paloma"?

And where is the organ grinder? There was one, for at least a few years, in Whittier. I know this because I was four when we went there, and when I was in the second grade, a good four years later, I could compare notes with my friend Gracie about him. Then he stopped coming.

He came always at twilight. Anne and I would hear him down at the corner, approaching slowly from Philadelphia around to Painter. It was a magical sound, and my heart still falters when I hear it with my spiritual ear. Whoever was in command of the house at that moment would understand, and put a nickel or perhaps some pennies in our hands, and we would go out alone and wait at the edge of the sidewalk. Up toward us (I see all this now in light flickering from the overhead lamp at the intersection, and long shadows, but that is fantasy pure and simple, for we would not have been allowed to stand outside alone in the real dark . . .) would come the small bent man with an organ strapped in front of him, and on his shoulder his little monkey. The man wore a soft pointed green hat, very dirty but with a feather in it, and the monkey wore a red coat with buttons, baggy pants, and a little round flat cap with gold braid, which he took off when he asked us for our coins. Sometimes the man would tell him to shake hands with us, and his fingers were cold and like bird bones.

First the little shadowy man would crank out a tune or two, depending on the time of day, how tired he probably was, and what our money might add up to. I know they were Italian, because afterward Mother would laugh a little about the way "O Sole Mio" or "La Donn' è Mobile" had sounded (she pretended to hold her ears when the organ grinder came, but always knew what he had played!). Then, for a year or two, he would go slowly on up the street. But it was the wrong time of day: people were closing their doors, pulling down their blinds. And he was really not in the right part of town for sidewalk frolicking. He found that he would have more luck down along the south and west edges, where the houses were small and shacky, and the people were more open than the respectable Quakers who lived on North Painter. Anne and I waved sadly as he turned away.

He would find my friend Gracie, though, and she was enough to cheer him and his monkey too. She was a stalwart mixture of her big Mexican mother, who still wore her hair in a long braid down her back, and her white father, who was said to be an itinerant butcher. She compared notes with me about the organ grinder, which it never occurred to me to do with my more proper friends, all of whom were Friends as well. The morning after the organ grinder had come, she would ask me tauntingly if he had been to our house, and I felt quite proud and jaunty that of course he had. We told how much we had put into the monkey's hat, and whether he had shaken hands with us. He always shook Gracie's. . . . She told me that one time the monkey jumped right into her arms, wearing all his clothes. That never happened to me, and I admitted it to her, but if one of the girls from the north of town had vaunted such a triumph, I might well have lied a little, at least by implication, and said nonchalantly, "Of course . . . me too . . . *twice* . . . of course. . . ."

Once when I did not have a single penny, and the house seemed empty of adult bankers, I left Anne on the sidewalk as hostage and ran to the house to grab a ripe avocado from the sideboard. The little monkey plunged into it, and surfaced like a green plum, with his eyes on top as black and bright as olives. The man laughed, and played another tune, but I know a nickel would have been more use to him.

I have seen pictures of slum children, pale and thin but gay, dancing to the music of an organ grinder in the slums of New York long ago, just about when my little sister and I stood shyly on the edge of our neat lawn and listened without moving to the wheezy music, and then waved good-by. How muted we were! But inwardly we vibrated like twanged cello strings to what the man and his companion had given us. After they left we would go into our warm house again, and Mother would play more music for us sometimes, and we would sing together. There was one book we liked especially, *A Child's Garden of Verses*, with really good accompaniment, the kind Mother could cope with. Snatches from it still slide through my mind at unexpected times: Oh, how I like to go *up* in the air, / *Up* in the air so bluuuuue. . . . I saw three ships a-sailing. . . .

But it was the organ grinder we still thought of, and perhaps sang to in our own ways . . . and perhaps still do. Where did he come from . . . and why did he come to such a tightly closed place as Whittier then was? After he withdrew into the shadows toward the lower part of the little town, did he find something to eat? There was the electric tramway which ran between us and Los Angeles. It cost more than the pennies he could ever earn on our street. Our family had a pass on it because of the *News*, but Anne and I knew he did not. And once into the big city, where would the tiny monkey stay, in all that dark noise? We discussed adopting him and his friend, but in a hopeless way. I talked with Gracie about the plan, and she laughed loudly and told me to forget it. All we could do was keep our ears open, and hope for the return.

It had nothing to do, then anyway, with the music classes with Mrs. Graham, in either three-four or four-four time but all sung at the same volume, the way young sheep blat, well fed, almost ready for the market. It had nothing to do with groups singing together as I knew them: church choirs, a wandering quartet intoning hymns in the Friends' church for foreign missions, even what I heard alone and more rarely together at home. Certainly it was far from Spain and Mexico and Italy. It was far from the Lower East Side. It was the piper's tune, played from the shadows of Whittier, and the tiny cold hand of the monkey still reaches toward me.

11

Dance of
the Slow Learner

It is impossible to think about going to school in Whittier
without thinking of the little college there, and it is difficult
for me to think of that without thinking of prejudice as it is
quietly and perhaps benevolently practiced by the members
of the Society of Friends. And since prejudice is not a pleasant aspect of life-in-general and of my own view of life as it
was in Whittier when I was a child there, I tend to avert my
thoughts from the whole thing. This gets me nowhere.

By May Day in 1913 we had been in the small Quaker
town for almost a year, and Mother and Aunt Gwen and my
baby sister Anne and I walked down the shady side of Painter
Avenue, and climbed up the hill to the imposing stone and
brick Main Building of Whittier College, to watch its young
ladies dance around a pole, weaving long Dennison Crepe
Paper ribbons in and out. It was a pretty sight, on the sloping
lawns. I doubt that we had been formally invited, but Father
as new editor of the daily paper had urged Mother to go anyway. Probably he had said grandly, "Tell them who you are"
—an injunction which lasted until his death more than forty
years later, and which would send us into whimpers of help-

less hilarity in the face of a parking ticket, a lost railroad fare, a rude headwaiter, a slipshod garage. . . .

We four ladies, crisp in summer clothes, drifted over the green grass, in and out of the shade, and perhaps there was fruit punch later, but I doubt it, and I came away with a vision of going to college so that I too could learn to dance around a pole and not get my ribbon tangled. Later, it is said, I told my mother I thought the young ladies were too fat and old, but all I can remember is their nimble circling in the warm afternoon light, and my decision to enter Academe as soon as possible.

This took longer than it would today, thanks to the unawareness in Whittier of any need for a truant officer, or any preparation for schooling before First Grade. Most children started when they were six, regardless of what month of the year they had been born in.

By the time my own younger daughter was three years old, I realized that new laws would hold her back in her grades one year, because she had been born in mid-March, and I was able then, which I would not be now, to cheat and bulldoze Whittier College into accepting her into its preschool nursery, run solely to instruct ambitious graduate students in the latest methods of child education. I told them who I was . . . literally: I was the rapidly aging eldest daughter of the town's respected editor, and willy-nilly my bright infant should be accepted in their clinic, one more wee laboratory rat to be studied through tricky one-way windows and guided through clever mazes. She was a sturdy human being, and it saved her a year of grammar school, and it was fun, occasionally, to speak of my daughter who had graduated from college summa cum laude at the age of minus-five. . . .

But when I was her age and beyond, there was no schooling provided except in the home, for children under six. Once, for a few months, two earnest or bored younger members of the Women's Guild of St. Matthias started a kind of day school. It was held in the Parish House where we met for Sunday school. Anne and I liked it, because people made a lot more fuss about us there than at home. The two teachers had read some Montessori pamphlets, and we *expressed* ourselves decorously, with wands lifted in rhythm above our heads, and plenty of Plasticene in place of today's finger painting.

Several of the Quaker children went too. It was long before the word baby-sitting had been coined, but a few of the more liberal matrons like Mrs. Maple and Mrs. Moorhead were pleased to hand their five-year-olds over to our well-mannered young ladies for a few hours now and then, to play with children who, after all, would soon be classmates in Penn Street. . . . Each one of us brought a piece of fruit for recess, and it seems to me we drank something from the Parish House kitchen. We sat on the steps in the sunshine, and one of the teachers would have us sing together as we gnawed and sucked our snacks. Things got a little rough now and then, in an exciting if forbidden way. Once Tolbert Moorhead hit Garland Swain, his best friend, about putting on the wrong rubbers for a rainy day. I was involved in this somehow, and enjoyed seeing two people banging at each other. Or perhaps it was that I traded my apple for a bigger one that had a worm in it, and did a little banging on my own? The venture did not last long, anyway. Paper cutting soon palled. . . .

A trial preschool grade was added at Penn Street School when my sister Anne was five, and I was finally in the First Grade at the ripe age of seven. It had been decided that there was no point in my starting at six, since I already read well and had nothing else to learn that year. This seems strangely illogical now, but Father apparently told the school board who he was.

I spent a fine stolen year at home, and reading fever mounted, and Anne and I were happy in the Back Yard, mostly under our orange tree, where we squatted for hours making tiny towns in the dirt, or reading *John Martin's Magazine*, a monthly nobody seems to know about now. We liked the sandbox too, but it was under Grandmother's windows, and once when we were pretending to be a man and his wife deciding something very important about the way our children were behaving, we heard Mother and the old lady laughing helplessly right above our heads, and removed most of our spoken dramas to the green cave of our tree.

In the last half of my first year at school, then, the basement at Penn Street was cleaned and floored, and cheered with cutouts of Humpty Dumpty and his peers, and the first public kindergarten in Whittier made its trial run. Anne was a charter member, and it added an extra excitement to my own blissful experience to be able to escort her to the basement door every morning, and wait for her at noon. I insisted, for a few weeks anyway, that she hold my hand on the walks. This made me feel doubly powerful and needed, and probably contributed to her latent resentment of me as the bigger and older.

She soon proved herself infinitely more advanced than I, in amorous prowess, a lead she was to maintain for the rest of her life, by falling deeply and wholly in love with a fat little boy who at every recess would meet her on his side of the high wire fence between the playground sexes. The two five-year-old people never touched or spoke, but simply stood looking at each other, their faces pale and unsmiling. The teachers peeked at this strange *affaire* from the windows, and Miss Newby reported it to Mother as being plainly concerned with love. But what else was there to say? By the time the tiny Héloïse and Abélard were promoted to the first grade, they seemed to have forgotten their almost palpable adoration, but I have never forgotten how mysterious it was, and sacred.

Miss Newby and her lifetime friend and companion Miss Raymer *were* Penn Street School, when I was there, and had been for many years. Once a big man came into Miss Newby's classroom to repair the wiring, and to my embarrassment she told us that he had been in her first grade, and that his *son*, now in Whittier College, had been in her first grade. I am not sure why I thought this confession was something better not made lightly. Perhaps it is because I secretly felt that never in all Time had there been Miss Newby's First Grade until *I* was in it, and that never had she really taught it until *I* was her pupil? It was jealousy?

She was the most exciting event in my life, after Aunt Gwen and Margie Thayer, and in some ways is still. I was seven years old, and should have been made to work mentally for at least four years before I finally started school. I had a lively and thirsty mind, which needed discipline and direction. Thank God I learned to read early in my life, or I might have gone permanently to sleep! But my reading was almost without pattern, except what I myself established by going from left to right on the eclectic shelves of the family library. (It was not until I was eight that the kind woman in the Children's Public Library showed me the thrilling satisfaction of how to use her card files, and from then on it was my special privilege to keep some kind of order in our books at home.)

Miss Newby was tall and firmly built, with grey hair, and nose glasses that snapped back into a black button on her bosom, and hung there when she did not need them. She had a clear high voice, never fluty or what I thought of as silly-sounding. She commanded our complete attention and respect, and I cannot believe that she ever got anything else. And we *loved* her. Nobody could ever have loved her as much as I did, but I had to acknowledge that other people shared some of my devotion.

She made us work, and held our attentions and energies like a skilled sorceress. We did not do things quickly. We planned ahead for every celebration of the year, like Halloween, Thanksgiving, Christmas, Lincoln's Birthday, right through the calendar, and we never suspected that we were learning anything dull like dates, colors, skills as we cut out pumpkins, turkeys, Valentines . . . made paper chains for our trees without getting paste everywhere . . . found that two blue Easter eggs and two more made the astonishing total of four eggs. . . .

There was one project that went on for at least three months, and probably most of that Great Year. We had a four-room house built of orange crates, two stories tall, standing on a low table so that we could keep an eye on whatever was happening. Miss Newby had a book about it, and every day we heard a little more about the life and adventures of Joe-Boy and his family, who before our eyes, and with our almost stunned help, moved into the empty mansion and gradually installed themselves comfortably with furniture we made, stocked their kitchen with tiny foodstuffs we molded from Plasticene, hung their walls with a changing art show from our crayons.

As I remember, Joe-Boy fell ill once, after most of the first graders had been home with Measles or whatever was "going around" Whittier just then, and we were able to diagnose his case from firsthand knowledge, and decide upon his treatment by holding a kind of medical seminar with Miss Newby as moderator. And as the climax to the year, Joe-Boy's mother went away (during this time he and his father planted a little garden in the lot next door—a large cookie pan with real dirt in it), and when she came home again she brought a new baby sister for our hero! Like magic Miss Newby and all of us rallied, and produced essentials like a cradle, a rocking chair, all made skillfully after our long experience with strawberry boxes, matchboxes, pillboxes, and crayons and paste and crepe paper. I forget what the baby's name was, but it was in Miss Newby's book.

Joe-Boy and his saga were familiar to my whole family, and I soon learned that it was polite to wait, at the lunch table on at least five days of the week, until Mother or Father *asked* me to detail the morning's events. "How is Joe-Boy to-day?" was the signal, and I realize now that it was given later and later at the meal, so that I often had to interrupt it to hurry back to my afternoon classes. Once Mother said to her husband, "How can any human being seem to enjoy doing this same thing year after year?" Father said that probably Miss Newby liked it as much as I did, and I think that is partly true, but that it was *us*, her ever changing children, and the way we lived with *her* in Joe-Boy's house, that kept her so fresh and eager every year for perhaps fifty or more.

Once Miss Newby was notified by either the police or the *News* office that an airplane would fly over Whittier. School was dismissed, and we all stood out in the grounds, the boys on their side of course, to watch the skies. I got permission to leave my class ranks and stand beside my sister Anne, to pro-tect her if she grew frightened. (Probably I insisted on hold-ing her hand, and hoped that she might cry a little.) The big Jenny, made of wood and cloth, finally clattered over us, at about five hundred feet, and we all sent up a shrill cheer, and the pilot leaned out and waved to us. It was a Moment, com-parable perhaps to watching a man walk on the Moon, except more immediate.

Long after my Great Year with her, Miss Newby was a kind of dean emeritus of the preschool training group when my younger daughter was getting her degree at Whittier College at the age of four. (She majored in drums.) Father suggested that I stop to see my goddess, still in her old house on East Philadelphia. He had talked with her lately. He said she spoke very simply and distinctly to him, as if he were a slightly back-ward seven-year-old instead of ten times that. She was set for-ever in that mold. . . .

I could *not* pay a call on her: I was older than any man or woman on earth that year, completely absorbed in my own domestic misadventures, and it was too difficult to get far enough out of them to be an adoring little girl again, even for a cup of tea. And besides, Miss Raymer had died. I could not see Miss Newby, without her there too . . . I tried to explain this to my father, but he only looked at me sardonically and resumed his reading.

Miss Raymer was short and stocky, so that Miss Newby seemed almost willowy beside her. Her voice was low and rather gruff, and she had an abrupt bossy manner which scared some of the younger teachers, but never her children. They went through her second grade as eagerly as they had through the first, more skilled in everything, thanks to Joe-Boy, and ready to lick wildcats *and* arithmetic. Miss Raymer was tough, and they loved it. She taught exactly as she played the piano for our marches: loudly, strongly, right on the beat.

There was an odd-shaped hall in the middle of the old school building, I believe with a skylight in it. Six rooms led off it, with partitions in front of their doors where the pupils hung their coats and left rubbers on rainy days. In the hall there may have been chairs, but I do not remember anything but the battered upright piano. When the weather made the Boys' and Girls' playgrounds impossible at recess, Miss Raymer would install herself at the keyboard for a good fast workout, and Miss Newby and the other teachers would march the breath, the devil, and the steam out of us, around and across the big hall and through the musty cloakrooms. Miss Raymer would play a kind of jolly ruffle, and we would go panting back to our rooms. It was a most enjoyable way to be alive and growing.

I cannot recall why I never had Miss Raymer in the second grade. Surely I looked forward to it. Perhaps I skipped half a grade? That was common in those days, with bright children, and I was considered bright: they were simply moved ahead one or two semesters, without regard to their own hopes, and apparently on the theory that the sooner one could get out of school, the better. Certainly I felt the same way, from about the fifth grade on, but there are flaws in it, as proved by one or two of my cousins who were *really* bright, and who found themselves out of high school when they were barely fourteen. They had simply shot through their classes, always with the highest grades, and suddenly they were helpless children expected to exist like near-adults in the university world.

This was never my plight, fortunately! Thanks to my mother's queenly dismissal of the public school requirements as unimportant to us Kennedys, I was absent as much as I was present after the magic of Miss Newby's class wore off, and barely made it out of high school when I was a full eighteen, with most of my classmates at least a year younger than I. So . . . perhaps Miss Newby deliberately promoted me to another second-grade teacher, or perhaps Miss Raymer had been shifted to the third grade that year; whatever happened, it is a complete blank to me. That is only fitting: even the gruff little bulldog partner of my idol would have been an anticlimax.

And then in the First Grade I had met Margie Thayer. We were to be Best Friends for almost a decade, which partly because of her was one of the richest in my long series of them. (Hmmm . . . interesting . . . significant: a psychiatrist ponders and looks quirkily at me. Yes, I nod with bland and sure equanimity: I loved a girl, when I was only seven years old!) Margie entered Miss Newby's class late in the year; she had been gravely ill, a year or so before, and was used to a governess. And suddenly there on the grounds at Penn Street I saw a girl exactly my height, chubby but not fat, wearing a little round straw hat with a black ribbon dangling down from its back. It was impossible! A hat at school! I walked up to her, drawn by her strangeness, and that was the beginning. She did not stay at Penn Street long, that year, but her mother and my mother met, undoubtedly with many quiet prequestionings of all their acquaintances. And then Margie came back for part of the Second Grade. The teachers watched us from their windows at recess, because Margie and I went off to the farthest edge of the Girls' Side of the playground, and built tiny towns, roads, forts, encampments in the soft dirt under a drooping sycamore or willow on the northeast corner. We reenacted every book we had ever read, and some never to be written, in a ten-minute recess, the way people can relive their lives in a flash as they drown. She was transferred to East Whittier School, because it was simpler for the Thayers' hired man to take her there and fetch her home, but we spent every weekend together, every minute we could.

My little sister Anne was the third member of this trinity, two years younger than we, and generally docile. We all read and knew the same books, and the minute we met we were out of any immediate surroundings and into a castle, a den, an island eyrie.

Saturdays were the best: no school; Edith mainly pregnant and glad to have us out from underfoot; Mrs. Thayer increasingly occupied with a suddenly paralytic husband, two adolescent siblings of Margie's, and a decreasing bankroll. Father would take us down Painter and across the County Road to the Thayer Ranch, and then pick us up at the end of his workday. Sometimes we would be asked to stay for dinner. Now and then we stayed overnight. It was almost as good as being next door to Aunt Gwen. We behaved with special nicety at table, in the big dark dining room with German baroque armoires and sideboards. We acted with the same discretion if we were staying overnight. Outside, we were on our own, the Wild Indians, and I feel safe and sure when I state flatly that no children ever had more fun than we . . .

. . . except that in this far focus I wonder about my little sister. She did everything we did, and when we had a mystical ceremony of giving one drop of blood into a dirty broken teacup half-filled with sour juice from some stolen oranges (in other words, a holy goblet brimming), she hid her flinches as bravely as Margie and I, when we contributed our ritual sealing of eternal fidelity. It was Cosa Nostra seen through the other end of the telescope, there in the attic of the Thayer hay barn. We were equals.

But there were other times when we were not, and I think they may well have corroded Anne's subconscious. If Margie and I were playing the Wizard of Oz and one of his conquests like Esmeralda or or or, Anne would be cast as Jellyanjam, the faithful Ozian servant. If Margie and I were deep in a Zane Grey fantasy, she would be the faithful Indian servant. She never kicked. She never revolted. But how could there not be some scar tissue, left from the cold truth that she was exactly two years younger than either of us?

Age is enormous, when anyone is almost without it.

And from that first sight of the girl just my age, just my height, standing there alone on the girls' playground at Penn Street School in her little round *Hat,* for goodness' sake, spread many an unsuspected ripple through all our lives. Mine was my own to cope with—and Miss Newby, Margie, all in one year . . . what bliss!

By the time I got into the third grade we were deep in World War One, and it is a little disgusting for me now to admit that I organized all the girls in my room and forced them, for a few heady weeks of dictatorship, to practice military drill during recess. My father turned up an old Army manual and let me read it, and I learned formations and commands and all the *hup*-two-three, and put my small troupe through a parade that astonishes as well as repels me as I think back on it.

The teachers would watch us from the windows, and smile and salute. I do not think that America has since matched the sentimental involvement of that war, and it seemed admirable for little girls to form squads and so on, just as it did for people like Father to travel around the county making short rousing speeches about Liberty Bonds, and overweight middle-aged men like Uncle Mac to stuff themselves into forgotten uniforms and run up and down hills in mock Sunday battles in the Home Guard. They carried real if obsolete guns. The girls in the Third Grade had their own broomsticks and made a snappy sight indeed as they presented them to the Flag, which of course *I* carried, as their Leader. . . .

After Miss Newby, there could be no brighter a star for another decade, and except for two faint little twinklers in the Third and Fourth Grades, Miss Merrick and Miss Brotherton, my teachers were a blur. I got along well with the rest of them because I liked their smiles, but without knowing it I had little intellectual respect for them. I admit blandly to a successful amount of canny shirking, when I was between eight and going-on-eleven. I was bored at school, at least in the classes. Thanks to Chickenpox and a few bouts of Measles I had gauged the logical periods of lassitude, malaise, fever, and then convalescence, and while I never tried to simulate these, through innate caution, I did manage now and then to appear to be extremely weary. Once I lay on the long couch in front of the dying fire, as I heard my parents come up the front steps after a small outing together, probably to listen to a friend play his fiddle and to drink a little port, and knowingly I breathed with the deep slow rhythm of sleep and did not swallow, and I let one pale long-fingered hand hang like a fading lily over the edge of the couch, into the fluttering light from the hearth. With satisfaction I heard my mother whisper, "Look at her! She's tired, too tired. She's growing too fast. Probably she should stay home from school tomorrow. . . ." And probably my father gave her the sardonic look which I grew used to much later in my life . . . and probably I did bring off the trick and stay home.

Then the day came when both Mother and I realized that I could not with honesty lie on the couch and read from left to right on every bookshelf in the house and still pretend to go to school. I was keeping up well in English, composition, all that. But suddenly I had flunked Arithmetic. *I*, used to my position as "best in the class," had *flunked*.

This was unheard of, as far as I can see, on either side of the family, and although it was gently blamed on an unusually lengthy bout of Measles, I well knew it was purely my own doing. It led to my spending a delightful month or so in the summer between Third and Fourth Grades, walking far down Painter each morning to have a lesson which I seemed already to have learned, so pleasant was the whole thing as I ambled along the silent street lined with old ladies behind their curtains and bushes and magnolia trees, and then sat, paying just enough but not too much attention, as the gentle elderly Miss Merrick told me of adding and subtracting and I looked at the paper skeleton on her closet door.

Her brother later opened a plant nursery where that old house was, and became necessary to more than his maiden sister, and I am sure he never knew that he introduced me, that fine summer, to the mysteries of human anatomy, all because once in an extravagant moment he had invested, by mail, in a life-sized colored foldable articulated male form. It not only showed all the bones in what I still assume are their correct places, but on sideways flanges which would slide under the bloodier parts were lungs, muscles, veins, subcutaneous layers, and finally the bright pink skin, and with all the obvious lower orifices carefully blurred by the lithographers.

I apparently learned enough arithmetic to skid me into the Fourth Grade and from then on, with precarious moments due mostly to the same cause, through my formal education, but I have forgotten almost everything about figures except to keep my checkbook straight. Always instead of seven-minus-three I think of that beautiful thing hanging on the door. I often wonder why Miss Merrick let me study it, but she did, and after a comparatively brilliant lesson I could move the skin layer back, and look at the muscles and veins, and then the bones of a hand or knee, and finally uncover the wild blue and scarlet convolutions of the bowels, the guts of the whole world. . . .

And in Fourth there was Miss Brotherton. All I can recall about her is that she was small and sallow, with large dark eyes, like some kind of tropical night bird. She made me feel that she was fond of me, which was pleasant, and I worked hard for her. In fact, I overdid it, so that finally she talked with my mother.

I was very keen about the Geography course, and no matter what country we were studying, I knew it intimately because, as I would tell the enthralled class in great detail, either my parents or my grandmother, or at worst one of my uncles, had *been* there. I described native costumes and habits vividly. I even dropped an occasional *bêche-de-mer* word I had misread in my *Books of Knowledge* and the *Britannica*, which of course I had been absorbing for several years. Once I told graphically about how my grandmother, on her last trip to Jerusalem, had walked down streets exactly like the little picture on page 247 of our textbook, where the walls were so close together that she could touch them with her outstretched arms. Miss Brotherton let me rave on, perhaps awed by my obvious exaltation, but soon after Jerusalem my mother had a short conversation with me. It was not harsh, but it made me see that there must be a difference between truth and fiction, at least in the Fourth Grade.

When I said that Grandmother had been in Jerusalem I was telling a lie. If I had said that I had *heard*, as I probably might have from one of the many missionaries who came to see her, that one could touch the walls in the narrower streets, I would not be lying. I could even say that I had *read* that, which was of course the truth. But it was foolish of me to say things that were falsehoods, just in order to keep everybody listening to me and perhaps envying me. I agreed, and lived more and more a silent life, as I withdrew from school and the people in it.

A long time later, Mother told me that Miss Brotherton had said that I was carrying on so flamboyantly because I was in a state of dangerous and desperate boredom, precocious perhaps but very real. Had I already gone into reading too far? What was there to do? I honestly do not know how I myself would face such a problem now, with Me on my hands. I was eminently healthy, and very open and well-mannered and thoughtful and gay and nice and everything, as far as could be guessed. Certainly I *felt* all that. But I was on a real spree of clumsy lying, more kindly called escape-from-boredom by Miss Brotherton of the wise dark eyes.

Mother's gentle but clear remarks to me about talking too much to impress other people were not quite right, for I knew I was simply telling *myself* all those stories. But I did not like to appear foolish, to others but especially to Me, an aversion which grew stronger with time. I went underground, academically, from then on and until I met the second Miss Newby, a teacher worthy of my true humility, when I was about sixteen. I was silently and really unconsciously supercilious about most of my teachers, and all of my classmates. Many of the children I went to school with were much more intelligent than I, but although we were about the same ages, I was far older than they in my acquired knowledge and my use of words. This cowed them, and impressed, even though it may have exasperated, the earnest women paid by the city to get me through the grades. I went into a kind of snooze, mentally, just alert enough to pass every test and then be flashingly awake for my own pleasures: reading, keeping two or three continued stories going to hypnotize my sister Anne into giving me her full attention as I spun them along, writing letters and epic poems and one novel. . . . Probably it was unhealthy to be so much more alive at home than at school. Certainly it is ugly to grow arrogant or anesthetic, even through ignorance and ennui.

Once school was over for the day, we never went to our friends' houses, because we were never invited. They in turn found ours dull stuff, with few toys, nothing but books to look at, babies to be quiet for. For a while after we all had bikes, we would ride up Philadelphia past the edge of the campus, and then coast down the hills. In the Spring we could roam the hills in a small pack made up mostly of non-Quaker kids. But mainly Anne and I stayed home alone, or went down to the Thayer Ranch to live in a dazzling world of faery.

In good weather, which meant most of the year, we stayed in the loft of Margie's barn, a wonderful dusty place of cobwebs and crumbling hay, and glinting sunlight through its wide loading door and its lacy decaying roof. Beneath lived the cow, some chickens, and all the rusting orchard equipment. Occasionally the dour Hired Man would let us watch him do the milking, and squirt the warm sweet stuff into our mouths as we knelt beside his pail.

In bad weather, and more as we grew older and the family fell on sparse days and there was no cow, no Hired Man, we lived a thousand lives in the upstairs of the big dark house. It was made of three low rooms with sloping roofs and many windows, and then a mysterious black attic. Everything was roomy, and the attic seemed to stretch far under the eaves. It was unfloored, so that we walked cautiously on wide planks laid between the rows of old trunks. Farther back in the shadows from the one electric light were broken armchairs, piles of faded magazines, stacks of paintings from Mexico, where the family had lived for many years, before Margie was born. There was a smell that I can bring to my mind's nose in a flash, and it is that attic: dust, and the decay of paper and silk and wood; the perfume of exotic vanished bodies once rubbed with rare oils, doused with drops from French bottles, powdered and rouged for roistering.

We had permission to open every trunk, and pull out its capes and robes and scarves, and *wear* them. How extraordinary! There were dozens of mysterious costumes, which the Thayers had shipped from Boston to Guadalajara to Alaska to Hong Kong in their wanderings. Sometimes we rewrote Louisa M. Alcott for at least two weeks, and felt authentically The Girls, with Anne doubling as Beth and Amy and none of us wearing clothes of their period but with skirts satisfyingly sweeping the floors behind us. Then we would take over L. Frank Baum, and add unsuspected drama to the Land of Oz, in turbans and veils and shuffling pointed slippers. Margie and I would be dressed that way, giving directions and changing plots as we went along. Anne would be Jellyanjam, *again*, no matter what her costume....

We all went on to Academe, in our own styles, and one time in college I actually found myself dancing around a Maypole, in honor of mothers of prospective students. By then I knew that I was mentally a dormant laggard, and I felt desperate about it, silently screaming to escape the trap I had helped build for myself. I managed to, with inadvertent help, and by now I know who my real teachers were, at least.

12

The Best View

From what I have read, it seems that the one-ring circuses that wandered over the North American continent as if it were a small park, during the last half of the nineteenth century, got along best if they called themselves English, no matter whether more than a couple of people in the troupe spoke more than a couple of words of that language, or cared more than a *sou* or a *centavo* where they were, as long as they could eat and sleep and fly through the air on cue. Most often they were known as something like Cutler's Great London Company, or Sanderson's Greater London, and perhaps it was not until the Yanks moved in on the trade that any tent show was blandly called Greatest.

These bands of jugglers and clowns and musicians, all of whom perforce knew the backside duties of caring for a handful of Ferocious Wild Beasts and trained poodles and such, as well as they did the two-a-day razzle-dazzle of the shows, sometimes with three full performances on holidays: they often dropped out, and were never seen again, and seldom mourned. I know of one clown, though, who was wept for at least fleetingly; and I thought with a small quiet pang in my heart of his grave, as I read in a casual paperback pickup of the way some of the best girls of the New Orleans brothels, after the Civil War, were recruited from traveling English circuses. Suddenly I was home again, in the wine valley in Northern California. . . .

There is a good little graveyard there, the kind for slow ambles along shady paths, with haphazard slow stops to read inscriptions on the markers, and observe past fashions in their sizes and shapes. Traveling headstone salesmen must have come through Napa Valley every five years or so, and for that next stretch of time every local grave might be topped with a limp-looking rose, its stem cut off too soon, its petals drooping as it lay prone before the scythe. Members of the Woodsmen of the World stuck to their symbol of an ax left cleaving into a realistic log, saying that man's work is never done, or something like that. Infants generally had some form of a crouched lamb for a topping. Two clasped hands were popular for a conjugal grave. The artistic *idée fixe* of many an itinerant stonecutter can be traced in our graveyard, given the one clue of its dates, and it is an almost docile way to spend a few hours, refreshing if one is not afraid to be reminded of his mortality.

Newspaper accounts of local deaths used to end, until lately, by saying that the citizen had been escorted to take his place in "the marble city," and like any small town, our cemetery has its rich suburbs, its solid center of respectable bourgeois, its slums. There is even a Skid Row, with some impersonal and nameless markers pounded into the rubble. And it was on the edge of this that we found the Clown.

His gravestone was a piece of redwood planking, marked with black paint which by then stood out like embossing on the worn surface. It had been struck into the ground, but lay now on its side, its base so eaten away by rot and insects that it was like dirty jagged old teeth. We stole it, from almost in front of the caretaker's office, dead sure that if we asked to repair it we would be involved in everything from ancient history to the last recorded laws about grave robbery. A little carpentering, a little retouching of the letters, and it was ready to be stuck into the ground. And the mysterious thing about our daring crime is that soon after the refreshed monument went up again, a little jar of fresh flowers was placed there, and has been kept full ever since. The caretaker remains silent about it, although surely he suspects who visits there. I prefer not to know. . . .

And this is how, from reading about the lost ladies in old New Orleans, I moved to the St. Helena Cemetery, and from there, willy-nilly, helplessly but with an agreeable ease, to a glorious few days I spent with a "Great London Circus" which was mine, ours.

It was before America went into the First World War, still referred to as *The* War by people who grew up with it. Probably it was in 1916, and once the troupe installed itself in Whittier, on a big lot on Greenleaf slightly north of the Pickering Hotel, it went flat broke and could not move on. It was stranded. My father, with his predilection for Lame Ducks, was the natural person to try to rescue it.

As editor of the daily *News*, he could and did give as much space to free advertising of it as his business partner would stand for. He bullied and blackmailed the local merchants to grant credit, and even to extend a few favors in the shape of bales of hay for the two elephants, and bags of flour and coffee beans and tins of tea for the canteen.

As in all such troupes, the two-legged members were skilled in communal survival, and my father was thrilled and astounded to find that the boss, a thin youngish man, with a bad limp from one of the first battles in 1914, was not only a good fellow but an expert at disposing of exotic dung produced by his little nonhuman menagerie. He spoke well, and wore a very small bristly moustache of a nice ginger shade, and carried a little stick under his arm, very British-Officer. I al-

ways saw him in immaculate soft country clothes or his uniform as Ringmaster at the performance, except once when he
and Father emptied a couple of sacks of manure under our
rosebushes and spaded it in, laughing comfortably about
lions and monkeys and trained pigeons. Then the Englishman was dressed like my father, in baggy overalls and a
sweaty blue shirt, but his little moustache kept him dapper
in my eyes.

He was not introduced to Mother, although if he had been
anything but an itinerant bankrupt circus manager she would
have liked him, I am sure. She was, as always, worried about
how deeply her husband was involved in his new romance,
financially if not emotionally. She knew that the circus was
staying in town much too long . . . and how was it eating?
How could it ever leave? If it did get to the East Coast again,
how could it cross the submarine paths to England? And did
the Old Country want a bunch of half-starved acrobats and
animals to care for? It is no wonder the poor woman felt
enough apprehension to dull her usual bliss at hearing a good
English accent, and Father was discreet in leading his floating
friend toward Charles Somerville's room in the garage, rather
than our living room, for a post-fertilizer nip of Scotch-and-
water.

Whittier was not a good circus town, and except for the
painful bliss the stranded troupe brought into a few of our
lives, it is sad that it happened to go broke there and not some
other place like nearby Fullerton, or Anaheim. To people of
the Gentle Persuasion, there was much that was garish and
plain unseemly about a group of wandering mountebanks,
dragging their dangerous caged beasts with them, flying
through the air in tights and spangles to the sound of drums
and trumpets. . . . Let them move along, go somewhere else,
was the general feeling in the town, and often there would be
only a few people at the performances, in spite of Rex's enthusiastic free advertising. And probably there was thin fare

in the canteen, if it depended too much on the generosity of the grocers and butchers in our citadel of brotherly love.

As all good circuses should, the Great London gave us a free and mammoth Parade, before anyone suspected that it would play more than its scheduled stand. It had moved into town during the night, in classical fashion. (Father was surely on hand for this always seductive operation, excusing his presence in the name of editorial duty.) There had been fanfare before: I remember bringing home a leaflet distributed at Penn Street School, detailing the educational benefits for us children: rare tropical birds and beasts, free for all to observe in their near-native habitats . . . the mighty king of the jungle and his consort . . . a giant python of incredible strength and length . . . two behemoths of Africa, live giant elephants gentle as a child. . . .

The Parade was scheduled to start from the Great Tent on North Greenleaf at precisely 11:30 on Saturday morning, to allow all the schoolchildren, all the farmers in town in their wagons, all the merchants, to stand on the sidewalks and see one of the most magnificent displays in the Western Hemisphere, direct from a triumphal tour of someplace or other besides its war-torn homeland, probably via New Orleans.

Mother and Anne and I, and I think Aunt Gwen and Isobel, stood on the east side of Greenleaf under a new awning in front of the furniture store. It was a fine hot day, totally correct for a circus parade. Precisely at the designated moment the calliope sounded from up the street, and a most remarkable pageant rolled slowly past us.

The Great London was a gem, a polished impeccable jewel of a little circus. Its costumes were clean and fresh, even in the cruel noon sun and under the critical eyes of the small town. The performers smiled, and looked healthy and gay. The clowns were funny and infinitely graceful as they flipped double somersaults along the edges of the street. A strong-lunged band of what seemed like dozens of uniformed musicians played at the head of the parade, rousingly, excitingly. While it caught its breath, still marching firmly ahead, the calliope at the far end would tootle and bleat musically. At the very head, of course, rode the thin young man with the ginger moustache, on a beautiful chestnut horse. His little swagger stick was under his arm, and nobody would know that he had a bad limp when on his own two feet.

And just before the calliope, as it whooped steamily along, came one of the great stars, better than the two elephants with men dressed in turbans riding them, the lion and his lioness in heavily barred cages with brightly painted tops, another wagon cage filled with, or at least occupied by, some scratching grinning monkeys, and the plodding broad-backed horses pulling everything, before they must go into the ring for the tricks! There before us was the drawing card of the whole breathtaking review: The Lady and The Snake!

We gasped with horror and astonishment, unable to look away. People surged into the gutters to get a nearer view.

In a glass cage, the size of the lions' but without bars, and with the wooden top and corner pieces heavily carved and gilded, a pale beautiful woman half-lay against a pile of brilliant velvet pillows. Her skin was the color of milk, and long thick hair of a strange greenish-yellow flowed over her shoulders and her couch. As far as could be seen through the plate-glass walls, the only other thing she had on was several yards of python.

It was the biggest snake in the world. It was alive, for now and then it would shift inside itself in a peculiar tight-loose way, almost peristaltic, and instead of one of its lengths lying over her belly, it would be farther down. She held its drowsy-looking face close to hers, and occasionally stroked it. For Whittier, at high noon, in 1916 or thereabouts, it was quite a show.

Even the music of the steam calliope right behind it grew

thin in our ears. Many people ran along the sidewalks to keep such odious beauty in sight, but Mother led us firmly up to Bailey Street and on home, for a delayed lunch. That last thing, with the *snake* and the half-naked *woman,* she told Father, was *too much.* He said that back at the tent, the girl had fainted, probably from the heat in the glass box. No wonder, Mother said without any pity. My father said that it had been hard to get her out of the snake, unconscious as she was. He had helped . . . and I suppose it was that casual admission of involvement with the circus people that froze Mother into a beneficent remoteness during the next week or so, for she washed her hands of the whole thing, and I was free to go to the matinées, and even several times to the night shows, without a single protest from her, when it was proposed by Father or Aunt Gwen.

Actually, I cheated, perhaps a proof that wandering artists exert an evil spell over little children. First I told Miss Newby that I could not come to class one afternoon because I was being *taken* to the English circus, when I really went all alone. By then I was known as the editor's little girl, and I got in free and knew just where to sit for the best view. Only a few people had come, but the band played as gustily as ever, and the clowns waved to me as they went spinning and tumbling around the ring, jumping on and off the patient broad horses. It was fine, worth almost any punishment, which to my surprise never materialized . . . for that sin anyway.

Aunt Gwen was as thrilled as Rex and I were about the exciting visitors in our little town, and was happy to use our passes every time she could, always with me along. We would buy one bag of peanuts, half for the elephants and the rest for us, and always I sat where we had the best view.

The strangest part about the whole strange caper was that I soon found I could sneak into the tent in the *mornings.* I simply went to the circus grounds instead of to school.

Miss Newby was so used to my mother's odd ideas of regular attendance that she never questioned my absences, and I was probably the only child in Penn Street School who never needed a "written excuse." My sly cunning, brought to a surging climax by the stranded circus, made me stretch my legs a bit more than usual, for in the mornings and after lunch I always went south on Painter from our house, as prescribed for the direction toward school, and then down Friends Street just far enough to throw almost any suspicious snooper off my trail. I then looped back on Friends to Bailey, and right on westward toward my place under the tent, where I could get the best view. Coming home again, once or twice a day, involved the same devious trek, but distance meant nothing to me when I was not only familiar with every hump and crack in the town's sidewalks, at least on our side of Greenleaf, but was caught up in an intoxication such as I have seldom since experienced.

It seems strange to me now that nobody seemed to notice at lunch, or at dinner if we were going to try to swell the pitiful attendance at the show, that my eyes had a different brightness to them. I could feel them snapping and sparkling, and instinct kept them hooded. It was instinct, too, that showed me where I could get the best view in all the tent, whether at morning workout, or matinée, or in the beautiful nighttime glare.

The best view was of the world-famous child flyer, the youngest ever to do a triple back somersault in midair or something, and I was in love with him. For me, he was the circus, Circus, one-ring stranded desperate Great London. So perhaps that is what I was really in love with, and not the flying boy?

A psychologist could have easy fun with the fact that this boy flew as a girl. He wore a wig of impossible golden curls, as long as Mary Pickford's, which floated out behind him as he dove downward toward the waiting arms, the tensed hands, on a lower trapeze, ringlets deftly tossed back as he climbed the spidery ropes for another swinging flight. How pretty she was. How beautiful he was!

The first time I saw her, I was speechless with envy, and I made myself into her, a free soul flying through the air of all the world, lovely, desirable, one minute a wandering Gypsy and the next a gossamer planet plunging to the sound of trumpets and drums. I watched her through two performances that day, for Rex was loaded with free tickets and Aunt Gwen took me with all her family of Nettleships. Perhaps two mornings later I found that I could sneak into the workouts, and I already knew the best place to sit, and although I can remember seeing a boy about my age, in black leotard, walk out and take the same stance in the ring as had the golden-haired princess, it did not astonish me at all. Of *course* he was a boy! How could any girl have been as knife-like in the air? And the next time I saw him in curls, I shared the secret companionably. Thus may be fixed the patterns of acceptance, in some natures.

When the little troupe moved on, after a stay that may have been six days or two weeks, I know many people were glad: the townsmen who did not like to have elephants and snake-ladies nearby for more than a few minutes or hours; my mother, who sensed a dangerous rise in her husband's quixotic pressure, and perhaps a new dimension in my life as a child. Father took us to the last performance, which was sparsely attended but with a better house than usual.

The uniforms and costumes sparkled. The band never played better. No dust rose from the tidy little ring, as clowns and acrobats tumbled and leaped upon the ever-ambling horses. The handsome ringmaster snapped his whip, caressed the lioness in her spotless cage, and kissed both hands of the snake-lady, who also did a trained pigeon act, very pretty, to the sounds of the Blue Danube Waltz. His little ginger moustache bristled, and his limp hardly showed.

My love flew through the air with skilled abandon. He wore a new costume, of pale blue tights and a spangled white tutu, and in his long curls were some diamond pins. His make-up was heavy, like a printed Valentine, the costly kind . . . or a cheap German lithograph of Saint Anne or Mary Magdalene. After his daring flips and floatings, he stood in the sawdust and bowed, looking very small beside the ringmaster on his capering horse, and suddenly he pulled off his curls and stood there like Galahad or Ivanhoe or Curdie, his short black hair shining in the spotlight.

I had already said farewell to him in my heart, but I was grateful for this one last salute to my love, which I knew came straight from him to me. While he and his circus were in Whittier, I had weighed as many aspects of my joining them as my small experience could call up, and I knew that it would not be the right time for me to leave. Mother was not feeling well, and might be deciding to have a baby. Father was not only running the *News* but taking lessons in how to graft and bud citrus trees. Grandmother had shingles. Aunt Gwen and Miss Newby would miss me.

The next morning I skipped school again, for the last time in many years, and walked my devious route to the circus grounds, to see if all the magic had vanished in the night, as it had come. The big lot was empty, smoother than ever before, with no holes to show where the tent pegs had once dug in, no sawdust to blow here and there. Never again would I hear a calliope to call me to the matinée and the night show. I felt much older, for a while, than I had expected to. It was my first deliberate farewell.

It is no doubt why the rotted marker in the St. Helena Cemetery had to be set up again. When a few people asked why we were bothering to repair it and repaint its lettering, there was no logical answer. When they asked why I did not do some serious research about the traveling circus and its members, I lied enough to say that the man who died there in our town had been a clown.

Yes, why not? And when the circus played New Orleans, his lady love, the bareback rider, stayed on in a fancy house. Joe grew thinner, and in the village under the volcano in the far far West, he turned his face to the wall and died. Of course. . . .

All I really felt sure about, when I was questioned, was that he had not been a little acrobat in a golden wig.

To the Memory of
JOSEPH W. BREWER
Died April 23, 1860
Erected by the Members of
Dan Rice's Circus Co.

Goodby Joseph

13

A Palace Incident

My first intimations of both elegance and sorrow came early in the American part of The War, perhaps in 1917. They seemed to belong together, for a while anyway.

In the beginnings of our life in Whittier there was a strong need among small religious groups to band tightly into themselves, and we felt it as a good solid clannishness at St. Matthias for want of anything better . . . like community importance, perhaps. We had a commendable choir, thanks to my mother's drawing-room contralto and Uncle Mac's barrack-room bass, with Mrs. Emory always making the altar bloom with scavenged flowers, and old Mrs. Atkinson, valiantly and slowly dying of bronchial cancer, at her companionably wheezing organ. We had excellent parties, with thin Jack Swain or plumper Matty Matteson being a well-stuffed Santa Claus, and then the annual Sunday school picnics in summer, with exactly three ice cream cones for every child: one chocolate, one strawberry, and one vanilla. On Easters, after we had made our best manners to the current minister at the door, there was a rich big chocolate egg for each of us.

Of course people like my father were very serious about their duties as vestrymen, but that had nothing to do with anyone under twelve. . . .

Aunt Gwen, of course, was an Episcopalian. How could she be anything else, since we knew her and she knew us, and we probably would not have met otherwise? And who else could be her dearest friend, not counting Mother of course, but Isobel MacLaren, Uncle Mac's only daughter? Both young women sang in the choir, Isobel in a small firm soprano, Aunt Gwen the female counterpart of Uncle Mac's spur-of-the-moment mingling of low baritone and basso profundo.

It was a fine sight to see the vested choir march ponderously into the little shack of a church, especially if we had watched some of their vestments being ironed frantically in our kitchen the night before. The people who were our lives were beautifully changed into near-angels, as they rocked a little from side to side behind the boy carrying the crucifix. Anne and I stared respectfully at them all, knowing warmly that under the flowing black and white lived Mother, Uncle Mac, Aunt Gwen and Isobel, and then groundlings like Mrs. Emory and other kind willing people. We always hoped that Uncle Mac would have forgotten to switch off the ship's bells in his handsome pocket watch, presented to him when he retired as Chief Engineer on a British shipping line to the far reaches of the Empire. It was lovely to hear that little bell ringing so sweetly and irrevocably from his surpliced middle, while not the twitch of a smile showed anywhere, and the service rolled on and his face turned a deeper purple.

His daughter Isobel was a Lovely Lady, Anne and I knew. I suppose that she was in her early twenties when we first met her. I was, and still am, caught in the sound of her name, Isobel MacLaren. Mother, the Anglomaniac, would have been happier if Isobel was not a name so blatantly from north of the Border, but she taught us right away how to say it: *Eye*-zo-bell, and not the ugly *Izz*-uh-bell we were used to in America.

Isobel was built in a compact way, and bit off her words with a near-snap of her firm jaw. She and Aunt Gwen were a good pair: both with Anglican accents that made them socially desirable in our tiny enclave of ethical behavior, and both well respected as Dutiful Daughters.

Isobel lived with her father (Uncle Mac) and her mother Barnie. We knew this birdlike dignified little woman was called that, even by her daughter, but we never addressed her as such, although as time passed we *referred* to her sometimes as Aunt Barnie. (Isobel had her soft lilting voice, but with more insistence in it.) Barnie must have led a largely self-sufficient life as the wife of a master seaman. She always stayed in the background, but it was fine to hear Uncle Mac say her name, rolling it out with the tenderness of a loyal if roaming lover over so long and rough a marriage.

The MacLarens seemed to coast always on rather thin times. I suppose there was a kind of pension . . . but they lived within a block of her younger brother Mr. Chaffee, and apparently she had often stayed in his other houses when Uncle Mac was at sea. All her brothers had left Scotland for Australia, it seems, and Down Under had made enormous fortunes. They had stables of famous horses. They had yachts. They were big spenders and knew how to be. And Old George held onto Barnie, and brought her to Whittier with him not long before we got there in 1912. He *needed* her.

I cannot know if he actually paid her and Uncle Mac for what they did to keep his whimsical investment in an elegant villa functioning as he wished. I hope so. There was a kind of jaunty subservience and mockery in Uncle Mac about it all, which used to make my parents snort impatiently. I do not even know if Mr. Chaffee brought them to Whittier or came there to be near their loyal help, the rich man following beloved and penniless immigrants from too many years of wandering, secure now in the close ghetto of Low Church Episcopalian retirement which he never touched except with his munificent yearly dues. How could I know about all this? The important thing is that the MacLarens were *there*.

I was always aware, in a disinterested way, that my family treated the Chaffees with a remoteness that was perhaps because of their economic differences, but more probably because they loved Uncle Mac and did not like to see him bend with such courteous good humor to the autocratic whims of the Australian brother, and see Barnie at Mrs. Chaffee's beck and nod, and see Isobel used as a substitute nurse and lady's maid for her fragile aunt. That is to say, the Chaffees, pronounced Chay-fees, were a different cut from ours.

The MacLarens lived in a small brown shingle house a minute's walk from the low but imposing palace Old George had built for his wife. This was on the beginning of the foothills north of Whittier, on steep streets named for the plain Quaker fathers and still lived on by the plainer citizens, down on the flats, but suddenly desirable to rich newcomers able to pay for pumping water and building retaining walls, and all that unnecessary display and frippery frowned upon by the first dedicated founders of the little religious settlement. If people like this Australian foreigner wanted to spend their money on a sprawling villa designed to coddle the mysterious invalidism of his invisible wife, let them! Let him with his gambling and his ill-begotten riches throw up the conceits of tropical plantings in a glass-covered loggia in the center of the house, like a heathen! The Friends withdrew from all this as if it were the Black Pox, or simply ignored it. I cannot know if the Chaffees were ever aware of their local isolation, nor if our indirect association with them, through the Mac-Larens, may have added to our own tacit enislement by the locals.

Tropical plants did flourish under the glass ceiling of the

center loggia, and on its four sides glamorous dim rooms lay
silently behind closed doors, with such a plenitude of bath-
rooms pretty and not plain like ours, and silky boudoirs with
little curvy chairs in them, as Anne and I had never dreamed
of seeing, even though we were already caught in the web of
princesses in the Green and Red and Brown Fairy Books and
in the spicy derring-do of King Arthur's knights.

The most astounding of all the empty languorous purlieux
of the Chaffee House, which we often tiptoed through as
Father grew more devoted to Uncle Mac and Aunt Gwen to
Isobel and therefore we could all go into the place when the
owners were away, and Uncle Mac was supposed to be keeping his eye on the elaborate plumbing and the exotic planting
and so on, and the most elegant of anything a princess could
ever have, was Mrs. Chaffee's bathroom.

Anne and I wandered through it, probably holding hands
in solidarity, as if we were in the most intimate secret apartment of Queen Glinda Esmeraldina, which perhaps we were,
for we saw Mrs. Chaffee herself only one time, and then
she was as if made of cobwebs on an enormous bed, nourished perhaps by three peeled grapes a day and a sip of yellow
wine. She smiled faintly and waved at us, with a grey-white
hand so thin it was like a filament or tentacle pushing out
from the froth of lace she lay in, and then Isobel led us
deftly from the dim room.

Later, when the lady left, to die somewhere from whatever
it was that had slowly changed her into such a strange
shadow, we went oftener and more freely into the house, and
it was always first to her bathroom, which of course we never
used for anything as carnal as our own relievings.

It was bigger than our generous living room at home. The
creamy skins of polar bears lay everywhere. Perhaps eight
or a dozen different kinds of tubs sat around its edges, all
running hot and cold water from golden spigots and sprays
and douches and such. (This was one reason why Uncle

Mac was such a jewel of a brother-in-law, after his life in the bowels of a hundred ships: he knew *pipes!*) Mrs. Chaffee needed all these tubs, to help comfort whatever it was that for ages had been wrong with her. Mr. Chaffee obviously loved her, and wanted to be good to her. He kept nurses there night and day, and they must have spent hours picking up the tiny colorless body and dipping it like an egg being poached into this perfumed water or that, while he had to be away almost all the time on business.

On good days her chair would be pushed into the loggia, to give her a fleeting look at the luxuriant jungle plants thrusting and twining steamily under the opaque roof (another useful accomplishment of Uncle Mac's, thanks to his years in tropical hinterlands: he knew *orchids!*). Usually, though, the poor lady lay alone in her great bed, between baths, while nurses slipped in and out of the cautious gloom in her chamber, and tested the waters in her many tubs.

Across the house from this shadowy apartment was a jolly room with a good smell, meant for men, for The Man. Father and Uncle Mac would sit there whenever the Chaffees were away. It was my first view of the leathery easiness of a small warm place where males, at least Anglo-Saxons, like to get away from females. It was cosy, comfortable. . . . I went in several times, then out, having observed sharply the books on the walls, the fine smell of tobacco and leather, not as bitter (nor as fine, I added loyally) as that in Charles Somerville's room in our garage . . . and my first seltzer-water bottle with its powerful silver squirter on the top of the bluish heavy glass. The two men would be sitting the way I never saw them at home, with their legs out, and big tumblers in their slow hands. Their voices were idle, and plainly different from other ways they talked. From the door Isobel might beckon to me, and I would leave unnoticed, an invisible and as yet unbothersome woman.

At the far end of the big flat house, carefully built so that

Mrs. Chaffee could go almost anywhere in it when she felt able to sit in her enormous silent wheelchair as a nurse pushed her from one empty room to another, there was a Sun Parlor, as glassed rooms were called in California when I was little. It was long and big and bright, with a generous table where perhaps someone had dreamed that a dozen lusty eaters and drinkers might sit. It had an air of waiting and waste, but I liked it because its glass walls went to the floor, instead of nose-high to me in our own such room, and because on the tiles in the dusty glare were succulents in pots, occasionally vivid with strange flowers which Uncle Mac knew how to make spring from their dead-looking fingers and stems. To me they were part of the palatial elegance everywhere. (Mother and Grandmother rejected "house plants" as a part of the prairie life they preferred to dismiss as undistinguished, or at least forgettable: Iowa farm wives kept geraniums and ferns blooming in empty tin cans on their kitchen window-sills, but the nearest the Holbrooks came to that was a pair of impressive cacti on the front steps of their village mansion . . . and once an impudent and rebellious offspring of the banker and his dowager, my Uncle Evans, stuck a red apple on every long cruel needle. . . .)

One bright winter day, in 1917, perhaps, with the sun blasting in through the westerly windows of the Sun Parlor, I roamed almost invisibly here and there while Aunt Gwen, the giant widow, helped Isobel, oh, Eye-zo-bell, unpack and do away with and distribute all the earthly belongings of her younger brother Fred MacLaren. He had been blown up or something—as, it was said to me later, Aunt Gwen's frail little homesick husband had been—on a beach or in a trench in France. He was still a British citizen, although later most of the MacLarens became Americans.

The young women moved slowly through the bright air. I watched them, from this and that position, and it did not seem to bother them. They went on quietly folding and sighing, and occasionally held each other in a silent passion-less embrace, as they dug through the two or three lockers the Crown had forwarded to Uncle Mac, last of kin and no doubt thankful to have womenfolk handy, to do this job for him. I knew a little of how they were protecting him, and Barnie too: strong sturdy girls there, raised to cope with life, to ignore any weak nonsense of whimpering and all that! Good British stock, both of them! They kept on almost word-lessly, in the best tradition of Empire, and pulled out mil-dewed uniforms and a few books and things, and then a gas mask.

I was shocked by its almost beautiful ugliness, which of course I had seen on posters, and I came in from my per-mitted edge of the action and asked about it. It was like a desiccated animal, with the strange tubes and stiff flaps that barnacles make on more helpless shells. It was colored a dull fecal brown (which was called khaki by the time the Yankees got into the War, and caused me some trouble at Penn Street School since I said *kah-ki* because Aunt Gwen did, but which was pronounced *kaa-ki* by the other kids . . .).

Then I crashed innocently through and into the intense controlled circuit of emotions and sorrows. When I asked about the hideous mask, and was told something or other, I suddenly pulled it on over my head, for I knew that I would seem to turn into a bug of some kind and amuse Aunt Gwen and Isobel, and get them out of their silence. Instead, those two greatest of all the giants in my life, goddesses of tender-ness and gentle shapings, burst into huge undisciplined sobs and wails, and rushed out of the Sun Parlor and into the farthest part of the great pretentious hopeless house, like thundering wild horses.

I stood there in the waning sunlight. I did not know why I was alone, or what had happened. The straps of the dead boy's mask caught over my ears as I managed to pull it off me.

And that is the last about the Chaffee House, I think, except for a kind of footnote: the invisible lady did die, although when and even why I do not know, and then Old George stayed more in Whittier, and when a cousin of mine was "let out" of the U.S. Army and joined forces with another one of Uncle Mac's equally wearied sons, in about 1918, the two of them, mechanically inspired and for the time being somewhat manic-neurotic-nutty, materialized a dream of George Chaffee's, of carrying around behind him on his compulsive jauntings a fully equipped little house, what an English gypsy would call a caravan, in which he could sleep and eat and otherwise live.

My cousin stayed with us. George MacLaren lived with his young wife and oncoming children. The two men were refugees from concerted violence, and in silent companionship they built the rich old Australian a beautifully engineered and designed behemoth which was, as far as I can discover, the father of all "mobile homes." He would take it out, either with only his chauffeur-houseboy or with the builders too, and they would get stuck on narrow mountain curves or in Death Valley sand dunes, and come back to Whittier and revamp the whole wheelbase, or the wiring or plumbing.

So . . . perhaps Mr. Chaffee was a good man. I think of his frail wife there in the faery-tower (through whose wish?), with all the soft waters flowing (but what else?). I think of his warm heady "office," with his jolly kowtowing brother-in-law, my Uncle Mac, using his elegant seltzer bottle in the whiskey my father undoubtedly took there and shared happily, away from us women like Mother and Grandmother and Barnie, even Aunt Gwen and Isobel and my little sister Anne and . . . yes, and me. Mr. Chaffee was perhaps all the things whispered about him in Whittier: a high liver, a gambler, a racing man . . . and he got those two shaky younger men through a peculiarly hard time, when they came back from the far shores of France. He saved them, by handing them an idea to perfect.

It is possible that I too helped release some war casualties from their immediate travail, the time I put Fred's gas mask over my little head and drove the brave young women sobbing out of the bright Sun Porch and into the dim elegance of the Chaffee House. I know now that their growing friendship entrusted them to that shared storm of grief, for they remained firm and loving all their lives.

And I remember getting the mask off. It was slower than pulling it on had been, perhaps because of my astonishment at what wearing it had caused, and it was horridly stuffy inside. Once out of it, I looked at all of Uncle Mac's weird blossoms against the glass walls of the empty room, and wondered for at least a few minutes what had really happened so suddenly in the palace.

14

A Pagan Ornament

A few days ago, in this my life far from the little Quaker town of Whittier, a Mexican friend came back from Ensenada in Baja California, where she had gone to bear her fourth daughter on her own soil. As soon as she was used to being home again, I went to see her in their cottage near St. Helena, where she and the girls live with her good husband.

He is head driver of the Valley's garbage trucks. He is a handsome quiet man with bad teeth, and if he was disappointed to find himself with another girl-child on his hands, he would never admit it, but smiled with remote tenderness as I pulled aside the swaddlings and looked at her.

As always, it seemed impossible that anything so defenseless could be here on this planet, able to breathe in and out and grow hair and all that. She was colored a rich subtle brownish pink, like the blushing egg of a Rhode Island Red hen. Her cheek, which I touched with a sigh of my fingertip, was like the egg's shell, and as warm. And in her small flat ears were the tiniest rings I have ever seen, something from a fairy tale. I had to touch them too, to believe them, and then I could not help giving a strong joyful laugh.

The baby heard it or felt it, and stirred a little, and the parents and the three delicious little sisters all began to laugh too, and we drank tepid cherry sodas to celebrate. It made me remember how long it took me to get my own ears pierced, and some of the reasons why. They were the results of all kinds of prejudices, strong both inside my own early homes and in Whittier. I yearned impotently for earrings then.

Later I forgot to think much about the advantages of such a short sharp operation, until one winter in Lugano when I wore a coat with a high collar which brushed from my right ear almost whatever bauble I hung on it, so that everything valuable I had owned was cut in half, and I was left feeling foolish, or at least careless, by the people who had given me the ornaments.

I told a Ticinese friend of this, and together we went to a jeweler in her hometown of Locarno. He did a rather crooked heavy-breathing job on my earlobes, and put into the little canals a moderately expensive pair of gold hoops, with his sincere wish for my safe recovery and another visit to his shop, when my ears could support a greater weight like diamonds or emeralds. All went well, as is usually the case, whether one does it with a sewing needle or an imprecise precision tool like the one the Swiss jeweler plunged shakily into my plump lobes. And I felt further back into my life, when I had moved from Whittier with my two little daughters, and installed myself, possibly forever, in a village in the wine country north of San Francisco.

Almost the first thing I did was to make an appointment to have the girls' ears pierced: they wanted it, and I wanted to prove that I was free, so I wanted it too, and we went to Dr. Brignoli. Surely a doctor with an Italian name would understand the simplicity and rightness of the whole thing, no matter how delayed it had been. . . .

It might as well have been a double mastoidectomy with

heart transplant on the side, for Anne and then for Mary. The doctor, a fine man who became our friend, was perhaps more Anglo-Saxon than his name would imply, and he developed what outside a medical building I would call the shakes. A nurse had to mop his forehead and his upper lip. The effort to steady his own hand was pitiable. He would lean back, even get up and stand back, and sight toward the target like a moon traveler confronting an uncharted satellite. He breathed heavily, as did the Swiss jeweler later in my life.

After we relaxed, in about a month or so, he told me that he never had done such an operation, nor would he ever again. When I asked him who did, for almost all of my girls' friends wore earrings, he said scornfully, "Grandmothers! And right away, first thing. But I don't have any call for it."

And right away I was back in Whittier, and I knew why he had no call for it: his patients, the people he took care of, did not *have* pierced ears, any more than did Honky Wilson's sick list in my first town. They were the middle class, not the immigrants. In our town of St. Helena most of the Italians were second and third generation, and if they had not turned away sternly from the telltale tricks of their Old Country families, in their pursuit of all-over Americanism, they still had great-aunts and grandmothers around to do the needle-work.

In Whittier, Honky Wilson took care of people like us, and only us, as far as I ever knew. He was not a Quaker, but he and the small handful of churchly doctors who were his amicable colleagues spelled each other on bad holidays and epidemics and during the War. The Whittier people who had pierced ears did not go to them. They birthed their own children, mostly in Jim Town but occasionally in shacks in the plainer parts of town, and it was a matter of course to pierce girl babies' ears at birth and run through a piece of silk thread, or a tiny loop of gold wire if the father was in funds.

I had two friends at Penn Street School who wore earrings. One was Bertha Wolf, a lovely sweet shadow who drifted past me before she died. She was the little girl who wore a scapular around her neck, painted with the Virgin and filled with asafetida to keep her alive. . . .

And Gracie wore earrings, almost invisible hoops. She was my *tough* friend. She came and went in school as if it did not matter whether she did or not, an idea foreign to everything other people seemed to believe, in that little place where Grades counted and a child went right on through High School without a hitch, if he came to school every day he could stand on his feet, and did not steal or lie too overtly, and wore passably clean clothes.

Gracie was our maverick, and something like predestination made me prefer her to all other schoolmates, except Margie Thayer, male and female, and potential neuter. She was strong and mean. She smelled bitter, a perfume which my mother identified for my infatuated nose as garlic, never used or mentioned in our own cuisine. She often disappeared, and later would talk tersely about sprees in Sacramento or San Francisco with her family . . . actually visits to close relatives temporarily in San Quentin and such places. She was rather dark brown. She cursed a little, which was the pepper on the egg for me. And she wore those tiny gold rings in her ears.

I admired Gracie and everything about her, passionately. I managed to lure her home a few times after school, but it never seemed to go off very well, and finally my mother said in a kind but firm way to me that it would be better not to bring her along with the girls who lived in our part of the town . . . Josephine and Eleanor and Eldine. It would be *better*. The last time I served an impromptu snack of cornflakes and milk and sugar on the piano bench, Gracie had splashed and splattered all over everything. . . .

I understood, with the fatalism of anybody trapped in childhood, and from then on spent what time Gracie would allot me in sneaking off the school grounds with her to the fly-spotted grocery a few blocks away on South Greenleaf, at recess, and buying red-hots and jellybeans shaped like little green cucumbers, with money given for more constructive purposes: an eraser, perhaps. It was a breathless life of crime, and I battened on it.

I talked with Gracie about having my ears pierced. She said her mother could do it, but that maybe I was already too old. I would probably bleed to death, or get terrible poisoning and lose both ears and all my hair. That is the way she talked. She was merely pointing out to me that I might bleed a little, and there might be some infection. Anyway, she asked, how would I get any earrings? I couldn't just go around wearing string. And what would my family do? It was plainly counter-indicated, if not hopeless. Girls like me did not have their ears pierced in Whittier, in 1915 and thereabouts.

However, I talked to my mother about it. (Why not? I loved her too.) She was firmly against it. It was a fashion practiced by backward races and heathens, she said, people in missionary lands like Africa. It was unsanitary: dirt was bound to get into the artificial holes in the lobes, and sometimes people caught terrible diseases there, which could even make their ears fall off and their hair drop out. At my age I might start to *bleed* dangerously. (Just what Gracie had said! Truth makes strange bedfellows. . . .) It was something nice people never did any more (which perhaps Gracie had said too?).

All the time my mother explained this old story to me, she was stitching daintily on another baby dress. She was a very bad sewer and everything fell apart soon after she finished it, but Grandmother had raised her to believe that a lady's hand should never lie idly in her lap, and my lady made a pretty picture as she matched her voice to the induced maternity of the whole scene. Her soft tones and the rhythm of her white hands and wrists partially convinced me that I should forget the whole unseemly dream and as soon as possible, or *now*. *None* of my friends wore earrings. (Gracie does, I contradicted silently.)

I gradually got around to mentioning the subject of pierced ears in a general way to Grandmother, and she dismissed them summarily as Roman Catholic. Foreigners and pagans —she told me as she kept her hands busy as any lady's with a neck scarf for an Eskimo—wear things like rings in their noses and even their lips and ears. Heathens in China and Pago-Pago try thus to question God's will: were they *born* with unsightly holes there? And so on. I nodded my head whenever she glanced up at me from her needles, sadly because of my own duplicity in loving a brown-skinned savage like Gracie, and I decided from then on to keep quiet and bide my time. It was true that none of my nice pink and white friends had their ears pierced. Who did, in all the world? Certainly not Mother and Aunt Gwen and Isobel Mac-Laren, my three deities, with Miss Newby.

When I was just past eight, Grandmother Kennedy came down from Washington for the winter with us, and it was discreetly pointed out to me as a subtle and malicious comparison between her and the more conservative side of my family that she had once, when a young lady, had her ears fixed to dangle jewels in them, but had long since given up such foreign and basically unclean ways. (Many years later, when I too was a young lady, that other grandmother sent me an earring she had saved from her frivolous days, a pretty cameo made into a pendant for my throat. I wonder how and why she thought about this sly remembrance. . . .)

By now I ask myself how many of the women who once outswung each other in the Penn Street playground wear baubles hung in their softly sagging earlobes. How long did they wait?

What has happened to the stern precepts taught them by their Quaker families and even their Episcopalian mothers? Have they let their little children submit to a trembling surgical caper, as I did in some vague revenge? When did they finally nerve themselves to a short gory appointment with a family doctor or a hopeful Swiss jeweler? There is something pleasantly ancient about being branded, even on request. . . .

15

The Haunts of
Sin and Iniquity

A friend of my father, one of Teddy Roosevelt's Rough Riders named Buck Denney, always referred to a hotel or clubhouse or theatre, of no matter what size or condition, as "a scarlet den of sin and iniquity," and then would go off into long happy chuckles. What he meant was that it was a nice promising place, and that is what I always felt about the Elks' Club in Whittier, which many of the good Quaker citizens agreed upon with me, but without the chuckles.

For me, it was where we had the most wonderful Christmas parties I have ever known in public. For them it was a foreign element of dubious bonhomie, and even of card playing and beer drinking and occasional routs of dancing. And it had been brought into town by my father, the otherwise fairly decent young editor.

Rex had a hard time starting it, I have been told. He and a few other mavericks in the little town, people like Uncle Mac and Matty Matteson, felt that the increasing number of young working men who were not members of the Society of Friends should have a place where they could meet, and no matter how incidentally do a little "benevolent and protective" work along with their socializing. Upon investigation it was found that in order to start a BPOE club in or near Whittier, a population of 5,000 must be proved. Legend has it that about four of the instigators of this whole shady deal snooped quietly through the one burying ground that existed in those far days, and managed to make up the required number of registered citizens. A club was founded, and when I was little it was housed in what I felt was a palatial lodge room above the Berry Grand Movie Theatre.

Three or four times in my life I climbed those elegant linoleumed stairs, and sat against one of the three dim walls in a tall chair quietly, to listen while the Roll was called. Once I think it was because my father was being made some kind of officer. The name of every member was intoned by the Grand Master or whoever was standing up while we sat, and when a name was slowly sounded three times, with a long pause after each searching pleading call, the Roll would go on. This was because he had died, the man who did not answer. My mother explained it to me, after the first such meeting, and I felt scared to go to the next one, with its sad waiting moments, but it always went off all right, because everyone else was brave, too.

The Christmas party was another matter. The churchlike chairs around the great room were empty of officers, and folding seats filled the floor space. Coveys of little children fluttered and swooped around their parents, or sat with acquired docility close by. Everyone seemed to have shiny hair, and as I remember it, all the little girls wore stiffly stuck-out white frocks, and long white cotton stockings with black Mary Janes. I do not remember the little boys, but I am sure there were a lot of them.

There was a great tree to the right of the stage area. (I don't recall this platform or whatever it was, from the more solemn meetings. Perhaps it was curtained?) The air was sweet with a wild-wood smell, and myriad sugar canes and twinkling things hung from the fresh boughs. And underneath was a mammoth pile, the biggest one I have ever seen, of carefully wrapped packages.

There was always excitement first: a real Punch and Judy show every year, and then perhaps a clown with a tiny white poodle that did somersaults over a wand, or a Fairy Godmother who emerged, all gauze and tinsel, from a dirty old sack a beggar carried right through our ranks after someone had heard him banging on the door at the top of the Lodge stairs. She could work magic, and throw oranges into the air, catching them carefully so as not to disarrange her long golden curls. There were untellable delights. And finally, given time for the old beggar or the clown to shift gears and make-up, Santa Claus himself would roar merrily on stage, and we would scream with untrammeled happiness to see him, once or forever.

The Elks of Whittier were no pinchpennies, in those days when business was beginning to look good for the out-of-towners and the oil-rig workers, and perhaps there was a little bravado there too, as a minority group brazenly planted in the quiet little Quaker enclave. Santa Claus was no local member who could stuff a pillow in his rented suit and say Ho-ho deeply. Santa Claus was a hired professional from Los Angeles, and he knew how to handle a controlled mob of excited bedazzled children with finesse and delicacy. Never did anything awkward happen. Never did a child cry or kick or throw up. (This is a rash statement to make so flatly, and probably it should read, "Never, to my knowledge. . . .") He had the Fairy Godmother to help him, and although the two of them with some four-legged help from a poodle might be playing all the parts of the beggar, the clown, the wizard, the witch, their pace was skillful and exciting to a split second in all our lives.

It reached its peak when the jolly god moved toward the great pile of packages, picked up one or two, and read the labels. Sometimes we went up to him, and he handed us, *each one of us* according to our names as he called them out, a beautiful present. Sometimes he and the Fairy brought them to us as we sat in a state of delicious quiverings beside our mothers.

I do not remember the present, ever. All I know is that it was for *me*, and that he gave it to *me*, himself. Once the Fairy was behind me, and tapped my head with her wand as I took the red and white package. The skin on my scalp burned as with an archaic and private and pagan stigma. Once I patted a koala bear that watched the ritual from the Fairy's arms. It glared a little at me, but did not bite. It seems strange that what was in my box is a blank to me. . . . There was plenty to eat, but that is forgotten, too, although it was probably of an elegance unfamiliar to us small-town children. What is important about those extravagant and by now legendary Christmas parties in the Elks' Lodge is that they were the first real debauches in my life, my introduction to the Scarlet Dens the old cowboy Buck Denney used to chuckle about, as I now can too.

It would be impossible today to throw such a naïve party. Even if there were a town small enough for a Lodge the size of the one in Whittier in about 1914–18, the children raised by hard-working absentee permissive parents would turn it into a debacle of bubble gum, half-eaten Popsicles, and deafened chaperones from the Ladies' Entertainment Committee, within minutes of opening the doors. There could not possibly be the silent awe that rose from all those vanished little people when the Fairy stepped dreamlike from the dirty cotton sack, for equally little people raised today on TV miracles. There could not be another poodle wise enough to stay calm and turn tail-over-top at the snap of a clown's finger, in the uncontrolled bedlam considered a sign of appreciation now when local merchants give a "free kiddies' matinée" for

Christmas on Main Street, with candy furnished by the Chamber of Commerce. I know, because I have been there. . . .

The other hint of orgies yet to come in my life was given me by the St. Matthias Church. Christmas again! We had really good parties in the Parish House, a lovely wooden shack. Everything was *gemütlich,* and in the best sense loving, as far as I myself was aware. We were more or less at home, and the familiar little hall smelled of fir boughs, with now and then a fine whiff of hot chocolate from the room which often served as bedroom and even kitchen for visiting priests. (Later this was more formally endowed with sinks and huge coffeepots and such, and the Ladies earned money serving a weekly lunch to the Rotarians.)

On the stage, which had the minister's Sanctum Sanctorum as Mother called it on one side, was a rather thin but tall tree, and compared with the Elks' Club spectacle it was sparse in promising decorations in the shapes of candy canes and wrapped packages. But the show was ours. There was no imported talent. Any child in the Sunday school who could or would recite " 'Twas the night before Christmas," or perhaps do a trick with a hat and a handkerchief, was dragged onto the stage and pushed one way or another through his stunts. It was a little like a prayer mission on Skid Row, except that we did not know it then: Pray, brother, before you get into line for the soup.

My sister Anne and I never "showed off," as Mother put it somewhat disdainfully, especially when our peers would recite and bring down the house. But once, when our family's Second Batch could stand on their own feet, my siblings Norah and David went uninvited up onto the stage and straight to the footlights, and then into a lengthy recital of every rhyme they had ever heard. My parents tried several times to call them down to the folding chairs again, and several more times the minister shushed them and even plucked at their shoulders, but the little people were possessed by a strange demon and stood there, holding hands invincibly and going right on with an act which the rest of us in the hot room could only applaud. They ended with an unseasonable poem which they recited in ringing and perfectly enunciated voices:

> *The moon shines East,*
> *And the moon shines West,*
> *But the man next door*
> *Makes the moon-shine best!*

Mother gasped, Rex cursed and leaped toward the stage, and the minister pushed my strangely exalted brother and sister into his office, for this was during Prohibition and even the mention of drinkin-likka was taboo. The house rang with helpless applause. David and Norah appeared beaming from the office by the stage, each carrying a red and white stick of candy, and right behind them strode Santa Claus!

Everybody knew he was Mr. Matteson, but he had almost as good a Hohoho as the professional at the Elks' Club, and whenever he was around, things went well. He saw that my serene siblings stayed close to their family, and restored the general tone of the evening to one of churchly joy with a request for the singing of "O Little Town of Bethlehem," before he headed toward the promising packages under the tree. I like to think that Mother's lovely voice sang out especially strongly, the night of the family's dubious limelight.

There was always plenty of food at the church parties. I remember it more clearly than I do whatever we may have eaten in the strange glamour of the Elks' Club orgies. There in the enormous room, where I could hear the three long sad names rolled out and nevermore answered, above the pipings of all the little children, the beautiful tree and the Punch and Judy voices and the self-possessed trained dogs and monkeys, things like ice cream took on a superb unimportance. But in the jolly warmth of the Parish House, hot cocoa, with cookies brought by the Guild's prize cooks, tasted exactly like Christmas itself, and above the sounds of the young ones seated in unaccustomed relaxation around the Sunday school tables rose the relaxed roar of the grownups, together once a year without need of discussing the church taxes, the new organist, or the quality of the communion wine now that Prohibition had closed in. . . .

By this time my roster of Scarlet Dens is rich indeed, and I expect to add to it as long as possible. I know that old Buck Denney let his description cover almost any place imaginable where from two to a thousand people could be happy together, shut off for a magical time from the drabness of life outside four walls of no matter what plainness or elegance. I am fortunate that I could begin my experimenting exactly as I did, in the first Elks' Lodge of Whittier, with its long shiny staircase and its free spending and cabalistic security, and then in the comparatively simple kindliness of the Church parties, sweet-smelling of Christmas tree and hot chocolate.

Buck the Rough Rider ended his life at the breakfast table, which was fitting. He was a redoubtable trencherman, very finicky about the quality of the quantities of food he ate, whether he was twenty-five and one of Roosevelt's Best, or eighty-five and the terror of Ward W at the Veterans' Home. One morning, while staying with some friends who like all the rest of us were hypnotized by his storytelling into inviting him for lengthy visits, he pushed his chair back a few inches from the edge of his plate of tender sausages, once-over-lightly eggs, and buttered toast, looked around him in apparent astonishment, and fell dead.

He would have approved of my second and later periods of exploring the Scarlet Dens, after the first innocent initiations. They were increasingly far from the sedate confines of the little town my mother and father used to flee with such dogged discretion: it grew time to follow them, into the world outside. . . .

Part III

. . . And Beyond

16

Fugues and Evasions

Everyone, no matter how much he likes the life he is leading, has an escape hatch. Often he is unaware of it as such. More often he recognizes it, or even invents it, to save his inner balance, commonly called his reason.

My parents, living in a pattern circumscribed and dictated by their backgrounds and their ambitions, occasionally fled Whittier in a vaguely nervous way, as if a dog were nipping at their heels. Inside the invisible walls of our good Quaker compound there was of course no alcohol, just as there was no riotous living. People who believed in "Plain Living and High Thinking" ate simple food in their own quiet homes, and two or three dismal cafés took care of transients, except for respectable drummers who could put up-at-and-with the Pickering Hotel. My father had to stay there when he was dickering for the *News*. It was grim, I understand, at least in its provender. It was not a place where a man would want to take his lady for a gastronomical frolic.

So Rex and Edith Kennedy would take off in the Ford now and then, for "dinner in town." That meant Marcel's, I think, and the Victor Hugo, and a couple of other places either downtown in Los Angeles or on the sportier outskirts. Occasionally Mother brought us back a tissue paper hat or a rolled whistle that would shoot out when blown, with a pink feather at the end, perhaps. We would discuss the menu at length, slowly and sensually. By the time I was six I knew several names of procurable California wines, and I can remember Cresta Blanca for its beautiful sound, although I have never tasted this brand. (Only a few years ago, when we dug out part of the abandoned cellar of the house I now live in, a half-bottle with the Cresta Blanca label on it rolled to the top of the rubble, and I brushed it off respectfully and then gave it to a collection of local artifacts. . . .)

When my parents went to the Scarlet Dens then available and pleasing to them, they ate and drank as they could not do at home, things like mushrooms under glass bells, and sometimes two wines, matter-of-factly, not the one bottle sipped occasionally for a family festival. A white wine and then a red! It sounded almost too beautiful, as did the way things were served by the waiters to each person, instead of being put in front of Father and then carried around by Bertha or Margaret or whoever was holding down the kitchen at the moment. Through my mother's long happy descriptions of her rare sorties, I grew to feel almost familiar with *la vie mondaine* as she lived it, and when the time came for me to visit my first restaurant, I was ready.

I was about six, I think. The D'Oyly Carte troupe was playing at the Mason Opera House. I am sure there was a lot of planning done, with overt disapproval from Grandmother for such extravagant tomfoolery, unfitting to our years, and it was decided that Mother and Anne and I would take the Electric to Los Angeles, have lunch at the Victor Hugo, and then go to the matinée of *Pinafore* and take the Electric home.

It is a wonder that I did not break my string like a balloon and float off before the day, so excited was I. I am glad I did not, for the restaurant was exactly as I had known it would be: white tablecloths gleamed more brightly than ever at home, and the silver twinkled more opulently if without our Irish hallmarks, and on each little table in the hushed room were several roses in a tall vase that made my little sister and me look up at them somewhat as we did to the star on the Christmas trees which so far had dignified our only debauchery. And kind waiters pulled out our chairs, which had already been discreetly heightened for us, although I do not know how: perhaps a couple of middle-sized baking pans covered with towels? Napkins were whisked open in the air, like stiff clouds, and then laid across our especially scrubbed knees. Mother was given a menu.

It was then that I tried my first deliberate step into the sea of public gastronomy. I asked firmly a question I had been practicing for a couple of days. It was based on everything I had learned from Mother's recountings of her flights from the family board. I said, "May we eat chicken à la King?"

It is quite possible that this caused a little ripple of interest if not hilarity among the staff, but all I remember is that we seemed to have a covey of black-coated men bending attentively over us for the next two hours, cutting all kinds of capers with the enormous silver chafing dish, the large glittering spoons, the general air of excited well-being. Mother probably sat back happily and watched the game. I took double enjoyment from seeing and tasting a dish she had often described to me as one of her favorite things in the whole world (I doubt this . . .). Anne very probably started, that noontime, her lifelong inability to do more than nibble at food in public places: forever she would ask for something special and then seem to sneer at it or push it away, so that it became family legend that her eyes were bigger than her stomach, or something like that. As I recall it now, I ate heartily, observed everything, and had enormous fun. The flame burning under the dish interested me. The hot plates interested me, and the simple but subtle flavors. The waiters interested me.

When we had to leave, after some kind of dessert I cannot remember, my sister folded her napkin with unusual nicety, and then asked the headwaiter, "Do these poor men have to wash all those dishes? May we help?" We swept out on this tag line, and as always, she had timed it perfectly to win every heart.

The rest of the day went well. I still remember Buttercup, who was indeed very plump and jolly. The best part was during the intermission, when Mother let me stand up on my seat to watch some of the audience go outside, and a tall Hindu wearing a large pale turban and a silky beard walked past our row. "*Jesus*," I cried out excitedly to my parent and the rest of the theatre. "Look! It's Jesus, all right!" This should have pleased my grandmother: one Christian impulse in an otherwise pagan fiesta. I am not sure that it did. My thoughts dwelt on other possibilities. I had tasted "sin and iniquity," and I wondered with impatience when I would next be able to eat chicken à la King with a flame under it . . . and perhaps someday much later order one or two wines to twinkle and shine on the impeccable linen of a Scarlet Den.

As far as I remember, we kept our orgies well removed from Whittier, during my childhood and forever beyond it. Except for almost secret temples like the Elks' Club and the Parish House for seasonal routs, and our own home for quiet little gastronomical celebrations when Grandmother was away at a religious convention and we could indulge in such foreign stuff as French dressing, there seemed nowhere to go in the town.

And Prohibition cut heavily through the lists of good places farther afield.

As local editor Father was wise enough not to be seen drinking in some of the dimly lighted ex-French ex-restaurants in the region, although he continued to leave the sherry and port decanters on the sideboard and buy pinch-bottle Scotch from runners stationed off San Pedro. Marcel's was hard hit, and I think it closed, after a shady decline as an "Inn," which in those drab days was synonymous with "road-house" and therefore with "speakeasy." A place I never went to until I was in my forties, the Goodfellows' Grotto, managed somehow to stay open and relatively unshattered, thanks largely to its loyal newspapermen and lawyers. The Victor Hugo, which I believe used to be down on Spring Street, moved uptown to Olive between Fifth and Sixth or something like that, and in a mysterious and obviously well-backed way it stayed elegant throughout the dismaying cultural crisis brought on the nation by doughty ladies like my grand-mother, who had fled alcoholic Northern Ireland only to land in the sodden Saturday nights of the Midwestern prairie villages.

The "new" Victor Hugo was upstairs . . . shades of the Elks' Club! The carpeting was soft and thick. Of course the linen and the mock silver gleamed and twinkled. The waiters, some of whom remembered us, or at least my little sister and her ladylike concern for them, seemed to scud along on invisible roller skates to whisk things before our noses. There was, within my memory, a lengthy prix fixe dinner which began God knows how but ended with a Nesselrode pudding, and my mother would always say faintly, "Oh, no," as I firmly settled for it, while she and Rex sipped cognac from their demitasses, in proper Prohibition style.

Once when we ate something under glass bells, one bell sealed itself hermetically to the plate, under which braised sweetbreads slowly died in their artful sauce, and the waiters puffed and groaned, and finally my father suggested that we continue with our meal and that a double grilled lamb chop be brought to him, *rare*. Another time I went to luncheon with a contingent from home. I do not remember any of them, because Miss Hope was there, and in my heart and eyes she was the most beautiful fairy princess of them all, a tall slender woman with a soft rich voice and enormous eyes, perhaps grey.

The noon buffet of salads and hot things over flames was always exciting to me, but that day I ate shrimps in honor of my lady.

We never ate shrimps at home. Most probably it had not occurred to Mother to see if she could even buy any. In Iowa they were undoubtedly alive in the good fishing streams, but if anyone ate them it was the Indians and people like that: "trashy." (Only a few hours ago, when Mr. Villa the fish man blew his horn along the street for us St. Helena ladies, I got some tiny defrosted bay shrimp from him for a Solari salad, and the elderly neighbor from across the street watched me with strange coyness and then squealed a little as she said, "Ooo, I've always wondered about those things! Of course I'm from Wisconsin." I told her they were delicious, but that of course she had millions of them in the streams at home, the fresh-water kind. She looked as shocked as if I had proposed eating a slice of her grandmother, and said, "Oh, we never eat anything but trout from our brooks in Wisconsin." Mr. Villa and I smiled invisibly at each other.) I had never, heretofore, put a succulent shrimp in my mouth, fresh or tinned. They looked in a distant way rather like curled snails, and I did not like anything that slid silently along, in water or on dry land. But Miss Hope was there, and in a gesture of which I am sure she was quite unconscious I served myself generously from the great pile of them in the silver bowl, let the waiter help me add mayonnaise, and walked to our table in front of the tall open French window.

Below us the gentle sound of Los Angeles traffic circa 1920 purred past. Somewhere nearby Miss Hope sat, speaking melodiously to the other older people at our table, her great eyes haunted and her long nose twitching in a way that later seemed quite familiar to me when I fell in love aesthetically with Virginia Woolf. The first shrimp was a test of courage and honor for me, because of my conditioned aversion to its general shape, but once I tackled it my whole life changed, and I knew that I would never feel anything but pure enjoyment again, on contemplating in any and all forms the subtle water beast, the scavenger. No ugly tale could turn me from enjoying it . . . nor ever has.

I like to think that Miss Hope missed sipping a glass of good white wine with her lunch, that magical day. I know that she was used to a less austere life than we all led in those strange times of the national disrepute of an age-old panacea. In Whittier I am sure she drank an occasional glass of wine with her family, the Lewises, when they all lived in our old house on Painter, and I know they drank a little sherry or whiskey at the Ranch. But that day in the twinkling sunlight at the Victor Hugo, when I really broke through a possible dietetic prejudice in order to prove my love, should have been graced with an important vintage. And perhaps it was.

A fine thing about "our" restaurant was that it was near the Philharmonic Auditorium, on Pershing Square. By the time I was ten or so, the Mason Opera House had lost its grip on the Angelenos, except for an occasional offbeat show, and people like Paderewski and the Marx Brothers played the Philharmonic, and there was the big new Biltmore hotel a neighbor on the Square, with a mile-long gallery hung with Art, and a hushed dining room and all that. We remained faithful to the Victor Hugo, and I often used to wish that I could stay and listen to the string trio sawing away on the birdcage balcony, and finish my Nesselrode, instead of trotting down to the barn of an auditorium to watch somebody like Marguerite Matzenauer belt out the Wagner.

Better than any Scarlet Dens, though, for all of us but especially Rex and Edith, was Valyermo. It was the enormous ranch of one of Mother's uncles by marriage, behind Mount Baldy from us, and then eastward over the empty desert. It took five or six hours to get there on a wild and even perilous ride once we turned out of Palmdale. Father counted on at least two flats or blowouts each way, and always carried two spare tires, water, oil, gas, and a shotgun. The last was in case he broke down at night, and the wildcats came in too close.

Mother hated discomfort more than anything except hard work, but she gladly ignored it for those treks. She returned from them happier and rosier than usual, and it is easy to figure on a calendar the two vacations that occurred just nine months before Norah and then David were born.

Anne and I went along on one of them, for almost two weeks, while Mother canned fruit at Valyermo. That was an annual ceremony, a ritual perhaps unique to middle-class life in those times. If Mother could not go up to the ranch, loads of fruit would be sent to our house in Whittier, and for days our own kitchen would hold the rites. And there and on the high desert it was unlike anything else I have known.

Great-Uncle Doctor was the boss figure. He was a former physician from Pittsburgh, and as I have heard it he never practiced after he married Margaret Oliver, my mother's aunt. Instead, he invested all the money he could find, in hundreds of acres of wild desert in California; he was determined to raise fruit there. He laid out his own wee family-town (where by now there is a real one with its suburbs and big industries!), and he lived there most of each year for the rest of his life. He was a handsome irascible man with a large white moustache, and Anne and I kept away from him, and never spoke at table if he was there. He and Rex got along well.

Aunt Maggie was a small witty woman, very active and lovely and kind. Like some few Irish immigrants of her generation, she was well read and well spoken, with a quick laughing tongue. She did her Christian duty and bore many children, and two or three of the big sons were at Valyermo when Anne and I went there, learning to raise prime apples and their own kinds of hell. One of them later became a tycoonish type, clever at manipulating the banana market from Guatemala and all that. Another died savagely, gnawed by a brain tumor. When we were there in Valyermo they were large figures who ignored us completely, since Anne was barely eight and I was going on ten. (They kept a good still going, and made better applejack than any Calvados I have ever tasted. I learned this much later, of course . . . and Aunt Maggie *never* knew of it. She and her sister Mary Frances Holbrook were steadfast members of the WCTU.)

There were always a couple of married daughters there for the canning, and a cousin or two, and the gaggle of women would gather after breakfast and then lunch, in what was called the Cook House. It was across the street from the Big House, where Uncle Doctor and Aunt Maggie lived, and down the street from the nice two-room cottages where all of us slept. It was an open-air hall, actually, with roll-up canvas walls inside the screening, so that it was cool and shady, like a beautiful *lanai.* There were several kitchen ranges in it. There were long scrubbed tables. Aunt Maggie directed everything, so that there were always enough clean pitted peaches . . . firm plums . . . late apricots . . . early pears, for the women to handle. There were helpers, and I think they were Indian women from the nearby foothills. Everyone wore long full blue aprons with wrist-tight sleeves against the spitting syrups, and all morning and all afternoon the Great Canning went on.

The smells were supernacular.

At home we often got to lick spoons or taste the skimmings from the jam pots, but in Valyermo, where halves and whole fruit went into countless jars, Anne and I sat under a shelf or behind a big sack of sugar, and absorbed through the tempered desert air what went on. In the next months we would eat from the jars, at breakfast and in our desserts and our rare tarts. We would recognize what we had known so intimately in the hypnotic ritual of Aunt Maggie's Cook House.

There were quick-growing cottonwood and sycamore trees everywhere in the oasis Uncle Doctor had chopped out of the desert, and it is strange that a city-bred Easterner could have known how to plan it so fortunately. A robust stream flowed through it, even in dead autumn. Parts of it were diverted into covered ditches that flowed swiftly to irrigate the thriving, spreading orchards. Another natural branch of it had been cunningly encouraged to pour past the Big House, with tall shade trees along the banks, and at one place it ran through a long low room, dim and cool, called the Spring House. It was a kind of buttery. Mary, the cook, let Anne and me go there with her when she needed milk or butter or chilled fruits, and we would kneel together on the stones that paved the floor, beside the water that rushed through on a wide shallow bed of pebbles, and pull out a tub of sweet butter, a big canister of the morning's milk, a bowl of cream thick enough to cut.

There was a new bull on the ranch. We were taken to see him, with Father driving Uncle Doctor in the front seat of the car. Father was knowing about farm animals, and had a special and perhaps fellow feeling for a handsome bull. This beautiful black creature was in a strong pen, far from everywhere, and roaring and pawing the sand. For hundreds of miles, there was empty sagebrush. The two men got out and circled the pen respectfully a few times, talking and pointing, but Anne and I stayed in the car. It was a small but awesome experience.

Once my little sister and I walked far up the stream, on a long Sunday afternoon when everyone seemed sleepy but us, and the ranch hands were fairly quiet in their bunkhouses on the other side of the creek, playing poker or harmonicas. We went with Old John, a man I cannot remember at all except that he was like Charles Somerville, very noble. He was a trusted but menial friend of Uncle Doctor: that is to say, he did not eat and live with us, but in a little cottage of his own. I think he had something to do about the pumps.

We went for quite a long walk. Then we came to a shallow pool in the gently moving stream. Old John sat on the bank, and Anne and I took off our shoes and walked carefully into the cool water, and then took off first our shirts, and then our short pants, and finally our underpants (Mother had designed a peculiar but handy uniform for our stay in Valyermo, of thin khaki-colored desert clothes, revolutionary at that time for little children still haunted by Buster Brown . . .). Old John watched us from the bank. We paddled. The water was clear and unmenacing. The light was dappled. Anne and I were innocents, and so I think was the solitary man who sat watching us. We trusted one another. But when we told at supper of our afternoon, glances flew like knives across the big table, the faint whiff of brimstone and evil tainted the air, and we never saw Old John again.

That was the only sad thing in the time we went along with Father and Mother on their escape . . . and we ate wonderful canned fruit and jam all winter, and in the next late Spring had a little brother.

· A nearer and possibly less hazardous escape hatch opened, soon after we came to Whittier and met Aunt Gwen. It was Laguna.

Laguna then was a village of maybe two hundred people in the winter and under a thousand in the summer, when a steady number of families with lots of children would move down from their comfortable homes in Pasadena or Glendora, and live in simpler but still comfortable "cottages" to the north of the settlement. (For the next three decades, we were the only people we knew who lived to the south. This may have been part of our own Escape-Hatch Syndrome?)

It took us two and a half hours, or more if we stopped for

vegetables or water in the Canyon, to travel the exactly forty-two miles between our doorstep in Whittier and our dusty porch in Laguna. I suppose that by now it can be done in half an hour or so, but I do not care.

Aunt Gwen's family, having lived in England, New Zealand, Japan, and I think once Borneo, camped the way most people breathe, and in 1912, or at the latest the next year, they showed us the way they did it. It was a new exciting look at the way we could live too, and with many modifications the way we were to be, for a long time, the minute we headed out of town for Laguna.

Rex was caught up in a real draft, a contained steady breeze of happiness, in the freedom at the beach. Even Mother loved much of it, and was a dogged and devoted camp follower. I look back on her part in the whole continuing adventure with great respect, admiringly. She was slothful and spoiled in many ways, physical and otherwise, but she understood the reality of the way we could be in Laguna.

We were completely cut off from any possibilities of social censure, for one thing! She was a strange combination of prairie princess (raised in an Iowa village where her father was The Banker and then, for many years, in boarding schools in Virginia and Ohio) and a Daisy Miller type, listening to Wagner in Dresden while her paid companion dozed off the last setup of laudanum. In other words, she was seemingly sophisticated but inwardly naïve. And she had enough strong sensitivity to accept all the sand, cliffs, flies, plugged toilets of being in Laguna, in exchange for our happiness and her own unfamiliar freedom, at times anyway, from neighbors and church and her chosen narrow milieux.

For a few years she and Aunt Gwen and Father ran a kind of weekend resort down there in the expanding cottage. They would head for it hastily, almost as if in a near-panic, tossing supplies and Anne and me into the back of the car, with everything prearranged to see several cronies and their wives there in a few hours or at least the next day, always Sunday because Rex had to put the Saturday paper to bed. In Laguna Mother, who seldom felt psychologically sturdy enough in Whittier to invite even two people to the house to eat unless they were blood relations, sailed through long messy noisy delicious meals, sometimes with so many diners at the table that it stretched, by hook or crook, from the kitchen door right through the dining room and the wide door into the living room. She would stand for hours frying countless batches of Mrs. Walbridge's "One-and-Only Genuine Unique Real Corn Oysters," with the inventor there beside her in the tiny kitchen. She would bring along monumental cakes she had baked or at least frosted at home with the current cook's help. She was a happy young woman, with her small-town laces loosened. . . .

In those times, and for more than another decade, there was only one way into Laguna: through the Canyon. A road went north from the village as far as Dos Rocas, where it ended at the stables of that then romantic estate. To the south there was a road of sorts, for five miles or so. It was called the County or Coast, and was maintained in a haphazard way for a few people crazy enough to live down there along the cliffs. Then it dwindled to a one-way trail, hard even for our Ford, into canyons and across gently rolling mesas back from the high wild cliffs.

In the summers a handful of desert rats and cowboys, all old men, would settle into a few isolated shacks along the trail, or pitch their tents, and raise some sweet melons if they felt like it. Father was drawn to them, as he was to all such foot-loose human beings, and often we would get into the car with him and hurtle cautiously southward to fill up the back seat with ripe cantaloupes . . . fifty cents a lug for the big ones, penny apiece for the runts ripening too fast. The old man would cut one open with his penknife and shake out the seeds and give Anne and me each a half. We ate them deftly and thoroughly, like monkeys, with not a spot to show for it when we got home, which somehow and of course we always did. Then it was fun to sort out the hardest first for Whittier, and divide the rest for right away and when all the people would be coming.

Mother always bit her lip nervously when we started out on one of these trips down the Coast, and never went along. As I remember the road, neither would I, by now, except perhaps on foot on a fine cool day. The rides were wild, in terms of man's hopeful control over matter, and without Mother along, Father would indulge in a few cornerings and suchlike which while not too obviously endangering our tender lives gave him some special satisfaction. A shadow of the trail we followed in our car still lies on the land, if one knows where to look for it along the slick smooth Coast Highway, and it is horrendous to think back on . . . and was probably much less dangerous than the six lanes of high-powered lethal weapons that now ignore it. Mother would stay at the cottage, then, and ready it for the expected mob: plates, hot water on the stove, milk, tea. . . . Usually Aunt Gwen was there.

Next the refugees would arrive, most of them from Whittier or nearby. Their voices and manners would be utterly different from at home. They would flirt a little, curse mildly, bellow over a story told for a change with the ladies present. Often they sang: Uncle Mac always was in voice for "On the Road to Mandalay," with everybody on the chorus . . . he and Aunt Gwen could transpose duets from Gilbert and Sullivan into everything from choirboy treble to basso profundo . . . now and then the rigidly remote Mrs. Walbridge would twitter out something about nightingales and dying maidens, and everybody would cheer her bravery. They were drunk on freedom. It was amazing. They were like alumni of a concentration camp, holding a reunion of the ambulatory survivors. . . .

I think my sister Anne and I were the only little children

at these comparative bacchanalia. We flitted about happily, invisible in our deportment and very well fed, on the fringes of the convocation. Mrs. Walbridge would have brought a huge bowl of chicken salad. Mrs. MacLaren had baked scones. There were usually a few freshly caught rock bass to fry . . . not like brook trout certainly, but more than edible. Somebody had stopped in Tustin on the way down for some loaves of fresh crusty bread, and a jug of homemade grape juice for the kids. . . . (*Queen Isabella* it was called, straight from the presses and much better than even Welch's, Anne and I believed.)

Edith was probably at her most open, during those first Laguna years, of all the fifty-some I knew her or was cordially acquainted with. . . . I think she was baffled by the cool fact that it mattered less than nothing to the people she was instinctively drawn to in Whittier, the bankers' wives and such, that she had gone to finishing schools and read Goethe and Balzac and lived in Europe: she was simply not a Quaker. She withdrew almost completely from our town as she grew older (which did not make life easier for the rest of us in the family . . .). In Laguna, though, and for a long time, she was gay, dashing, amusing, the rare bird Rex had caught. I know that she was often harassed, at the beach, by problems like hungry or sick children, tree roots clogging the pipes of stinking water. But spiritually she found her own release in those long-gone Sundays, full of tumult and hard work and communion. And Father did too, in concomitance as well as on his own, and of course conjugally.

Laguna nudged Valyermo aside, Anne and I grew older and new siblings flew into the nest, and for several more summers Mother and Aunt Gwen kept the beach enclave alive. Good renegade Episcopalians and a few disavowed Southern Baptists and plain heretics spent their gently riotous Sundays there, and then took off through the Canyon again to their appointed Monday tasks. Anne and I stayed on. We did not yet know that we too were refugees, which was just as well for everybody concerned.

We had plenty of friends and even lovers, in Whittier. But they all went from school or business to their withdrawn unknown homes, in our little town of brotherly love, and we went to ours. It seemed natural, the way life was. But it did not lead to communication, sharing of food and trust and affection. And that is what my parents, and all of us, found in other places: a secret meal in a remote roadhouse near Cucamonga and the vineyards; a weekend in the dry murmuring air of Valyermo; the heady quiet of Laguna nights, and then its roistering Sundays.

The problem still exists, of course, and perhaps even more so. People must escape now and then, to survive. If there comes a time, as seems probable, when there is no place to go, what does a man do? The alternatives are not pretty, at least to me. But I am fortunate to be able, occasionally, to wrap the security blanket of my far past about me and rejoice, not only for myself but for some good ghosts.

It has been written of ghetto children that they cannot go back. I know differently.

17

Flora and a Few Fauna

My mother did not like animals. She seemed to have an utterly hollow spirit toward them and about them. She did not mind them when they were invisible, but when by chance she came in contact with one, in a fleeting passage on a street for instance, she shuddered off. We had no friends who kept house pets, except for one couple seldom seen, who had an unattractive small shivering fox terrier which was always hidden when Mother called.

(Call in this sense did not mean to telephone, but to pay a call in the afternoon with hat and gloves, or to go out on a rare evening visit with my father. They especially liked the people with the carefully cabined dog. The husband played the fiddle sometimes for Mother on these visits, over their highballs, although it plainly embarrassed my father as an unmanly attribute, better suited to Christmas caroling when the St. Matthias choir would climb onto an old truck and sing into the chilly air, with our friend squeaking along on the melodies. His wife died finally of alcoholism. . . .)

So we had no pets, as such, until we moved down Painter to the Ranch. Then we had what were called Outdoor Dogs or

Ranch Dogs, with whom we carried on an almost furtive courtship and allegiance. We never had cats. Mother was a felinophobe or whatever the word is, and although there were occasional cats around the barn when we had a lonely milker living in its attic, a lurking shadow of a man who needed company, none ever dared get near the house because of Edith's fear of them. It was legendary, of course, that if by chance she went to a house where a cat was permitted to live, it would immediately leap upon her lap, and she would tremble and bite her lips and later be sick. I have seen this happen once or twice. Very neurotic, but what can children do about it, except go without?

That we did. It seems a shame: I like to live with other creatures, and so does my sister Norah, born nine years after me. My sister Anne did not actually like animals, I think, and may even have been as horrified by them as was our mother, but she asserted her independence from such freakish behavior when an adult by tyrannizing a succession of overbred and highstrung spaniels and poodles, and occasional "outdoor" cats who provided her with good conversation and kept down the Sausalito and Nevada rats. (One of them, named Augie, still lives in an electrically warmed and otherwise elegant cat house south of Carson City. He is as big and heavy as a lynx, and king of most of what he bothers to survey. When feeling especially fit—he is now about one hundred as cats go in human chronology—he will stand up and box and feint deftly, for laughs. Once he has heard the titters and guffaws, he will sit down again, smiling benignly.) In other words Anne, when grown up, treated animals much as she treated men, with a cool need for vengeful power, so that either species would bow to one lift of her graceful slender wrist, one flick of her index finger of either hand. They danced when she said to dance, and they worshipped. It was painful but interesting to watch, and I always felt as if I were peering at our mother through the wrong end of the telescope.

My sister Norah has a more direct approach to living with both dogs and cats, but in it I still sniff out the rebellion: she is great pals with a dog, for instance, and gives him robust whacks and big resounding slaps on his muzzle, while he looks adoringly at her and shivers sensuously. He will sleep like an enormous scratching lump on her bed, beginning at her feet and ending, mostly, alongside her, snoring, farting, nibbling wetly at himself. She too seems to feel great satisfaction, and perhaps part of her is thumbing a quasi-respectful cocksnoot at Mother, who literally found all four-legged people disgusting.

I have no idea about birds in connection with Mother, except for one strange experience with a canary a neighbor left with us while my parents were away. I was about eight, I think. I followed all the directions, and tucked lettuce between the bars, and the old lady missionary who was watching over Anne and me, and the cook-of-the-moment, enjoyed real outbursts of singing from the back porch. The bird was called Dickie, which seemed fatuous to me even at the time. He had a piece of dry bony stuff he pecked at happily. He made many small odorless turds on folded paper, which I had the special privilege of carrying away and so on, being the oldest child. He ate seeds, in one end and out the other I soon observed, peck-peck from a little white cup. At night the old missionary put a pretty cloth over his cage to protect him from the balmy air, and in the morning she whisked it off, since I was too short to be given this other special privilege too. He would look sleepy and soft.

It was a pleasant vacation for all of us, I would say, but the minute Mother stepped out of the topless Model T as if it were at least a landau, an evil wind blew straight from the front porch to the back, and in a half hour or so, after some good kisses and embraces and a little present for everyone, I went out to the back porch and Dickie lay claws up on the bottom of his cage, dead as if he had been shot.

All my insides turned over, and I gave out some unseemly cries, although I had already learned that as the senior child it was my special privilege to maintain stiff lips, upper and lower, and teach the younger ones how to show control. Rex and the missionary took care of Dickie, and the next day my mother explained about drafts and so on to the neighbor, but it was a sad moment for me, and perhaps why I have never again been able to face birds in cages with much poise.

Once in about 1932 I lived across from a small zoo, in Strasbourg, and I became almost dangerously depressed by the half-frozen cranes and buzzards and suchlike standing in their prisons, with their feet in the ice and their shoulders hunched under capes of snow. . . . And once my own children inherited a budgie who flew in the house on a bright day when we lived far out in the country. We decided he had been trained by a prisoner, perhaps even the Birdman of Alcatraz, not quite a hundred miles away: he would snap out commands like "Get me a lawyer . . . Call the priest . . . I wanna divorce. . . ."

This peculiar vocabulary dwindled, and in direct ratio my girls grew more fond of him, so that two years later when I had to move from St. Helena down to Berkeley, to give my younger child the dubious benefits of a somewhat better schooling than she could acquire during a lull in local Academe, we had to take the large cage and the ex-con back and forth with us every week, since I was determined to keep a toehold in St. Helena. I would leave Mary at her school by 8:15 on Monday mornings, and then drive eastward into the Berkeley hills, there to unload the car, all down endless hillside steps: clean laundry, leftover roast beef, and of course the cage, with the bird letting out squawks which had long since slurred off from his first impeccable commands. And then for five days I would sleep in the same room with him, carry him up the hill on Fridays to the car, and start for Willard School and St. Helena again. My girl loved him. I loved my girl. But I do not love birds in cages, and in fact have little emotional interest in them on the wing.

Long before we bought the Ranch, in 1921, we knew the lady who owned it, Mrs. Hazzard. She was eccentric, it is safe to say. Among other things she cherished a parrot named Lara. To the north of the exotic jungle which was later to become our home, with its tangle of bushes and trees which Mrs. Hazzard had smuggled into our subtropical climate from every part of the outside world, was the Thayer Ranch, where Margie lived. Whenever we stayed at her house one of the most exciting things about being there was that Lara might fly in.

She was a large bright-hued bird, correctly for her family line, but I do not remember any erectile crest on her head. She never got near enough us to be touched, but would sit in a pepper tree and laugh loudly, Haha hah *hah,* when we tried, only to amuse her, to say her name exactly as she did. "Lah-rah, Lah-rah!" we would screech hoarsely up at her, and when she was in a good mood she would yell down at us, "Lara! Hey, Lara! Haha*hah!*"

If someone in the Thayer house heard this monotonous ritual, and telephoned to Mrs. Hazzard that her parrot was there, Lara would refuse to budge for a day or two, and would still be sitting in the tree when Margie and Anne and I hurried down Painter from school. Yes, there she would be, our giddy-coated friend, and "Lara!" she would shriek harshly at us, full of merriment, and "Hey, Lara Lara Lara!" we would call up to her, even before we dashed in for whatever had been laid out for us on the generous Thayer pantry ledge: cookies, bread-and-butter, some apples. If nobody had alerted Lara's mistress, though, she would listen to us for a few minutes after our arrival, and then with a scornful cackle she would jump clumsily into the air and flap home again. She added the spice of unpredictability to our lives.

Margie's Ranch also gave us the straightforward friendship of a fine and noble collie named Jim, and of several silvery Persian cats with long fur who paid us little heed, but lay beautifully under rose bushes or on the wide chilly porches of the Big House. Margie's two older sisters, Marian and Frances, sometimes sat in the sun in the back yard, a good undefined space between their house and the Hired Man's, shaded with great pepper trees, and while their freshly washed hair dried in the dappled sunlight, they combed slowly at the placid cats stretched over their knees. This was a job for grown-up girls, not for the Wild Indians, as we were called. We watched now and then, and then went off to rougher pleasures. Usually Jim came with us.

He was a big dog, with a handsome coat which perhaps Frances and Marian brushed too, but which we took most of the burrs out of, especially after he had helped us with something like making wigwams. This was a trick he had perfected, and I know that he often regretted his skill at it.

On Mrs. Hazzard's ranch there was a newly planted orchard of little orange trees (which were to grow to giant size while we lived there, and then to be torn out cracking and giving almost human cries, to make way for the subdivisions of some forty years later). Between the rows of baby trees long rows of corn were planted every year, and in a way which would now be called quaint the drying stalks, plucked of their ears of kernels, were leaned together to form pointy stacks, before they were hauled away for fodder. And Jim Thayer knew how to turn them into wigwams, or perhaps they were more properly tepees, if there is a difference.

We would push open a few of the bottom ends of the cornstalks, enough for him to stick his long nose in, and then he would dive, make himself into a kind of wheel, and turn round and round until there was a good dusty smelly place pushed out, plenty big enough for a girl or boy. When he knew it was right he would come wheezing out, half-blinded by the dust and dry stuff from the stalks, and we would pat him and embrace him and make a great fuss in general. He would beam and go on dutifully to the next potential tent.

At least, he did this for a few fine times. Then it grew harder to work up enthusiasm in him. We had to beg, and wheedle and bribe him. It must have been a wretched job, and we knew that we ourselves were incapable of it. The second or third year, we had grown bigger and he had grown older, and we recognized with mutual respect that a chapter of our lives was closed.

All this casual friendliness between animals and people was part of the Thayer Ranch while we still lived up in Whittier, and one we never dreamed would be, or at least could be, part of our own lives when we moved down Painter to Mrs. Hazzard's dilapidated overgrown place. And meanwhile we had plants and flowers in town, or I had . . . and I took it for granted that what was for me was for my little sister Anne too.

Mother, whose favorite position was propped up with many pillows on a good couch, had an astonishing knowledge of botanical names, and although I doubt that she had ever buried her hands in good loam in her life, or kneeled to nurse a tender pansy plant, she could rattle off words like *pittosporum* and *citrus sinensis trifoliata.* Who were we to question?

When I was almost a woman, or roughly between thirteen and perhaps thirty, she confessed casually to me that whenever a visiting foreigner like somebody from Iowa asked her the name of an unfamiliar plant, and she did not know it, she would say that it was a form of acacia, since there were hundreds of them, from the giant redwood to the flowering mimosa, and she felt safe. I know now that she cheated with more than acacias, but it was fun to bring home twigs and leaves, and show them to her. She would be on the long couch in front of the living room fire, when we lived in Whittier, and then on the long couch alongside the fire at the Ranch, and she would look at the specimen and say with unique languor, "From an *Acer rerum,* of course. I didn't know there were any *aceraceae* in California. . . . " Sometimes she would add kindly, "What makes maple syrup?"

In general, though, an orange tree was an orange tree, and grass was grass, and those are the first two growing things I remember clearly, although somewhere in my dimmest consciousness are the rows of tall eucalyptus trees bending and creaking in a sea wind, in Ventura where we stayed for a few unfortunate months before Father bought into the Whittier *News* in 1912. Wind, fog, cold: I know that it was a mean time for my mother, and that what I think I remember is really what I gleaned from her later sarcasms about it. But the tall beautiful trees are my own, somewhere far back.

In Whittier, there was a small lawn in front of our big brown-shingled house, with a straight cement walk splitting it to the front steps and two patches of pesky Bermuda grass on either side. I suppose it was a proof of respectability, but it was always a nuisance, for Rex refused to put in a sprinkling system as most of our neighbors did gradually, and he must have mowed it himself now and then, although I do not remember this. Maybe some of the hobos in those days did it now and then for a handout. The turf stayed springy, but we seldom played on it. Instead we went into the Back Yard, a fine private place perhaps fifty feet wide and somewhat longer.

The Front Yard was open to the street, with a spindly privet hedge between us and the neighbors to the north, and dwindling past a few rose bushes to the south and into the half-wild orchard where Aunt Gwen came to live not too long after we arrived. (Perhaps a year? Six months? They were not real until she was there. . . .)

In the Back Yard, which had a high latticed fence on Aunt Gwen's side and at the edge of the Alley, there were two or three healthy orange trees. There were other things, of course: equally healthy Cecil Brunner roses climbing over the long pergola that led from Painter to the garage, and a fine trumpet vine over the woodshed that leaned against the garage, and a blackberry bush, harsh and healthy, over the Alley fence. There was also a thriving high privet hedge cutting off perhaps fifteen feet of the Back Yard by the Alley, behind which Rex grew small batches of chickens, rabbits, and even ducks. But in the main the Back Yard belonged to Anne and me, and the orange trees were our own.

We had a sand pile. We also had a fairly crude wooden slide, always ready to put splinters in our behinds, which Father had been given in payment of a back bill for advertising. It was a mean thing, but I loved it, and performed daring feats on it for visitors, while Anne watched admiringly and with what I learned later was an innate resentment. Under the orange trees was the best part, though. There we soon smoothed off the ground, so that even Bermuda would not grow where we squatted happily; where we made invisible rooms and even whole palaces in the hard clay soil; where we could leave our toys except in the worst winter rains. (Compared with modern cheap plastic and metal gadgets for children, ours were sparse and extremely simple: a ratty little wagon, some handmade blocks . . . a doll a year at Christmas.) The dark green leaves came down like magical walls, still letting in the sunlight, and we felt safe and very happy. In the winter the branches bent with fine fruit, called Navels and Valencias in spite of Mother's more rolling syllables.

The first year we lived in Whittier, there was a bad freeze. There is a picture of our biggest tree with a coal-oil heater burning in complete futility under it, and the crop of young fruit turned to sherbet in its skins. I remember that Father took out his pocketknife and cut an orange in half, and it was solid ice crystals. He laughed shortly, and it was a mysterious thing that on our first Thanksgiving Day at the Ranch, seven years later, he walked across our ringing gravel driveway into the Thayer orchard, pulled off an orange savagely, and once more cut it in frozen halves. He tossed it on the ground. "Happy Thanksgiving," he said, and I knew even then that it was a sad blow to him to have our first real crop ruined, along with every rancher's in the county. People had told Rex he was a fool to try to raise oranges. He should stay up in town where he belonged. Editors of small-town dailies were not fruit growers. This was proof, they would say. By noon dinner, which happened only on Sunday, this day, and Christmas in our family, he was his usual dignified and innately philosophical self again.

Besides the grass and the orange trees, there were some bushes growing against the Whittier house along the driveway under the kitchen and dining room windows, which I always liked, although they were spindly and in general neglected. They were purple begonias, and the tutu skirts of the little ballet blossoms were a creamy white. If Anne and I pulled out all but two of the threadlike stamens with their yellow tips, we had tiny dolls with slender green necks and heads . . . no arms, of course, but so finely clothed, in the full cream and purple costumes, and the slender legs and their little slippers, what need was there for anything more?

Next to the row of begonias was, by some accident, a sturdy and also neglected and therefore scrawny bush of something that smelled good when a leaf of it was bruised. It was possibly a lemon verbena . . . or a rose geranium? Or perhaps a form of acacia? Something else grew against the front of the house, and I think it was geraniums, still one of my favorite flowers so I do not see why I feel so vague.

In the strip of ground between the public sidewalk in front of our house and the street were two trees which grew taller while we lived there. One was a camphor tree, and its leaves smelled good and, if bitten, reminded me of having a cold, for we used camphorated oil as a trusty panacea, at least whenever Grandmother was in residence. The other tree was mysteriously referred to as a bottle tree, and I was told, but surely not by my mother, that when young it could be planted upside down just as well as with its real roots in the ground, and that it would grow. I often looked hard at it, with a continuing disbelief, and meanwhile it made a fine shade, under which the iceman's horse liked to stand in summer. We in turn liked to stand near the back of his wagon, while the iceman chipped off the shape of ice we needed. Sometimes he would scoop the little chips into our hands, before he put tongs into the big chunk and trotted, dripping, down the long pergola to the back porch.

Once we had been told not to pick any chips off the road itself, and when Mother saw from the glassed sunroom that Anne had already crammed her mouth with them, she swept out like a quiet hurricane, snatched a long supple twig from the privet hedge between us and the neighbors, and headed for my horrified little sister, tearing off the leaves to make a mean switch as she moved. Anne let out a wild cry, and bolted straight down the driveway pergola, with Mother after her, and as I think about it I am sure that never before or after did I see that large indolent woman move so fast. The iceman was coming out to the street. Anne streaked past him, howling, and he stood there laughing and snapping his big tongs in the air. Mother said something breathlessly about being embarrassed, and he laughed some more and climbed into his wagon and clopped northward.

I suppose Anne was pinned down in the garage and given a couple of small switches over her legs, which was as far as my mother ever went in corporal punishment. I remember that later she told Father about it, and that she herself was ashamed to have gone leaping out onto Painter Avenue to chase a helpless infant. What must people have thought?

(*People* did not even know, I am sure, of that traumatic experience in our lives. I could count on my hands the number of people I ever saw walking up or down the sidewalks in our block, and as for four-legged ones, there were *none*, except for the casual visits of the iceman's horse.)

There were many trees along our block, and some of them are still there, giving Painter a quaint elderly air in the sprawling new town with its neat curving subdivision streets and its carefully chosen planting: trees must not grow past a certain height, nor shed untidy leaves, nor cast too deep a shade upon the dwellers' petunia beds. When we lived in Whittier, our street was a horticultural shambles, planted according to unknown whims and convenience, so that great shaggy peppers would crowd out the two peaches some practical resident had stuck in next door, and the sidewalks were a constant hazard underfoot, what with the treacherous pungent pepper berries one time, ripe fruit the next.

All this made delicious scavenging for people like Anne and me, still fairly close to the ground. It also added to occupational risks, for during a few years I spent most of my waking life on skates, and the roots of all the trees along the sidewalk would manage overnight, in the right weather, to heave up a new lump here and there, to trip me and send me into one more bloody collision with the cement I sailed over, and even with the trees themselves.

One time when I was trying to work up a little speed on my skates, on the uppity sidewalk between our house and the Fays', I hit a place where a new pepper tree root had heaved up the pavement after the last rain, and I left a good slice of my knee there. I raced back to the house, and demanded from my mother a little white box I had seen her push together that very morning at the breakfast table, probably finishing some pills. She handed it to me without question, too used to seeing me with torn stockings to notice that this time one of mine was thoroughly blood-soaked, and I ran as fast as I could to the spot where I had fallen, to pick up the fair-sized piece of myself I had left there, and take it home to be bound back into place. There was no sign of it. Had it withered so quickly? Had a greedy bird swooped it up like a mouse? Had ants swarmed onto it and made it vanish? It was the biggest piece of my body to leave me until I had to have my tonsils out, and then much later a couple of vermiform adjuncts, and I have always wondered in a somewhat atavistic way about whom and what I may have fed. I know I returned the box to Mother, and told her why I had asked for it so brusquely, and she held me to her in a quick soft sadness, but laughing a little. My knee was mean for a night or two, but at least I did not have to take a bath every day while it made a new skin, and I could wear socks instead of long stockings.

There were many plants growing then in Whittier which are now curiosities, and hard to procure from fancy nurseries. There were guava bushes, brought by the Mexicans I suppose, and loquats and kumquats brought by the Chinese. There were Gold of Ophir roses tumbling over outmoded backhouses converted into toolsheds before the march of the American flush toilet. There were rows of crepe myrtle, which I was told by my Anglomanic mother was Queen Victoria's favorite plant, but which I have always felt was of an unfortunate color when in bloom, like incipient gangrene . . . a bruise that may begin to rot.

There seemed to be many fruit trees. On our corner, where Aunt Gwen came to live in the farmhouse, there were peaches and apricots, and I think a couple of almonds, and of course the Gold of Ophir spilling over the back shed. And on the northeast corner, across from her, were handsome date palms and, in the Moorheads' yard in the back, a beautiful tree of saucer peaches, which are almost unknown to most Americans today.

I have tried to find out about them. I suspect they were Chinese. They were without doubt the most delicate fruit I ever ate, and I am told that they are impossible to ship from one country or state, or even one village, to another.

When they were ripe, Mrs. Moorhead would lay some on a tray and hurry across the street to our house with them, and we would eat them at the next meal. The best way would have been to peel them at the table, so quickly did they turn brown and bruised, but fruit was always skinned and cut up and heavily sugared in little dishes, in our basically Midwestern cuisine. Almost surely we poured cream over the peaches, a deserved treat. What we liked best, though, was to stand under the tree when the Moorheads were picking. Anne and her first lover, Tolbert, and I could eat whatever fell to the ground, for at once it would be too wounded to save for even an hour. The fruits were perhaps a fat inch wide and half an inch deep, of a tender green, and with a wee seed big as a baby pea in the middle, as if it had been pinched in there to make a pincushion. I swallowed several seeds in my gourmandizing, but said nothing and suffered not at all. The skin peeled off easily, in one or two pieces, and the flesh was of an ivory white, but already discoloring from no matter how light a pressure.

Almost as fantastic a delicacy were the loquats which grew in several places in our part of town, the northeast side. (Philadelphia marked this mystical distinction to the south, and Greenleaf to the whole west, and it is true that the houses, the plants, and the people differed greatly because of those two streets. For instance, on Painter south of Philadelphia the planting was different from up north, except for Aunt Gwen's house on the north corner and then our big place, both of which had a definitely classless look. On South Painter the houses were smaller and older and the people who lived in them were "plainer," less assertive. Such distinctions perhaps do not hold to the basic tenets of brotherly love in the Society of Friends, but they existed in our Quaker town as they do in other places, and were recognized and obeyed. There were a few noble loquat trees, and even magnolias, on South Painter and even west of Greenleaf, but the bushes were lowlier, to match one-story houses. All the streets, humble or not, had good names, though: Newlin, Comstock, sounds of the founding fathers, who almost surely had not foreseen any social distinctions in their considered pacings-off of the gentle sloping meadows that fell from the foothills toward the bed of the Rio Hondo . . . and the future Jim Town slums. . . .)

Once I was reported to my family for swinging up into a loquat tree, to impress a gaggle of small friends below me more than to snag any of the beautiful but only half-ripe fruit. An old lady was peeking at my unseemly thievery and conduct, and she telephoned to Mrs. Moorhead, not wishing to deal directly with a person of another church from theirs, and our good Quaker neighbor talked with her usual gentle tact to my mother. I was called on the carpet, after lunch and before Father left for the *News*.

Grandmother agreed fully with the old lady of the loquats that girls of my age should not get up in trees, like rough boys, where they could be seen with bare skin showing between their underpinnings and the tops of the outlandish newfangled socks I was wearing. Girls should wear proper stockings, in or out of trees, and as high as their legs went! (Grandmother and Edith had a running feud about this. Socks, the older woman felt, were a foreign affectation, a danger to health, and very immodest on any female past the age of perhaps five. Mother kept right on putting us into the high thick black or white leggings as soon as Easter approached. "Those children's knees are blue with cold!" Grandmother would snort with a dramatic shudder and clicking of her teeth, at the beginning of each such season of freedom from winter underwear and garters and long stockings. *Blue with cold* became part of the Family Language, meaningless to anyone who did not vibrate to its subtle mockery and affection as Time changed its first disapproval.)

I do not remember what penalty I got, but I stayed out of that one loquat tree. (It still stands, and I passed it not long ago and looked at the house behind it, in memory of that sanctimonious old snooper. . . . She was right to protest my thievery, but my modesty was my own problem. . . .) There were plenty of other places where I could snitch good fruit and nuts, but probably nothing tasted as delicious in a puckery way as the unripe loquats that far day, and even now a ripe one has a *verboten* savor to it, and even from my own tree in the side yard of my house in a little town removed in every way from Whittier.

My friends and I ate dates that fell onto the sidewalks, and although my parents spurned the ones I brought them, and I would not like them now, they tasted real and therefore right, although they were nothing but seeds. Much later I would thrive on dates in some thin student days in France, when that country's government was buying them for near-nothing to encourage Algeria or perhaps Morocco. I told myself that an Arab could ride a camel for countless hours with a handful of dates to sustain him, and that I should be happy to do the same, on shanks' mare. I liked dates very much then, and still do, but the real reason is that I got to respect them on the sidewalks of my hometown. And when we moved down to the Ranch, in my twelfth year, there were exotics like the many bushes of guavas, so delicious ripe in the hand . . . and pomegranates, fun to eat because of all the spitting that must go on . . . and more dates, also a spitty fruit if one is in the right company and eating the kind ours were, with big pits, little flesh, a lot of harsh skin and a fine flavor—*Whittier sidewalk* dates!

As I look back, we really ate almost anything that we could put in our mouths without being burned or stung, and swallowed everything that our bodies would not reject. It was a good education for my palate. At the Ranch, thanks first to Mad Mrs. Hazzard and then my equally agrarian father, we had beautiful orchard and citrus fruits, and artichokes, and asparagus and every kind of vegetable that would grow above ground (the soil was impossible for roots like parsnips, thank God . . .). Peaches, apricots, plums, mirabelles, prunes, the guavas and dates, strange little things called roselles . . . they all flourished in our Chosen Land, as did the pigeons, chickens, turkeys, pig, cow, Hi-Ho Silver the horse, dogs, cats, children, and other people.

My mother not only never had an animal inside the house, but she did not like to be made aware of any great dramas going on in other nearby places, like a calving cow or even a setting hen. What is more, she did not want us children to participate in the barnyard activities. Once the cook came in and whispered to Rex, and he left the table. I knew that Bessie was having a baby, and I was dying, in my own words, to go out there and watch, and perhaps learn something about myself and other things. But it was impossible, or so it seemed then: Mother was plainly sickened by such basic actualities, which she herself had indulged in pleasurably and often, and she needed us to stay close by while we all ate decorously at something like tapioca pudding, and she tapped her toe.

The outside animals, though, were a fine lot. Rex was their master, and he was too casual for my own taste. He let one of our best dogs drink milk all the time, simply because there was a lot of milk, and the dog got a bad skin condition and the vet said to stop the milk, and the dog kept right on getting it because Rex thought milk was good for people. That was stupid. The dog scratched and looked worse than scruffy and miserable. But Rex liked him very much, and it would not have occurred to him to change either his mind or the poor beast's diet.

The only time I remember losing an animal, except for the ones we ate along the way, for that we did with almost complete detachment, was when my father decided that Hi-Ho

Silver was too miserable to go on. He was a superannuated nag who, we were told and almost believed, had been a movie hero, the first and *genuine* Hi-Ho. He was a silvery white. Rex rode him through the orange groves, but not often enough, and he stood impassively in his very nice private quarters for years and years. We would show him to visiting children and he would toss his head a little and give us his profile. But he simply stood up too long, like an old clerk in the yardage department of a decaying department store. His hooves gave out. He was miserable. Rex was miserable too. (This was later in his life, and I have always thought that he identified himself with the horse. . . .) He arranged for a friend of his, a retired colonel of cavalry who ran a small riding school, to come for Hi-Ho and dispose of him. No glue-factory stuff, no dog factory: a bullet through the temple and an honorable deep grave. With military dispatch, the Colonel drove in with a truck for our friend, and I stood for a few minutes with Rex in the long driveway as the trailer went toward Painter Extension, and then I faded left, to leave him alone with his real sorrow.

When we moved to the Ranch there was no such shadow of the future in our minds, and we felt acceptive if not actively puzzled by Mother's inability to tolerate animals, but got all we needed outside the house. There was Jim Thayer, and for several more years, there were the beautiful silky Persians at his Ranch. At ours there were the comparatively undistinguished watchdogs and barn cats and all the other native birds and beasts . . . except of course for Lara, who left with Mrs. Hazzard. We always had an owl or two in residence, big ones who lived in a dark barn somewhere but who liked our grand trees. They were said to be dangerous, but never bothered anyone, and their calls at night were straight from the romantic books we fed on. There were mourning doves now and then, and happily they no longer distressed Mother, who once when she was ill at the Painter house had become too tearful over their sad sweet notes, and even begged Father to shoot them . . . which he did not. And there were many birds now almost unseen near Whittier: orioles, red-wing blackbirds, very bright hummingbirds.

Father liked to play with bees, whose communal life fascinated him almost as much as did the rampant monogamy in his pigeon cote and the equal freedom of choice in his rabbit hutches. He had a friend known as the Bee Man, who used to wear a lovely veiled hat when he showed Rex how to introduce a new queen to a hive, and helped take out the honey. Rex wore gloves, all right, but spurned the hat (too feminine?), and said that no bee would ever sting him, which apparently was true.

We caught several new swarms from the rich air when the orange trees were blooming, and Anne and I were allowed to beat on dishpans to make the humming wild clouds settle somewhere, to be coaxed then into a hive. We must have had too much rhythm, or at least volume, for we had a continuing community for several decades in the hollow north wall upstairs around the chimney, and they could never be interested in any more practical place to put their honey. Often we heard them buzzing over some state event . . . a new queen, perhaps? . . . and their special warning hum was a sure signal that within a few seconds we would feel an earthquake, very common in those days when too much oil was being sucked out from under us. And after we all left the Ranch, and the bulldozers came to raze the tottering old house, we were told that honey actually spouted from its north side and ran down the front walk and out onto the long driveway. . . .

In the wall between the living and dining rooms, and in the downstairs ceilings, there were invisible but active kangaroo rats or perhaps tiny chipmunks, who never gnawed on anything audibly, but ran about and occasionally squeaked. They did not bother us, nor we them, since there seemed no tenable way to send them away. Mother, who disliked things like ticking clocks and dripping water, thought them quite funny, since they were invisible, except for once when she had put down her novel as she lay on the couch. There on the white plaster ceiling near the fireplace was a grey wet spot, and as she and Father and my younger sisters watched, it grew from the size of a saucer to that of a pie plate and then to a platter, while they laughed more and more and shook their fists impotently at it. I was always sorry I missed that sight; I was probably up at the Thayers', reading Zane Grey with Margie. But the spot could never be covered, by any paint known to man, so I could see the proof of the chipmunk's sudden loss of control as long as I lived there . . . and share vicariously the moment of high scatology in our family history.

And everywhere outside, fruit ripened on trees and bushes, and vegetables flourished, and flowers grew as casually as weeds. We brought them all indoors, for varied nourishments, and kept cats and dogs outside for like reasons of survival, and lived in a state of blissful compromise between Mother Nature and Mother Edith.

18

A Footnote on Fauna, Largely Secret

It is sometimes hard to separate discretion (intrinsic self-protection) and deception (lying, cheating), in a child's gradual process of fitting himself into this world. As soon as I saw that my mother disliked and even feared all animals but the human (and could well forgo any of those not linked to her by consanguinity, except for her husband), I simply did not mention them to her, and made sure that they never set foot or paw or wing inside our house, in case I felt even fleetingly within her own pale. As I recall this discreet non-communication, probably as deliberate on my mother's part as on mine, I realize that all along, from my own beginnings, Father was tacitly backing me in my actual deceptions. This was not mentioned, however, until I was a raddled fifty or so, and bringing cats and dogs and pots of geraniums into the house at the Ranch, after Mother had died and I had returned there to help run things.

There was one time when my mother felt a flash of regret, I think, for her intrinsic detachment. It was about two ducks somebody gave Father when I was nearly six. He and Anne and I took care of them in the little space between the Back

Yard hedge and the blackberry fence that ran along the Alley. That was where Rex always had a few thriving rabbit hutches. He read government pamphlets about not only feeding his family but making his fortune from their pelts, which he and Charles Somerville, our best tramp, cured and stretched in a revolting way on the garage walls. The meat was delicious.

It was different about the two ducks, though. They lived in a big screened box, in which they turned fast from the fluffy, small stage to glossy mammoths. Father sank a bucket into the ground in front of their house, so that they could take a good dive now and then even if there was no room for paddling. When he came home in the late afternoon from the *News* he would signal to Anne and me, and without any undue fuss we would meet in the Back Yard for an exciting few minutes, never mentioned, never referred to, *secret.*

First Father would run fresh water from a hose into the little swimming pool. Then he would let out Mutt and Jeff, and while they stretched and made trusting sounds and finally took turns dunking themselves, Anne and I helped clean out their box and put in new alfalfa hay and so on. Then came the best part, when Father produced a couple of heads of tired lettuce that he had picked up on his way home. He would break them into big chunks, and give them slowly to the two handsome quiescent birds, and it was like a trick of magic to see the way the pale green salad vanished in a flurry, a tiny frenzy, of beaks tearing and snapping and the throats gulping. It made us laugh with amazement. In a flash everything would be gone, and Rex would push the stuffed couple back in its house, and we would go decorously to ours. It was never necessary for Father to advise us to keep quiet about such things. Without knowing it we were already caught in the nets of caution. . . .

And then on Thanksgiving Day, instead of eating a turkey we ate Mutt and Jeff, without any forewarning to Anne and me. After all, how could Mother have known that we were perhaps forever entangled in the lives of two ducks she had never even seen? And Father too: it never occurred to him, who had often watched us feeding the rabbits we were soon to savor at Sunday Dinner, to remind us that ducks too are raised with a purpose. So Anne and I had no idea that the two delicious brown birds on the platter in front of our father were our friends, until well after we had all been served and he said something casually about having done a good job of raising those two ducks So-and-So had given him. Then my little sister and I behaved in a trite, banal, and also classical pattern and had to put our forks down quietly, with our throats closed and our faces pallid. Pieces of Mutt and Jeff lay on our plates. . . .

Some sheepish explanation must have gone on between the two grownups, because Mother cried out in pity for us: how dreadful . . . she had not realized . . . oh, how sad! Father probably muttered self-protectively, in his chagrin, that everybody *knows* farm birds are food, something like that. It is sure that he and Edith were really regretful for our sitting there so shocked and pale . . . but the birds were well prepared and the festive meal went on, and I suppose Anne and I revived enough to eat the "special" dessert at least. It was plain to us that people have different feelings about things, and we never mentioned Mutt and Jeff . . . nor were we ever again involved emotionally with the rabbits-chickens-turkeys-pigeons that in the next decades graced our table, after their well-fed lives in our Back Yard and then the Ranch.

We had another secret friend in the early days with Aunt Gwen: her dog, a dignified but mischievous character always called Pat Nettleship and not just Pat, liked Anne and me very much. He had a fine peppery smell. He was short-haired, mostly white, of medium size and a vaguely terrier build. One of his ears was crumpled and definitely black.

Of course he never came into our house, not even onto the front porch, but when Father took Aunt Gwen and Anne and me to Laguna, to install us for the vacations or just to catch the breeze, he always rode on the back seat with us sisters. If the weather was cool and breezy we would hunch down together in the bottom of the car, the three of us warm and snoozy under a filthy lap robe full of burrs and stickers, and stained with spilled cocoa and who can tell what else, from a hundred picnics. We fitted together like three yolks in an egg.

Pat Nettleship began to wait tactfully behind the low hedge that divided our front lawn from Aunt Gwen's wild dying orchard on the corner, and for our Sunday Afternoon Drives, arranged to leave Grandmother alone in the house for her family letters, he soon figured a way to slip, sly as a fox, into the back of our car after Mother had been installed on the front seat. Anne and I never let out a peep, from the first time we found him there. We simply spread the lap robe over him and hoped for the best. When the weather indicated it, we would gradually disappear down into the bottom with him, while Rex sped dashingly along in our merry Ford and then Maxwell and finally Oldsmobile.

Pat Nettleship finally did himself in, as far as our secret rides went: one Sunday he suddenly stood up on his hind legs, with the lap robe over his head and shoulders like a proper shawl, and put his front paws on the back of the front seat, and beamed pantingly down between my parents. I suppose he felt a wave of well-being? It must have been justifiably unnerving to both Edith and Rex. He kept control of the skittish car and then her, and she sobbed and shook, and he headed for home and hot toddies for them both. Anne and I were told sternly not to let such a thing happen again, and Aunt Gwen's dog understood.

One time Mother managed to laugh about a four-legged creature, though.

On the west side of the Alley, next to Aunt Gwen's big lot, was a good Quaker named Peter Trueblood. He had a cow, and chickens, and a mule. I do not remember him as anything but a wonderful name (he had a son, I think, named Rufus, which was even better!), but I can still hear the sound of his mule coughing in the night. Father said he had swallowed too many barley beards, and that they had stuck in his throat (and that we should not eat any ourselves, which we always did in the Springtimes, when they waved on the hills back of the college and had a wonderful sweet tiny kernel in them . . .). And one night at dinner, there was a great excitement, for we heard a heavy stamping up our four or five front steps, and almost at the same moment Rex sat staring wildly down the length of the table and past Edith to the big front window on the porch, and then Mr. Trueblood's mule who stood there looking in at us let out an enormous cough, a long braying wheeze that rattled the pane. Mother leaped to her feet, and apparently whirled around to see what Father was staring at, and gave a real yell, not at all ladylike, and rushed weeping and shaking into the living room and onto the couch.

I remember two more things about this dramatic moment in our experiences with the wildlife of the Quaker jungle: Rex gentled the scared mule and led it back down the steps and to Mr. Trueblood's, and then threw some more wood on the fire in front of the couch and got Mother into long and happy laughing, which Anne and I heard from our bedroom at the top of the stairs, through our own continuing and well-muffled giggles and titters.

There was another side to the hidden hunger in us to communicate with other creatures, and it was completely silent. By now I am not sure that Anne needed it, or at least used it for excitement and comfort, as I did and still do. But there were many things all around me that made not a sound, and that need not betray either themselves or me to my mother's aversion to them. I think that some of these voiceless things I knew how to find, when I was a child in Whittier, have long since disappeared from the hills and arroyos and sandbanks where I knew they would be. There were trap-door spiders! There were horny toads! (There were even wild yellow violets and an occasional mariposa lily, before *people* started moving in. . . .)

There were a few girls about our ages who lived within a couple of blocks of us, and every Saturday morning unless it was rainy or too hot we would meet at Eldine Hamm's, on what is now part of the campus of Whittier College, and head almost feverishly for the hills. They rose steeply to the east of town, in beautiful rolling rhythm, and although there were little arroyos in them for the occasional water-shed, their natural covering of thick grasses kept them from any erosion, and they were not dangerous for us. They were unfenced. They were ours. In the Spring, for at least one fine Saturday, the wild weeds would be so thick and juicy that we could slide down the steepest hills in wooden orange crates, in almost waxed toboggan runs we made. Later, when the weeds were coarser, they were still good to lie in and to run through, for countless weeks, before summer dried them out.

This joyous pack had no real leader, but I was admitted to be the best of any of us for finding the secrets, like the subtly hidden one-room palace of the trap-door spider. I knew how to show how the little door worked, hinged as it was with bolts of invisible cobwebs, and perfectly fitting. I could open it with a stem of wild wheat. . . .

Once I dug up a whole trap, which out of the soft warm earth of April looked like an ugly piece of dog dung. In my hand, though, I held a silk-lined cave, baited, waiting for the curious fly. Then with one deft flick the door would close . . . victim and mighty spider silently together in the softness . . . shades of Bela Lugosi . . . shades of Nabokov and pale fire! Aunt Gwen, always my guide in such matters as life, birth, and death, told me sadly that I could never go back, never replace this astounding bit of skill, any more than I could touch a fawn and have its mother still love it, or pull up a *Brodiaea* bulb and expect it to grow again after I had nibbled at it for its taste of garlic. Don't even touch the trap door with a piece of grass, she advised me urgently. . . . We have our own smells, she said . . . and she took me to the Biology Room at the College, where there before my eyes was a trap-door spider's lair, cut neatly down its middle and lying on cotton under glass. I studied it. I think I could draw it now. It was a silent forgiving friend, and my first excitement at its mysterious beauty was forever tempered by humility.

The horny toads were almost as quiet, although they made patient scratching sounds if I kept them too long in a paper box, under the orange tree in the Back Yard that had the lowest branches, and therefore was best adapted to preoccupations best left unobserved. I forget what time of the year was the right one for finding the little creatures. They liked dry hot weather for wandering. The sandy gravel in the bottoms of the gulleys was a favorite place for them, and they looked so much like it that it was only the pulse in their throats that betrayed them to my keen eye. Now and then one would hop clumsily across the sidewalk as we came home from school. I would put it in my pocket, so that nobody might step on it in its bewilderment, and then transfer it to an old shoebox Anne and I kept ready for such mixtures of compassion and curiosity. We always put in a little fresh grass and a Mason jar top filled with water, and I would try to catch a few gnats or flies, but nothing was ever touched, and after a few days we would take it up to the edge of the hills and watch it shuffle away.

Horny toads are strange leftovers from another world, neither dragon nor frog, and not lizards certainly. They have an intense stare, or so it seems to a human being, and they are as dry and impersonal as a long-dead leaf. They are pleasant to the touch, not cold and serpentine, not warty, but rather like the hand or cheek of an ancient person, still alive and warm under the cool horniness. I never had any feeling that they minded my keeping them for a time, and I hope I was right.

Common flies were occasionally a pest when I was little, and nasty swatters were part of the household equipment wherever we ate or sat or cooked, in the summer. I trapped a few, to watch them, but found them dull and repellent even though I knew about their extraordinary eyes, and their delicate front hands, from *The Book of Knowledge*. Once Grandmother told me that God had created every living thing on Earth to help us be stronger and nobler Christians. We discussed the rightness of such things as birds, cows, perhaps even people. Then, taking great care to modulate my manner so that I would not sound impertinent, I asked her about the housefly. She was not daunted, at least visibly. "The housefly," she said with great conviction, but unconvincingly, "was put here to make us better people, by *trying our patience*." This is perhaps the nearest she ever got to admitting that her God may have been a little less all-wise than usual, at least once.

Bees and wasps, and especially mud daubers, were much more interesting, and I came to know quite a lot about them. It now amazes me that I was never stung until I was sixteen, when a wasp got caught up my sleeve as I was riding a captious colt in what is now the Emerald Bay area of Laguna Beach. For a minute I was on a runaway, an inter-

esting experience which I am glad is as unique in my life as
the sting that started it. . . . I was completely out of control
in my pain and astonishment, and the pony knew it. . . .

Once I got deeply involved in breeding and studying
mosquitoes, thanks to Aunt Gwen's help in letting me keep
my smelly jars of them in all their stages on her back porch.
It was my first heady taste of research work, done for a
class at Penn Street School called Citizenship, which taught
me more about how to build a septic tank and what might
happen if I did not, and how to prevent the spread of
malaria, and also how to salute the flag in almost any situation, than any course I have since attended. I lapped up
this free and fascinating information the way a thirsty pup
drinks water, and meanwhile all my pets were largely silent,
which was wise and best in our household, dedicated as it
was to the nonrecognition of the lower species.

Very rarely Anne and I, in possession of a tiny white
sliding pillbox perhaps found in a wastebasket or given to
us by Dr. Wanberg, our Danish dentist-hero, would sneak
up to our room a voiceless ladybug or two. Mostly, though,
our cached catches were dry and dead: moths, a battered
dragonfly, once a tiny bat. We would close our door, which
fortunately was always acceptable in our family, and tip
the find onto a white paper on the floor, study it from every
angle, turning it over delicately with one of Mother's finest
hairpins.

And all this was done with guile, with mutual connivance,
with plain dishonesty and cowardice, some might say. We
never mentioned such floutings of the house rules to anyone,
even Aunt Gwen: we already had in us the germs of mis-
trust, of suspicion. We never spoke of Mutt and Jeff: we
were already two-faced. We kept quiet: we were already
selfish.

19

The Separation of the Senses, or Not

One of the best things about my childhood in Whittier was that several people in the last few generations in the family had been easy marks for book salesmen. Prime culprit was my grandfather Holbrook, Grandmother's husband, who died in about 1910 after a long sedentary life of reading, which of course one does not do as well behind a plow, or riding a tiger, as one does in an armchair.

Grandfather had managed to evade active combat in the Civil War, it was hinted, by buying one of his brothers, the family rake, to fight for him. He himself had been sent to help survey what was the Territory of Iowa by *Lincoln*, it was also hinted more proudly. He carried with him a small trunk filled with books, and gradually it also became the strongbox for all kinds of banknotes and treasures brought to him by people who could not read or write, for safekeeping: he was an educated young man and therefore he must be honest. Fortunately he was both, and he took care of every request his illiterate companions made, and later became the first banker in the new state of Iowa, mostly because he still had quite a bit of other people's cash on hand and they needed him to sign their names.

He always disliked his position, and called himself a usurer from the moment he began charging interest, as did his eldest son after him. He stayed away from the little bank building in the village of Onawa the way a man will avoid an abattoir if the sight of blood makes him faint. He sat most of the time in his book-lined study, at home. He read catalogues from England, and Boston and New York, and gradually the walls of the whole house filled with good, bad, and quietly indifferent publications.

There is a nice photograph, the kind Lewis Carroll used to take, of a lovely young girl curved over his shoulder as he sits plumply in a large chair, his neat beard already white. (Mother was the Afterthought of nine children, and his only living daughter.) Behind them rise fine fat shelves of books. Beside them is a little table with a bowl of apples on it, and a decanter of port . . . two rituals of every evening, according to Edith much later. Grandfather would peel a piece or two of the fruit, with a silver knife of course so that it would not turn black, and cut it into eighths. He would pour the wine for himself, and toast her with the first slow glass, and then give her an occasional sip, never to be mentioned once outside the library. The coal fire would chuckle along, and the two refugees from Grandmother's stern Puritanism would read themselves away from the freezing little village on the Midwestern prairies, and into gracious indomitable England, or Père Goriot's meanness or Voltaire's cruel wonderful wit.

Most of the Holbrook books went as much farther west as they could go, when we moved there in 1911. In Whittier, a year later, the first thing my parents did was to have a respectable chimney and fireplace built, one that would burn real wood and stay warm night and day, that would light up a room and sweeten the air. The second thing was to build sturdy bookcases all around the living room, for our "sets," and such.

That was perhaps the peak in English-American publishing of Collected Works. Some of our editions were truly fine, in typography, illustrations, paper, binding. Others were plain shoddy. But, and that was the joy of the whole thing, everything was right there, bowdlerized or not . . . and usually *not* in what my grandfather had bought from his sequestered easy chair. We had, for instance, three or four different editions of *A Thousand and One Nights*, one partly ripped to several pieces in what might have been anger (my grandmother's?). I read every word of every edition with absorption, of course, and early was puzzled by the liberties publishers and printers seemed to take with what I knew instinctively was the basic stuff.

We had the "definitive, complete and authorized" editions of Dickens and Thackeray, both of them handsome and sturdy, with all the original illustrations. There were the Waverley Novels, not illustrated, and Charles Reade and Captain Marryat and Jane Austen, and Lords Bulwer-Lytton and Disraeli. There was *The Decline and Fall,* and a complete Charles Kingsley. Tennyson and Burns and good old Irish poets, and Longfellow and Bryant and Poe, were all there, and Washington Irving of course, and everybody else already pushed into third-rate high school anthologies by the time I advanced that far academically. There was Chaucer with a "modern translation," page for page, and the same for one of our several editions of *Don Quixote* . . . a very good way to sink one's teeth into Spanish, if not Middle English.

For some reason (perhaps because of Mother's having gone to two boarding schools?) there were duplicate copies of Gayley's *Classic Myths,* which was double luck for me. That book may have been the favorite, at least over the longest period, of any of the hundreds I read in the first part of my life. Our editions were fat with little engravings, line drawings, pictures of amphorae and shields and tear vases. I knew much more about Jove and Apollo and Wotan than I ever cared to find out in my own professed religion, and if I had been asked, which never happened, I could have outlined many a mythological tree, complete with all its strange fruits and devious reproductive habits. I kept one copy of the book in the orange crate at the back of the closet in Anne's and my room, to read aloud to her as we huddled snugly under the racks of school clothes that smelled of starch and probably some sweat. By now I am vague about the reason behind the reason for Achilles' bad heel, or what kind of wax Ulysses put into his sailors' ears, but until a few years ago I could have told anyone . . . if, that is, I repeat, anyone had asked me, which never happened. I cannot regret my silent knowledge, though. It wove a sturdy straight fabric for all the rest of the embroidery.

Mother carried her inky father's disease in her life's bloodstream, and kept on buying books after he died, the helpless prey of passing salesmen, catalogues, auctions. She often got hooked on pretty poor stuff, since we already had whatever Classics there were in English, but still she provided me with real escape reading: all of Richard Harding Davis as well as Kipling, *The Best Short Stories from Collier's* as well as Russian Immortals. . . .

We had a few things like the preciously bound volumes of Ruskin's *Sesame and Lilies*, and *The Nabob* (did Daudet write that?), and of course Elbert Hubbard's publications, which my mother would toss scornfully to me as they turned up in the mail, always adding that I should put them on the top shelf behind the living room door instead of in the wastebasket. (We never threw away a book, as far as I know, irrespective of its worth . . . and I still find it almost impossible to do more than pass my own along to another potential reader. . . .)

During some thin years when my parents were trying to adjust their earnings to their expenses, which must have been heavy, given the steady rise in our private population and our peculiar standards of basic necessity (for instance, Father shipped his six-foot white enamel bathtub from Michigan to Whittier, when he had not two nickels to rub together), we depended largely upon Grandfather Holbrook's literary leavings for our entertainment. And there was always the Bible; when Grandmother was in residence that was my main fare, and it did me no harm. She also invested occasionally in peculiar Christian publications in sign writing: she was as gullible for a Protestant publication as her husband had been for half-calf unexpurgated Ovids. . . . I would puzzle my way through these mildly interesting books, where the word "I" was always an eye, and God was a dark cloud with a hand coming through and pointing right at me, and I probably learned to read, a little anyway, from those shoddily composed texts.

I suspect that Mother never mentioned some of her monthly purchases. I am sure she made them from her own pocket, for she and Father believed in Woman's Independence, based first and foremost and always on the premise that a female should know how to use money and have some of her own to practice with. It must have been a little dismaying to my finicky dam to see such poor stuff dribbling onto the more shadowy shelves in the living room, but along with the collections of magazine fillers came "completes" of people like O. Henry and, gradually and after my initiation, Conrad and Shaw and Galsworthy.

I don't remember seeing my father read many books when I was young, although I know that he kept a sharp eye on magazines. I saw him mostly at table, in bed, and in our current car. We ate together, although he often managed to

avoid the disciplinary aura of breakfast, first by retiring behind the newspaper nearest to hand on his morning pile of
them and then by bolting for his office. Nobody read at the
other meals, of course. And when Anne and I got into bed
with Rex, on Sunday mornings while Mother was singing
at Early Service or more rarely while she had to lie alone near
a new baby and he probably felt deserted, we never read.
What need? He told wonderful sleepy stories in those early
years. . . . And naturally he never read when he was driving,
which he did every day of his life as if it were a thrilling new
adventure.

Mother read whenever she had the faintest excuse not to
be doing something else, and kept a fat supply of English
novels beside her, whether she was lying in the long stiff
"Directoire" couch in front of the fire, or on her big bed
upstairs. She carried on a lifetime *affaire* with any and all
English men of letters, with one exception, Mr. Trollope.
Anglomanic as she was, she still could not swallow his
mother's criticisms of American manners, no matter how
secretly she may have agreed with them, and she held this
firmly and with female illogic against the literary man himself (although Dickens' similar views did not bother her).
This is too bad: Mother could have sailed forever through
those cozy endless volumes about parish tea parties and
aristocratic amours. . . .

I cannot remember how I learned to read. I am sure nobody
said, "Now we are going to . . ." and then proceeded to show
me the trick. Everybody in the house who could follow a
printed sentence read aloud. Grandmother read the Bible to
me. Mother read whatever she was reading, if I was within
earshot . . . the Los Angeles *Times,* an old copy of *Punch,* a
page from whatever novel she was into. Father read head-
lines at the breakfast table. In the kitchen Mother would
read a recipe to the cook and try to explain it and then I would,
from memory, show the cook the words again. And of course

there were always the books Grandmother bought, with a big eye meaning "I."

I did stay out of school until I was seven, of course, but by the time I was going on five I had reading in my own hands. I started to practice, apparently, on one of the Oz books, and whether it was because the story was pagan fantasy or not, my grandmother asked Rex to send me to the Spare Room, because I seemed to have to read in a high slow keening shriek.

This was a special treat for me, since Anne and I were not allowed in the cold ugly room (dark green with mahogany), unless Mother was ill or something like that. Usually it was occupied by various Holbrook kith and kin.

I lay voluptuously on my stomach on the big bed, blissfully alone, and I felt a thrill which has never left me as I realized that the words coming magically from my lips were mine to say or not say, read or not. It was one of the peaks of my whole life. Slowly my eyes rode across the lines of print, and the New World smiled. It was mine, not something to beg for, book in hand, from anyone who could read when I could not. The door opened, and without hesitation I walked through.

I feel quite sure that first book was *The Wizard of Oz*, because there was some cynicism on Grandmother's part when I announced that I had finished it upstairs. She sniffed, and rightly, that I already knew it by heart from hearing my mother, and was simply repeating the words. To prove her wrong I did what now seems to me an odd thing, and I removed somehow from her sacrosanct apartment (the third addition my parents made to the new house, a large bed-sitting room and bath and dressing room off the living room, with a softly sliding door which we never opened uninvited) a tiny book called *The Imitation of Christ*. Its soft black leather binding and its size had long tantalized me, when I went into Grandmother's room to fetch her glasses or handkerchief, and apparently I palmed it quite easily. I scanned it aloud, upstairs, and then went right to Mother, to show her that I could indeed read something I had never known before, no matter what it might be. To my surprise she laughed helplessly through several pages of my innocent inflectings of Thomas a Kempis' far from frivolous suggestions for a contemplative life. When she could stand no more, she embraced me strongly, and then took the darling little book to replace, the next time she was near her mother's desk.

She told me she was very proud that I could read, and suggested that I ask Grandmother, after supper, if she would like me to try a bit of the Old Testament aloud. That should prove my point. And so, apparently, I did, for after that I often read the Bible as Grandmother knitted hideous khaki-colored socks and mittens for the Poor Tommies and then for Our Boys. She would not stand for any singsong or carelessness, very good for me, and when she asked me sharply what I thought a new word meant, and I had no answer, I was sent straight to the dictionary, which I learned to use long before I started school.

That gigantic unabridged book first stood in a corner of the living room, on its wrought iron stand. Then, since most of our semantical discussions happened at table, it moved slowly through the inconvenient front hall to the dining room, where it stayed in the corner farthest from the kitchen door, in front of the cupboard full of things we never used, like a dozen Wedgwood service plates and a soup tureen nobody but Rex could carry, full or empty. When we moved down Painter to the Ranch, Mother tried again to keep Webster in his somewhat more proper place, in the Sun Parlor beside her desk. Gradually the great book on its stand slid into the end of the living room, and then around the corner and into its rightful place beside the tea wagon, behind Father at the head of the table but where Mother could keep a cool eye on whoever had been sent to use it during meals.

That was usually I. For a few years I needed a little stool. Later I handed this on hopefully to Anne, but she felt the whole process an unseemly interruption of her gastronomical enjoyment, and was much smarter than I about getting out of such things. I actually enjoyed the whole process very much, and did not mind being excused from the table at any time, to find the puzzling word like a little monkey and hear my own voice reading about it to the hushed diners. It was a heady and welcome taste of the limelight to me. "When in doubt, consult the dictionary," my family said, and at the first three words and a nod from one end or the other of the table I was out of my chair and on my footstool, turning like a well-trained librarian to the *G*'s or the *V*'s with a skillful flick of my hands.

The Unabridged was our only book of words I remember, except for a Biblical Concordance in Grandmother's private library, but there were several atlases on the bottom shelves in the living room, and a battered set of the *Britannica*, and equally beat-up copies of the World Almanacks which sifted back from Father's office at the *News*. And in the southeast corner of the big room, where grownups never seemed to sit, were Our Books, on all the lower shelves.

A big French door folded zigzag into the corner from the Sun Parlor, and made a fine private place on the floor, for as long as daylight lasted . . . and when Mother caught on, there was a clear light at night on top of the bookcases. When nobody was on the Couch we used pillows from it, although Grandmother disapproved of this as unhygienic, her own word for enjoyable or even sensual.

Of course Anne and I had lots of "sets," given our heredity. Two I liked from the first slow mouthings were called something like *The Five Books of Knowledge* and *Pictured Knowledge*, the latter in two thick volumes. They were badly printed and no doubt worse written, but they kept me happy through

countless rereadings, and from their clumsy engravings I
got to know the shape of a whale, the convolutions of the
inner ear, the way wheat is separated from its chaff in India.
And there was a really good collection, in perhaps fifteen
well-bound volumes, called *The Junior Classics*. It started
out at about the same age I did, with a book for people five or
six, and went on up into intoxicating worlds which I skirted
cautiously for a few years, and then plunged into and cast
behind me lightly, as child's play, having already found out
about the twelve-year-old stuff when I was seven or eight, and
not because I was precocious, but because I was omnivorous.

I read the way alcoholics drink, from dawn until Fall-
down Time, and from left to right on the liquor shelf. I took
care of *The Junior Classics* every few months, avoiding only
the last couple of volumes, which had a little love-stuff in
them, very embarrassing and boring to my sister and me.
(This aversion to sex play lasted until I was almost thirteen
and was reading *Westward, Ho!* to Anne. When we got to the
last couple of chapters, where our hero deserted us for a silly
young lady, we laughed loudly and made rude noises and
never finished the book. We had of course been jilted . . . but
it was more convenient to believe that it was *he* who played
the fool. . . .)

We had a complete set of bound *St. Nicholas* magazines, as
well as our monthly numbers in the mail. Mother had
triumphantly dragged them home in several cartons and
baskets on the Electric, after an intoxicating auction at
Holmes' Book Store in Los Angeles, and I dabbled at will in
them after my first hungry and thorough gallop through
them, and for the next several decades knew where to turn
for almost any fleeting satisfaction, from a full-page drawing
of an empty snow scene which actually contained fifteen
housecats, to an essay on maple sugar.

There were deliciously increasing numbers of the fat sturdy
"annual" from England called *Chatterbox*, perhaps Anne's

and my favorite for a good decade or so. We got *Father Tuck's Annual* every Christmas too, but found it less satisfying.

We had all the Oz books, gradually. They were, as Grandmother had skeptically remarked about my first reading from one, known by heart, but they stayed fresh and wonderful for a long time, as did all of the Lang fairy books. Then we went into series like the *Five Little Peppers,* and liked them passionately for a time, but found that they grew tedious after five or six readings. We had all of Louisa May Alcott, and those books did not pall, as long as I continued to read in either a belly-warming horizontal or circular crouching position in various corners of the Painter house and then the Ranch. Other series, like *The Little Colonel* and *The Motor Girls* and *What Katy Did,* were good at first but not worth a second go. Mother refused to spend money on them, wisely, but we borrowed them from Margie Thayer or the Library.

There was a set of J. M. Barrie, of course, but not on Our shelves. I went to it like a moth to the flame, and read as always from left to right, thereby catching a few glimpses of the English scene which most young lovers of Peter Pan did not suspect. This did nothing, however, to put me off that boy. I understood him. I also understood Wendy, and the big fine dog whose name I forget for now . . . Nana? I did not think Wendy's parents came up to snuff, ever: colorless creatures compared with mine.

I was by about nine well into Tennyson's version of the Court of King Arthur, and I knew every knight and lady by respectful name. That poet may have been the Walt Disney of his time, in a literary sense, but he suckled me on fine rolling verse, and made my heart pound as any young heart should. And so did the endless and now unreadable prose of Walter Scott: I lived many lives more than our twenty or so volumes of his novels would indicate, and am none the worse for it, I think.

Once Mother and Father went away for a week, and of

course when they came back they brought us each a present: Grandmother; a lachrymose lady missionary who was a protégée of hers and took care of us as a special concession during that time; the cook-of-the-moment; and Anne and me. Once Mother had got out of her duster and veils and so on, and Father had brought in the suitcases from the back of the Maxwell (it must have been a Maxwell, because we got rid of the Model T when I was seven and I was already almost going on nine), we were figuratively lined up, palpitating like half-starved but discreet sailors waiting for our Sabbath tot of rum. We had been good, each in her own fashion.

And Grandmother got a new pair of gloves, perhaps ("Nonsense!" she would say crossly); the lady missionary got a fine handkerchief into which she would cry a foolish tear; the cook got something like a little coin purse with a small sum in it; Anne got an Indian doll with beads on its forehead which could and did come off almost at once; and I got my own copy of *Ivanhoe*.

This made me feel sick. Undoubtedly Mother had seen me working toward that book in the Waverley set, and before she left she told me in several different ways to wait to read Volume 14 or whatever it was, because secretly she knew she was going to give it to me. But while she was gone I could not stop. I was on my way, and suddenly the next volume in my drunken path was that one, and I read right through it with a wonderful breathlessness, for the first of several times, and then plunged on. By the time Mother put the beautiful little edition of *Ivanhoe* in my hands I already knew it by heart, word for ringing word, Anglo-Saxon curse for Norman oath. I knew more about being Jewish, and cared less about being noble, than I had before. I had, in truth, been blooded.

I think that I never told my parents about this compulsive trickery, committed while they were off roistering somewhere, wherever there was in Southern California to roister in about 1916. Grandmother and her unpleasant protégée and the cook all said Anne and I had been very good girls, and Anne and I went to bed, simmering gently with the feeling of being secure again, with Rex and Edith home. She pulled all the beads off her Indian doll and put them into a little tin box where she kept important stuff, and I started happily on my second bout of *Ivanhoe* within a few days. I had to read fast, so that I could keep up with myself and not lie too much when I told Mother about it. That was easy. The knight was really a knight to me, perhaps the way Tarzan and Superman have been more recently to other children of almost every age. I leaped passionately alongside him, and never told my mother of my helpless bit of cheating while she'd been gone.

There were two more books I did cheat with, stupidly and guiltily, and neither one gave me any good feeling, because they were not worth my pain. They had been hidden from me or forbidden to me, otherwise unknown happenings in our family, and that of course made their reading imperative, by hook or crook, neither of which I was comfortable with.

One was called *Poppy*, and I think it was by Berta Ruck. The way I remember her name at all is that later I learned that she was really called Mrs. Oliver Onions, which is unforgettable. *Poppy* was overtly hidden from me in a most childish way, by my mother, after it had accidentally been mentioned in my hearing as a dreadful disgusting horrid shocking book. I found it immediately, and read it with waning curiosity in a couple of hours (perhaps a new method for speed reading could be based on the fear of being caught in the act?), and then replaced it in its silly cache behind a set of Edgar Allan Poe on the second shelf to the right of the fireplace. I think Poppy was a drab in South Africa, whose wrists got ringed with cold grease from the dishes she was always washing in buckets and pans and tubs. Maybe she did worse things than that, but how could I know, and what did I care?

The other book I sneaked was *Donal Grant,* by George Macdonald, and I still am not sure why it was declared out of bounds. I knew *The Princess and the Goblin* and all the rest of his parables, and *At the Back of the North Wind* by heart, without any attention at all to anything but the wonderful story on every page. I was the little boy, shivering alone in his bed. And I was Curdie following the mystical thread and finally plunging his hands into the bowl of burning roses, and I was the princess who loved him. I never quite got to the point of being the goddess. . . . But I *was* the little boy shivering to the sound of the North Wind, and I was almost that Wind. The man who wrote to me about it all was my own storyteller, and when I found a paperbound copy of his *Donal Grant,* with illustrations even I dismissed as unworthy, I took it into my private pattern.

To my astonishment it was removed, by either my mother or Aunt Gwen, who was mixed up in this important adventure. I was surprised, and then outraged, and of course spent my next hours and days ferreting out the book, to try to discover why it had been hidden from me.

I did find it. Apparently it had belonged to Aunt Gwen, and she took it over to her house on the corner, and put it, almost as stupidly as Mother had put *Poppy* behind Poe, under the silken pillows on the little love seat in her parlor. I went to it like a bird dog, fitted myself into the strange stiff piece of furniture, and read it in perhaps three feverish sessions. (By now I can't help feeling that both Aunt Gwen and Mother knew exactly where I was and what I was doing, but the secrecy was always respected . . . and also I am sure by now that they had hoped to protect me longer from the fact that Macdonald did not always write about little people like me.)

The story, which I could never bring myself to read again, was about a young Scot, an educated but still poor and humble villager, in love with the lady in the castle. This would not do: aside from the rigid class distinctions, she was already married to the laird. There was an aeolian harp that sang in the endless winds of the moors around the abandoned castle. Years went by. Donal finally broke into a deep chamber at the bottom of the chimney, and there on a great bed, chained legs and arms to the posts, lay the skeleton of his lady, with the tiny bones of a child between . . . well, there somewhere in her upper femurs. Donal Grant's hair turned white, while the aeolian harp thrummed in the castle chimney.

I admit that I was pretty well shaken, myself. The whole thing was a far cry from the sound the North Wind whispered through that little crack, before she took the thin sick boy away. . . .

But what really unsettled me for a long time and perhaps forever was the language. The novel, two columns on every badly printed page, and in tiny print at that, was written almost entirely in a Scottish dialect, I suppose now from the Highlands but am too scared to find out. It cured me forever. Go into a Gaelic lilt or a Marseillais thump or an Oklahoman drawl and I am out the door, as long as it is on paper. In the ear it is a different thing, to be supported at certain times and only when both valid and justified. But on paper, perhaps because of my early guilt at sneaking, it is insupportable. "Bra' bricht nicht" is no worse than "y'awl" for me: I retch. And I rear back defensively when anyone writes "wimmin" for "women," which is the way "women" is pronounced anyway: it becomes dialect and therefore tinged with panic for me, and the immediacy of being uncovered in my sinful first reading.

I put *Donal Grant* back where I had found him, and of course plumped the pillows like any hardened sneak, and never mentioned the caper or the book. It is always disconcerting to try to cover a recognized farce, but Mother and Aunt Gwen and I carried it off blandly, and I returned to the safer pastures of the "sets."

There were two more books which were not forbidden to me, but which my parents never realized I was devouring as a wasp does a ripe fig. One was a big thick thing called something like *The Care and Feeding of the Child*. The other was *Nostrums and Quackeries*. The first was always available, for Edith Kennedy consulted it for all her living children, as mothers turn to Dr. Spock today. The second was on my father's bookshelves in his *News* office, and on the delightful Sundays when he would take Anne and me down there to give Mother and Grandmother a little rest, I would head for it as tactfully as possible.

First we would prowl through the back room, with its biting smell of ink and newsprint, one in puddles and the other in piles or giant rolls. We would sniff around the job-paper room, which had high walls of wire, perhaps to keep out rats, and Father would give us each two sheets of white onionskin, three of scratch, one of copy, all colors and textures, in every size. It was fine to be there with him alone in the great smelly shop, with the Miehle presses like sleeping elephants and the linotypes poised ready.

The Front Office, after Father moved from the one-room plant on South Greenleaf, was chopped off into little places where the Business went on, with the reporters on the other side of the aisle, and Rex there with them, but in a kind of cubicle between them and the Back Room. And in his room, about seven feet square, was one book I developed a kind of hunger for, because it was so forthright and so iconoclastic. It was called *Nostrums and Quackeries,* and I have long wondered why my father kept it, for I never heard him sound off in one direction or another on the subject of medical nonknowledge.

I loved it. I still have it, but it is far away by now, and all I can recall of its format is that it was probably a vanity press job, with generous numbers of bad photographs of cough syrup labels and trusses and suchlike. It was on slick paper, not at all what I was used to in my dash through the Complete Works. It had a racy desirability to it, and I cannot imagine what Father and little Anne were doing while I snatched at its temptations on every available Sunday. I managed, however, to establish a firm cynicism about medical fancies from it, whether current in the 1890's or now, and cannot feel it did me as much emotional harm as the sound of Donal Grant's harp.

At home there was always the *Care and Feeding* tome, which fell apart when I was about twelve, I think partly because of my careful but prolonged readings. It was illustrated as fully as one could do in those days of Hem-&-Haw: there were diagrams of the male and female bodies with only a few regions turned foggy, and there were extremely murky photographs of newborn children just *after* the private parts had been covered and the cord had been pinched off (off of what? That is what I deftly managed to surmise: off of or *perhaps* even *out* of the mother-body, silly!). I saw in this book, really my Bible for several years, horrendous pictures of children being weighed and measured, always from the back side, children who had for one reason or another not had proper food. I had proper food, because my mother and father had it to give me, so I would never have had that silhouette, or so I assumed.

And there were even more interesting pictures of every kind of childhood malady considered inevitable in the United States in about 1900–1920. There were ratlike tiny bodies covered with all kinds of spots, and I could identify every one of them. I could even smell them. I knew when the children would scratch, and when they would throw up, and when they would get a little chest rattle. In fact, almost before I myself succumbed to these plagues, which were considered basically beneficent then, I knew how I was going to feel and what I could look forward to, because of the book Mother had bought during her first pregnancy, to know what to do about colic later and morning sickness right then, and to glean a few hints about what to do if she had a baby somewhere with nobody around . . . a hansom cab, a canoe. (This is a common female fantasy, I am told.)

I soon knew at least as much as she did, in theory anyway, about "what to do," and was sorry not to be included in the act when Norah and then David were born upstairs, but the information that continued to concern me most intimately was how to recognize and contend with *Measles, Mosquito Bites, Bruises,* and other things obviously part of my own human condition. Later, when I was unanimously appointed Chairwoman of the Board to assist with the new additions to the family, I was also ready for *Teething, Diaper Rash,* all that equally routine pattern. One thing led to another, of course, and with the help of some outside reading I was conversant with *Laudanum Poisoning, Rabies, Leprosy* . . . I felt exhilarated and very healthy and powerful.

I am always sorry, when I meet a good person who has no need, no wish, to read. It is as if he had lost a leg before he knew he had one: he swings along nimbly enough, but he is not whole. The last thing he needs or wants is my pity, but he has it, just as fine keen-minded children do when I see them unaware of anything but the television and movies and the illustrated weeklies. . . .

One of the best-known of our modern seers, Marshall McLuhan, said either ten minutes ago or perhaps a decade that with the first use of movable type for print, probably in the Gutenberg Bible, there happened "the separation of the senses, of functions, of operations, of states emotional and political, as well as of tasks."

I think I know what he meant. I prefer, though, in a way

both simplistic and egocentric, to feel that with my own discovery of the printed word I came into focus. I had no need to know how to read, in order to tell sound from taste, and sitting on a toilet from walking on a path, and love from lies. And so on. But from the minute I could read, I was not "separated" but whole, of a piece, and not only with other people but my own self. And it is probable that being able to look at print and recognize it has kept me in one piece, since that first far day when I lay on my stomach, alone with the new world on the Guest Room bed. Perhaps separating everything is what makes it possible to put it all together again?

In Whittier, our "sets" and "series," the Classics and the trash, the borrowed once-is-enough books from the library and even Margie Thayer . . . all those phony cures for cancer and falling hair in the book in Father's office, and Poppy with her greasy wrists, and the dead baby at the bottom of the wailing Scottish chimney, and of course Rowena and Rebecca smiling it out on the jousting fields of Race: they helped make one more sensate and occasionally coherent person, or so I like to assume.

20

Notes on
Following the Gleam

There are almost always several plausible causes for a result such as my early interest in eating and drinking. Perhaps an important one for me was the fact that my little sister Anne had a very finicky digestive system. It made me aware of how one person can eat this but not that, when another can eat both . . . how one person will push a plate away and even then be sick, while another will polish it off and feel rosier than ever.

Later in our lives Mother told me that the first two years with Anne were heartbreaking. Nothing suited her insides, and she cried weakly for hours, and grew almost rickety, like a starveling. By the time I was aware of her as a person sitting in a highchair at the breakfast table, when I was going on four, all this anguish was part of the family pattern, and although she was by then a rather plump and very pretty female, her emotions and her guts were already a capricious team, and as her appointed protector I was strongly aware of that.

From the highchair on through her whole life Anne ate in strange waves and cravings, in unpredictable whims, now half-starving herself with a small sensual smile for the worry she caused, now gorging hysterically on something she knew would result in an illness which would disrupt the lives of everybody around her, and thus hold on to the frantic attentions she had sensed in her first months. This tortured pattern finally ended with her ugly death, when she was fifty-five, from massive intestinal cancer. It seems clear to me that organically, chemically, biologically she should never have been coaxed through her first two years, when she was trying so hard and innocently to escape. And all this is one reason why I soon became hypersensitive to how such a thing as an egg can be manna to one person and a searing time bomb to another.

Then there was Grandmother's Nervous Stomach. It undoubtedly influenced my whole future, with its dictatorial rumblings and belchings. I was apparently born with a need to put words together, but without my first eleven years of gastronomical awareness when Old Mrs. Holbrook was in residence I probably would still be swimming in unread iambics instead of puzzling over the relationship between food and love, painting Zen-begotten abstracts instead of observing the glandular reactions to a pot of dark broth in my hungry guinea pigs, my loved victims. I would not be this *me* but some other, without my first years in Grandmother's gastric presence.

She was a healthy Victorian neurotic, who of course had never heard the last word, and she lived well into her eighties and was eulogized correctly as a Good Woman. That would have seemed only fitting to her, had she heard the funeral service. She took it for granted, from all one can surmise, that because of her upright Christian life she *was* good: she knew there was a sinful difference between that and anything else.

She came to America from Ireland when she was almost eight, in the kind of sailing ship that carried all the men in one big room and the women in another. It was during the Potato Famine, when the Crown tried to keep people's minds off their empty bellies, and their tongues quiet, by making cheap liquor even cheaper. The real reason Grandmother's family was fleeing is said to be that her father talked instead of drinking, and hated Queen Victoria a little too loudly and articulately for safety.

The crossing was long and cruel, and finally the small girl was the only female left on her feet in the big noisome room, where all the cooking, on the one stove in the center, had to go on along with every other human need. She made soups, stews, slops. She helped when a passenger miscarried. She ladled tea from a bucket to the moaning seasick women in their tiers of bunks. And in the worst of the voyage she fell on her wee knees and called aloud to God, promising him that if only he would get her onto dry land again, she would not only stay there, but she would sign the Pledge and never touch liquor in her life. (She kept her faith in the last part, but was persuaded in her late fifties, after much prayer, to make one triumphal return to County Tyrone and Dublin.)

After marriage and nine children, she poured her creative strength into her church, as all women of her class were supposed to do, and instead of youngsters at table there was a steady stream of missionaries. My grandfather would excuse himself blandly after carving the roast or the birds and presiding over the vegetables, and go to his book-filled study and the decanter of excellent port. Grandmother set a bountiful board, secure in her position as the most literate gentlewoman as well as the most devout for perhaps a hundred leagues around, on the Iowa prairies, but my mother has remarked that if it were not for those starved Christians forever underfoot, she would probably have been nourished on nothing but gruel and porridge, since her own mother considered any physical enjoyment a sin unless it was in the name of the Lord and therefore her bounden duty. In this case, it was indeed her duty to nourish the men of the cloth, with things like roasted pheasants and fresh custards, but certainly they were not meant for carnal pleasure, especially her own.

Once or twice a year she went to Battle Creek, in Michigan. The religious atmosphere was correct there, and she reveled sternly in the "treatments," which consisted almost solely of enemas, as far as family legend has it. Mother, who was taken there twice to break her boredom as a young lady stranded in a remote village where there were several times as many bars and brothels as there were churches, told me when I was twelve or so (or at least of a proper age for female confidences), that one morning she pretended to feel too unwell to go to the regular prayer service, and was caught sneaking down a hall toward a sunny balcony. "What, bilious again?" the nurse said with shock. "Another *lavage* for you, Miss Holbrook!" and within minutes Mother was firmly involved once more with the miracle-working apparatus.

Grandmother's Nervous Stomach today would probably be called a menopausal symptom best treated by a change of scene and a rest from domesticity, which is exactly what she prescribed for herself. Her stays in the cornflakes kingdom grew longer with familiarity, and continued all her life. They were a respite first from connubial activity, once she had bred herself out; then from running a kind of hotel for hungry men of God just back from Alaska and China and Guatemala; and in the last part of her life a vacation from us, the Kennedys.

And vice versa.

Grandmother had come to live with us soon after we moved to Whittier, as prearranged, and my father often spoke with gratitude and even affection of her, for without her moral and financial help he might never have weathered the first years there. She was a good solid part of our family life, and Anne and I respected and trusted her, without ever feeling what I think of as love. It was like living within sight of the Rock of Gibraltar. She and her daughter were often chilly, the outward sign of their long hostility, but they never bickered or exchanged ugly words, and Rex presided like a wise Chanticleer over his hennery, smoothing feathers with discretion and occasionally showing his spurs.

Once when it was clear that Grandmother was moping and peckish, he found that she felt she could no longer keep up her almost lifetime membership in the Women's Christian Temperance Union, because of the decanters of port and sherry that stood right through Prohibition on our sideboard. He had a lengthy talk with her. She is said to have announced that either the decanters went or she went, and it is also said that he replied, gently, "Then I must say good-by to you, Mother Holbrook." And she stayed, and so did the wine, and she renewed her Union dues.

Occasionally, or at least often enough to set Mother's right foot vibrating, Grandmother would concede to the urgencies of her innards, and on the advice of her Battle Creek internist ("Better out than in," he had counseled her) would bring forth a slow rolling bellow of a belch, without a word of genteel apology, or the bat of an eye. This was usually at the table, perhaps in immediate protest of a dish she found "fancy" or even "foreign," and even when I was little it astonished me that such a rigidly correct old lady would do something, with such apparent satisfaction and impunity, that would have sent us upstairs and into Coventry at once.

It is plain to me now that my grandmother's gastric peculiarities nurtured all our latent sensuality and gourmandise, even poor wambly little Anne's. We loved to eat together. ("We must not love anything but God," Mrs. Holbrook would say to that statement.)

We had a fine time when she was not there, mostly in the dining room. Nothing made us secretly happier than to be told that next week she would have to leave for Battle Creek, or even for a week or two in Long Beach for a religious convention. It made our mouths water. No more pale bland overcooked unseasoned barely palatable food, adapted to her gastric requirements as established by the Sanitarium diet kitchens! No more Boiled Dressing on watery lettuce! No more "plain" stewed hen, with meaningless dumplings in a gravy equally without either taste or color. No more stewed tomatoes with pink soggy bread in them!

Of course our gastronomical sprees were kept innocent, because of our tender years as well as our parents' naïve palates, but we were deeply aware of Father's pleasure when he cut into a thick broiled steak on the special wooden board with runnels in it, and a well at one end to catch the juices. We knew that the watercress around it had been picked by him and Uncle Mac and probably Aunt Gwen the day before, from a secret bend in the Rio Hondo. And the red wine in the glasses was from a little vineyard over near San Gabriel.

From almost the beginning of our life in Whittier, I was allowed to have a stemmed glass when Grandmother was away, with water and a little wine to color it. I liked it, and sat, correctly not speaking unless spoken to, thinking about how different my parents were, according to who was at the table and what was on it. It was plain to me that there was a mysterious connection, and I planned to study it.

One way was to get into the kitchen, to see what I could make happen to the people who ate what I gave them. This I managed to do when still young enough to need my little footstool from the dining room, where it stood beside the dictionary stand for me when I looked up words, mostly at lunch before the paper had gone to press. I was allowed to stir things, and then to beat eggs. On Saturday mornings Mother sometimes produced a cake, if she felt like it, and then I could not only help to measure and mix things but "lick the bowl" afterward for a reward. I enjoyed all this. I was part of a drama.

When I was perhaps seven I made the first of my two worst gastronomical blunders, at least for several decades.

I had learned how to make a basic White Sauce, which was a staple in our house until Grandmother died: we seemed to eat a lot of creamed vegetables, and creamed things on toast, tuna and chipped beef and even sliced hard-boiled eggs. I think Mother felt that something on toast with that sauce over it was *fitting* in the middle of the day, and the endless procession of cooks through our kitchens never said her nay, for what could be easier than this quick mess? And the first thing I learned to do alone was to keep our sluggish flood of it going, all made correctly with a minimum of butter, almost no salt, and a generous amount of both flour and milk. (But compared with the same thing today, it was surely more enjoyable: the milk was Mrs. Worsham's best, the butter was sweet and honest, and the flour came in a hundred-pound sack from the mill near Anaheim. . . .)

I fell easily into the deepest pitfall in a beginner's path, when Mother suggested that I make something to serve on Sunday night when she and Rex would get back from a long drive. It was a heady prospect. It was my first great assignment. I was alone, the Star. I got down the biggest cookbook on our very puny kitchen shelf, and read a recipe for Hindu Eggs, since it had been gently pointed out to me that there were several hard-boiled ones ready to use. They could be served sliced on toast, covered with White Sauce. But in what I think was the trusty *Settlement* ("The Way to a Man's Heart"), an exotic dash of curry powder was to be blended into the flour. And of course I thought that if one tiny spoonful could add such Oriental glamour, several large ones would be even more exciting.

The sauce was smooth and dark, and the smell from its double boiler was different from the usual one, more interesting. Everything seemed to go well, that is, until the first taste at the dining room table. There I had erred too, not to have sampled it first. But what could I have done by then to remedy the ghastly business? It is Family History, wrapped in a kindly fog of mockery: the night we drank floods of cooling milk milk nothing but milk for Sunday supper.

My second dire disaster was when Mother was still resting from the birth of Norah, so I was almost nine. Now, women are walking about within a few hours of travail, but in those days it was the custom to stay in bed for about two weeks, if one could afford it. Great-Aunt Rebecca Oliver in Pittsburgh, who gave birth to sixteen living children, never set foot outside her apartment in the enormous house for exactly ten weeks, each time, on her husband's orders. I am sure Edith Kennedy would gladly have followed such an affluent pattern if possible, but as it was she did manage after the new sister's arrival to lie in bed or on the chaise longue for almost a month, because of the surgery she had survived during her pregnancy. And it was fun for me to help the nurse prepare her frequent trays, and sniff their dainties.

Mrs. Thayer, my friend Margie's mother, often sent a little naked squab up Painter from her ranch, and it would be roasted in a tiny pan with plenty of butter, and then laid upon a piece of toast with all the crusts cut off: fairy food! Or the nurse would whisk two eggs and pour them into our smallest skillet, and in a flash they would be on a heated plate in a perfect omelet: a miracle!

She was a nice woman and did not mind me, for she taught me how to butter toast properly and fill the jam pot, and scavenge for a fresh Cecil Brunner bud to lay on the napkin I myself had folded. (Mother always seemed to have babies when roses were in bloom.)

One morning when Mrs. Hamilton or whatever her name was had plans for an afternoon to herself, we made a cornstarch pudding to help the cook-of-the-moment, with a special bowl of it to be taken up to Mother at precisely four o'clock, alongside a glass of cool milk and two small sugar cookies.

The nurse saw that everything was correctly placed on the tray, except for the milk and the pudding, which were to stay in the icebox until the last minute, and then she left for her "free time."

At a little before the hour for my mother's Four O'Clock I took a long proud look at the pudding, which Mrs. Hamilton had turned out of its bowl into another prettier one. It was suddenly impossibly stupid. It was leftover White Sauce. How could Mother tell, by its appearance, that it held the finest sugar, a good dash of vanilla extract, the top cream from the morning milk? I thought of a few flecks of cinnamon or nutmeg, but that meant standing on the high kitchen stool to reach for them: strictly forbidden. I listened to what my palate told me, and dashed out to the blackberry fence, and there on the sunny west side I found a puny handful of berries that were not dead-ripe certainly, but looked black and luscious. I made a balanced ring of them around the mound of dreadful white stuff, and it bloomed. It was mysterious, transformed, exciting.

This was apparent when I carefully got the tray up to Mother's bed, for she exclaimed with pleasure, and pulled me to her and kissed me strongly. She ate one bite, with a berry on top, pronounced it delicious, and I went downstairs, since for some reason only Father sat with his wife when she ate in her room. The new sister was in a frilly bassinet, safe at the end of the enormous bed, probably snoring like a healthy mouse, for she seemed eminently well set for the future. If the thick silver copy of the Apostles' Bell rang from beside Mother's pillow I would of course leap upstairs, since the nurse was off carousing as wildly as one could within the Whittier city limits, but meanwhile I had three books going at once in my private corner on the living room floor behind the French door, and there were two back issues of *The Youth's Companion*, which Grandmother continued optimistically to subscribe to for Anne and me, and which we continued discreetly to find dull stuff and small potatoes compared with what went on in *St. Nicholas* and the wonderful best-of-all never-matched *Chatterbox Annual,* which Uncle Park got for us from England.

By the time Father came home from the *News* and whatever else he may have been attending to, and then Mrs. Hamilton came in, and the cook turned up from somewhere outside the city limits I am sure, all Hell had broken loose. Our doctor Honky Wilson was there, running up the stairs with his black bag and running down again to telephone to the druggist, and the baby was crying *Hunger* and the question was, Should she drink what was in those great white flowing melons? Mother was covered with red terrible welts, a kind of hives they were guessed to be. She was in real distress from their dreadful itchings and the heat they sent over her generous body. It was plainly an abrupt food poisoning.

Emergency treatments went on in every direction, and when things seemed to be quieting, and the baby's demands had been turned off temporarily with some diluted dairy milk, there was a Meeting in the dining room, to which I was invited for the first but not last time in my life. Mother had not left even a faint purplish smear in her dish to prove what I had done, but I told almost the whole story of my compulsion to change the appearance of the cornstarch pudding. All I left out was that it had looked too much like leftover White Sauce. I felt that detail would be disloyal to Grandmother.

Then we all went upstairs again: Father, Honky, the nurse perhaps named Mrs. Hamilton, and I; and Honky said to Edith, "Nothing to worry about . . . blackberries."

Mother held out her arms to me and onto her great white pearly bosom, yes, pearly again, and it was difficult for me to assure myself that I was the oldest in the family and therefore past crying loud and hard.

Many years later I made a third and much more dangerous

kitchen error, but that second one was the hardest emotionally, and of course it taught me too many things to put on paper. It did not stop me from changing patterns and colors if I found my creations ugly, although I am sure that I have never garnished a pale pudding again with any kind of berries . . . nor have I ever made one.

One of my happier discoveries, which Anne appreciated as much as I, and then Norah and David and cousins and our peers, was not equally appreciated by Father and Mother. It was for *us*. When we had permission to indulge in it, on nights when there would be cupcakes for dessert and after a coincidentally well-mannered and therefore pleasant dinner, our parents would go tacitly into the living room by the fire, after Mother had pushed the kitchen door wide enough to say that the children would be a little longer at the table, Bertha-Margaret-Ruby-Cynthia—whoever.

Then each of us would put his little round cake into his empty fruit or pudding dish, and begin a serious and mostly silent ritual.

The top button of the cupcakes must come off in one piece, deftly spooned out, and Anne and I often helped the younger children, for we were as sure-fingered in this operation as any surgeon, and could lift out the intact delectable morsel with suavity. Beginners did not make the hole deep enough in the cake, and if we liked them sufficiently to want to see them again we would permit them to hollow it out a little and then quickly eat the crumbs. (Crumbs were a sign of the amateur, the uninitiated.) Then sugar was sprinkled generously into the cavity, and cream was poured slowly into it, to the brim. This was a long process, what with all the passing of necessities, and depending of course upon how many of us there were.

All the cream had to disappear. More sugar was put in, more cream, until it began to seep out onto the dish. Then we stopped, put on the tops, which when the cupcakes were at their best had a delicately sticky golden crust on them, and once more we dripped cream over the whole soggy sweet wonderful mess.

It was worth everything we had gone through: the forbearance during Dessert; the long waitings while the damnably thick cream worked its way down and out, carrying the melting sugar along with it; the occasional tedium of having to be helpful to smaller siblings or older thrill seekers.

We ate those exquisite titbits silently, with our own reverence, and I knew the satisfaction of a creator, even a secondhand one since I had not made the bases: cake, cream, sugar. This took away some of the latent pain of the bad blackberries, and the untenable lash of my Hindu Eggs. I could go on undaunted, like a minion at King Arthur's court . . . Follow the Gleam, Merlin's Gleam . . . which in my own case seemed to be the reflection from a well-polished kettle or skillet. . . .

Sometimes people who really do not like to eat in front of others or even alone, and who dislike to admit that there can be any art to it, ask me and not without malice if my early concern with the pleasures of the table could have been quite *normal*. Was it not, they say, perhaps a little . . . well, *sickly* . . . for a child to be so aware and make such a fuss?

I never made a fuss, as far as I can remember, in those beginning years. I simply knew from the first taste, from scratch, that a real mayonnaise was good and Grandmother's Boiled Dressing was a gastronomical horror and desecration, and I preferred mayonnaise, which I got now and then at Margie Thayer's ranch and when my dam was gone. When the other stuff was set before me, I ate it with familial courtesy and resignation.

My main answer is that while many things led me to ponder on the intertwinings of our needs for love and warmth and food, it was no more astonishing for me to like to cook than it was for one of our much brighter cousins to know every American railroad timetable by heart by his twelfth year . . . and that does not mean freight alone, but passenger trains. It does not mean Santa Fe and Penn only, all that big stuff, but short lines between Denver and Colorado Springs and suchlike.

This cousin, one of the nicer people I have been tossed against in the continuing storm, was rightly thought to be smarter than all of us put together, as his strange compulsion increased into his early teens, and nothing was ever asked about *his* being normal and all that. And one of my current friends at Penn Street School was eating every pencil and crayon and piece of chalk she could make off with, and then would let us see all of the colors that came out of her in a day or two, in the Girls' Toilet, for a penny apiece. As far as I know, she was considered a nice normal child, and she grew up to be a pillar of the Society of Friends.

I am the first to admit that one intoxicating angle of my early eagerness to substitute for the family cook on her day off was the extra attention it brought me. It made me feel creative and powerful, and that is possibly the truest reason for my continuing preoccupation with the art of eating.

As the oldest child, I was given more and more responsibility, but all the real attention was centered first on little ailing Anne, and then on the new dependents as they came along, and of course on Grandmother when she was rumbling and belching regally in residence, and always on Mother before and during and after her confinements. I had to fight for my place on stage, and I soon discovered, no matter how melodramatically now and then, that almost everybody smiles passing beams of pleasure if a little girl, or even a jaded old one, can turn out good scrambled eggs and a commendable oyster stew, a crisp well-seasoned salad, even a cupcake. That was my way to show that I was there *too* . . . and perhaps it still is.

21

Streets of Gold Forsworn

Several times when I was little and Grandmother was away, Bishop Johnson came to our house for Sunday night supper after a diocesan call in Whittier, and this pleasant habit lasted for many years, until he was too feeble. I always liked his portly benign presence, but I do not recall a single meal we shared: scrambled eggs or oyster stew, probably, and a glass of wine. So easy was the inner family weather when he was there that my mother never went into her customary flurry about what would be served at table to "strangers." The Bishop was a fraternity brother of my father's. He had the simplicity of good breeding. Later I went to a school named for him, and began to wonder a little about his legendary devotion to his mother, and why he had in her memory made a chapel for so many daily prayers on such impossible kneeling benches, but when he came to our house everything was innocent of question, at least for some time.

Once, after he had left, I listened to my parents discuss at length his version of the next life, in the Heavenly City. Yes, he had said in confidence to them after supper, the streets would indeed be paved with purest gold. The houses might be too, with walls of porphyry. Everything would be flawless to look at, and filled with love and understanding. There would be no wars and squabblings and illnesses. Rex and Edith went on chatting about all this, and I could tell that they considered it affectionately but as if it were a touching dream. The feeling I got was: Do you really think Bish (his private name with them) believes all this? Jerusalem the Golden? Peace? Heaven? People walking around smiling and saying, "Well, hello there, Uncle Abraham, Aunt Millicent!" Rex and Edith laughed quietly.

I returned to the secret (except for me) vision of my little sister Anne. It seemed more realistic, or at least more plausible, than the Bishop's. Inside her head, she told me, was a tiny perfect town. It fitted exactly into her skull, the whole top of it above her eyebrows, with a blue cloudless sky always, and trees and flowers of pure jewel-colors. The tiny houses were white, with paths leading between lawns and things like strawberry beds to the picket gates and onto the one curved street. The roofs were a soft red. The shutters were green. There was a pointy spire above the church on the village square, where happy children played. Their voices sounded like silver bells. There were no shops or animals . . . no bicycles. Mother and Father were there somewhere, and of course Aunt Gwen. It never occurred to me to ask if I was too, but by now I rather doubt it.

Her close-kept town was a Grandma Moses painting or a Breughel, seen decades early for her, and although she did not think of it as Heaven it was my little sister's refuge and Happy Home, where she wanted to be and most probably was. I almost never talked of this dream with her, respecting its privacy, but I was very aware of it, and I envied her.

For some of the same reasons, and perhaps a little because I did not want to incriminate myself as an eavesdropper, I never talked with my parents about Bishop Johnson's golden conviction.

Nobody ever asked me what I thought or believed, when I was little, and it is just as well, because I had no ideas at all on, for instance, the subject of a future life. I was unable to *know*, as did Anne and Bish with their visions. I had nothing to muse upon and to question gently, as did my parents. I seemed to believe in nothing, or even Nothingness probably, like an oyster or a seed. I knew that some people loved me, and that plants and animals grow, the way I was doing, and that I loved them and some people. But it was impossible, from as soon as I began to think, to envisage a pretty tiny village as mine, or a great city with streets of gold or, most of all, happy reunions with people and flowers and beasts I knew were already dead.

That is one reason why it was a fine thing to live where I did, on the immediate edge of a tightly knitted community of Quakers, bound by their religious faith to conquer the wilderness and to stay in it with their own dignity. I had no plans for a future, as did Bish and my little sister, but I knew that Whittier was my place to be, for a time anyway. I was *there*.

The streets went straight in the town, but then zigzagged with more beauty when the pavements ended in the near hills and riverbeds and orchards. Few houses were white, and there was not a red roof or a green shutter anywhere. Brown shingles and ugly stucco were the rule, except for an occasional shambly old farmhouse like Aunt Gwen's, and the dwellings were big or little according to their location and the social level of their people. The sidewalks were in many places good enough to roller-skate on, and how could I want more than that? The streets were not yellow at all, but black with occasional coats of tar. As I grew older I could ride my bike everywhere but down to the intersection of Greenleaf and Philadelphia where stores and a few cars were. It was an intrinsically good place, especially then and until I could fabricate a more reasonable facsimile of What Next, which was probably what my sister and the Bishop meant anyway.

Of course by the time I was being prepared for Confirmation, I was less nonchalant, no longer the grasshopper singing while the ants dug and delved. I tried to be serious, to think about my soul and where it was going. I dreaded the whole business of finding out, if our prescribed Episcopalian course was the only one, and aside from my growing inner confusion there were two good reasons for my qualms.

One was that I had never been baptized when a baby, because my Grandmother, the Campbellite, believed in Total Immersion, and my mother was a rebellious and renegade "Anglican" and put her trust in a mere signing of the Cross on a child's forehead. We children waited, then, until Grandmother died before we could be made real Christians, and anyone seeking that state in our church must be baptized with holy water before going on to a public confirmation of what is assumed by the age of reason of twelve or so to be true Faith. Therefore I would have to go through two ceremonies almost together, whereas my fellow members of the lengthy classes to prepare us for Confirmation need not stand up before a font meant for puling infants, and in long white socks and a foolish Sunday dress be delicately sprinkled. Bishop Johnson would do the whole thing, and have supper with us later, which made it more bearable to think on, less of a social humiliation.

The second reason I dreaded the business was that my Uncle Park, then and long after one of my favorite people, had put off just as I had the moment of being baptized, waiting to defy his doughty mother until she was safely in her tomb. He came to spend the winter with us, as often happened, and tactfully was dissuaded by our current minister from attending all the Confirmation classes given twice or more a week for the young people. But he was almost sixty, and he had waited long enough. He would join me in church.

The prospect of stumbling up to the font, along with a few sucklings in their mother's arms and a man old enough to be my grandfather, and then having to head for the chancel with him and several of my peers: it weighed on me. I listened to everything that was being taught about the benefits and privileges soon to be mine, ours, with dull and largely anesthetic ears. Plainly Uncle Park and I were far too old to be baptized, and if we had got as far as we seemed to have done on the job of merely existing, why did we have to stand up like two clowns, he with his beautiful little white goatee and I almost as tall as I would ever be, and have Bish do the babies first and then sign us with a damp cross, and *then* kneel at the altar rail and have both his hands on our heads? I knew a lot about the meaning of the Sacrament, or assumed I did . . . the duties of being a Christian, all that. But I was dismayed to find myself apart from everything I was being taught. I also felt mildly noble to admit to myself that I was being vain and pettish to brood about the cold fact that some of my friends would titter into their gloves to see me there at the font gawkily with an old man and some babies.

My outraged human vanity led me helplessly into an incoherent anger, and finally a real doubt about the existence of God Himself. If He did watch over his flock, and protect us, why must I face my immediate future of embarrassment? Why must I pretend to kneel with bowed head before His power? I had lived a happy life without being baptized, and would gladly promise to continue the same carefree unblasphemous pattern, full of trust and obedience, if I could skip Confirmation too. . . . A part of me was frightened of this growing attitude, in a primitive way, and I never spoke of it. But I did make one strangely inept attempt to hint to my parents that I had something on my mind besides the next meal.

One night after dinner, when we sat for a while at table if Father did not have to rush to a meeting, and talked about things that were forbidden while we ate, things like schoolyard or internecine squabbles, death, taxes, politics, I remarked with sly candor that I was fairly sure Bishop Johnson always gave me a special handshake. Of course I had heard that fraternity brothers, and Elks and Masons and people like that, knew secret ways of communicating. And Father and the Bishop belonged to the same college club, and Father was both an Elk and a Mason and perhaps some bishops were too, and it had certainly seemed to me that the last time the Bishop came to supper he had, when he held my hand for good-by at the door, pressed it in a certain way.

"I am sure he gave me the secret grip, yours, just a little changed for girls," I said solemnly to Father, and I was going to add that it seemed foolish, since I was already more or less initiated, to bother with Baptism and Confirmation and all that.

But my parents looked at each other and laughed, very nicely but thoroughly, and in a kindly and dismissive way. I went up to bed, after the usual politeness. I knew that I had missed the point, somehow. I could still feel that strange pressure within my palm: index finger up higher than usual toward the thumb, the little finger outward, and then two sharp short downward shakes, or something like that. How fine it must be to belong to a secret club, and learn all that in private, not out in full view!

Uncle Park continued to prepare himself, with afternoon private talks in the Parish House and a cup of tea later with the rector's wife, and I went on listening stolidly to my instructions about how to be a Christian. I felt I was learning some inner strength, but certainly it was not the kind toward which I was being led.

The day came. We made it to the church, in two loads: first Anne and me, with little Norah and Aunt Gwen, and then Uncle Park and his wife, and Mother, all ignoring the ghost of Grandmother in their own ways. Uncle Park looked as natty as a portly dragonfly, in a grey suit with a fawn-colored vest and the handkerchief of purest white folded expertly by my mother. Aunt Virginia used her own fine bit of linen to mop away an occasional tear as he belatedly joined her faith. I was at one of my life's lowest points, dressed like a skinny child when I felt as old as anybody within sight. I am sure Anne was going to be baptized too, but not confirmed, but I was so engrossed with my own problems that I was numb to her being there at all.

It was too late for emotions, good-byes. Ritual must be clung to in such moments, and I knew exactly when to take off my gloves, kneel, stand, all that. And I was pretty sure I knew what would happen.

Bishop Johnson, old by then and magnificent in white and purple, his great amethyst glowing under the wrist ruffles of his special pleated surplice, and preceded by one of my friends carrying his crozier, took his place inside the altar rail in his special chair. The baptizing was over. Several of us went up to the stained pine rail Uncle Mac had often cursed at, because even he could never tinker it enough to stop wobbling, and part of our instructions had been not to lean against it in any way but especially toward the Bishop, or we might go sprawling at his feet, an unseemly prospect on that day.

The Bishop went through his appointed duties. When he came ponderously around to me for the last time, I was saying to myself, *I do not can not will not agree to this contract. Strike me dead if I am wrong.*

I was supposed to close my eyes as the priest's hands were laid upon my bowed head. Instead I looked up, saying as visibly as a silent cat can say that she is thinking of a mouse, or a sardine, that I wanted the altar to cleave open like a great egg, and strike me dead with one godly bolt of lightning. "Strike me dead!" I said. "If there is a God, let Him prove it now!"

The Bishop went on down the row of young people who had not lifted their heads with open eyes as I had done, but it seemed to me then, and later, and even now a little, that his hands stayed for a second with a secret message upon my prickling scalp, not one learned in any fraternity I knew of. Gently he lowered my head. He knew what I had asked for, and why I had been refused. I closed my eyes, condemned forever to doubt, but glad not to be dead yet.

He came as usual to supper, a mildly hilarious one because Uncle Park was happy to have his long wait over, and as far as I know I never saw his Reverence again . . . certainly not in the decorous arcades of the school he founded in his mother's memory. I feel sure that as he laid his fat knowing hands upon my head, that dreadful day, he was telling me that I would find my own version of his Golden City, my sister's tiny village to be held in a porridge bowl, and a dozen others.

22

Petitions, Manifestoes, Broadsides, and Such

One more proof of the influence of heredity as well as environment upon even the tenderest child may be that when I was about seven I wrote my first of several basically political pamphlets. Not only was my father following in his ancestors' footsteps by running a sternly nonpartisan and often censured daily newspaper in a small partisan town, but on the other side of the family my great-grandfather Oliver had fled Ireland one mile ahead of the posse for printing and circulating scurrilous messages pertaining to Queen Victoria, then eminently unbeloved in County Tyrone and environs, but with a strong police force to back her dreams of empire. This may be why it seemed natural for me to lend some authority to my first passionate plea for justice, by printing it on a sizable piece of paper and having both my sister Anne and the current kitchen slavey sign it along with me.

My father and mother, who read it at the table after we had all eaten lunch, gave it unsmiling attention, although much later I learned that it really touched them. They discussed it at some length, with Anne and me there, and the cook listening through the little plate door in the built-in sideboard between us and the kitchen. They agreed without compromise to our demands, although there was some quiet discussion about alternatives to the proposal.

Our whole premise was that we loved oranges, that they grew on trees in our own yard, and that we would never be able to swallow them again, or even think of them without gagging, if Mother continued to give us our rare "cleaning-out" of castor oil beaten into the beautiful juice.

This was a dreadful custom, undoubtedly springing from her Iowa childhood when an orange was such a treat that it was offered along with the oil as a kind of bribe or reward. With us, newly arrived in a land heavy with citrus fruits, the story was different, and it seemed plain to Anne and me that we need not ruin one of our greatest pleasures by this strange carryover from another culture less fortunate than our own.

Our parents were sorry, they told us immediately, for submitting us to a dreadful experience which had to them seemed merciful. It would not happen again. The family bottle of castor oil would remain unemptied in the downstairs medicine closet in Grandmother's bathroom, along with the camphorated oil, the small sample of Hind's Honey and Almond Cream, and the Mentholatum.

On our side, having been freed from our basically gastronomical panic, we must make a few concessions. If we ate properly, there might never be another need for a Cleaning-Out: California seemed easier to live in, with all its vegetables and fruits, than had the somewhat gut-bound stretches of the Midwest in winter. On the other hand, if things came to a sorry state with either of us (and we must remember that Anne was inclined to be bilious . . .), we would have to drink a large glass of citrate of magnesia, and TO THE BOTTOM. This might spoil our delicate palates for lemon juice (all this was explained to us with straight faces), but at least the oranges would remain untainted for our continued enjoyment.

There was some solemn bantering between the two grown-ups about things like Cascara Sagrada, Syrup of Figs, Phenolax. No, it was decided: citrate of magnesia, freshly made up by the pharmacy, would be the alternative to the ghastly emulsion of. . . .

And the subject was closed. Rex said he would like to keep the Petition for professional reference or something. Anne and I were excused to go to the kitchen to tell the cook what she already knew . . . SUCCESS!!! . . . and my nice parents may have shared an extra look of tenderness.

The next time I remember our being forced to the point of a public statement of our anguish and protest was in about 1917, after the little sister Norah had been born. Fads and vogues, like popular tunes, traveled much more slowly then than they do now, in a week or so of radio and television boosting, and the style of wearing "bobbed" hair started by Irene Castle was a good five years in hitting the West Coast, at least in its smaller enclaves like Whittier.

Edith may have said something joking, or even wistful, about getting rid of her long silky black hair. Perhaps she said it to Aunt Gwen, whose hair was thick and springy, as they tended the lovely baby, while Anne and I watched them enviously. However, we got the word, it burned into us, and after much discussion in our room after the lights were out we decided to risk writing another broadside.

We realized that we should not overdo our luck. But it seemed like a long time ago that we had published the sheet about orange juice, and all had gone exceedingly well on that historical day. And this was a desperate situation. What if the two women, without telling anyone, took the Electric into Los Angeles and came back looking like enormous bristle-necked unsexed blowsy eunuchs (or words to that effect)? Did Father know of the danger? And above all, who would add a grown-up signature to our petition? (We were not too sure of the new cook. . . .)

We composed it in our bedroom closet, where we did many other private transactions. We kept the prose simple and terse. It said something like, "We, the undersigned, do not want Mother and Aunt Gwen to get their hair bobbed, now or ever. We cannot stand the thought, and will not stay here if it happens."

I realize now that I used my little sister like putty, pushing her this way and that in fashions I did not know were subconsciously worthy of all the resentment she later felt toward me. I was my own best press agent, and it was easy to get her apprehensive enthusiasm about the whole project, before we printed it in colored letters, signed it, and then took it sneakily out the back door and down the path to the garage, where Charles Somerville lived. He came home from work, as janitor in the *News* office, about five o'clock. He was there, working on a big pile of the dried tobacco leaves he hung in swinging bundles from the ceiling of his room, for his pipe. He welcomed us, asked how Baby Norah was doing, and then read our paper slowly, several times. I suspect that I hoped with part of me that he would veto it. I felt that we were daring too far. I was apprehensive, I remember clearly. Finally he uncorked a little bottle of ink, got out a pen from the wreck of a desk Rex had found him for his room, and signed with great flourishes and curls.

I forget everything else about the petition: presenting it, when, where, the reaction. But Edith Kennedy never bobbed her hair, and neither did Aunt Gwen, and only once was the caper referred to, when I appeared after my first marriage with a haircut my mother did not quite approve of, and she said mildly that it might be time for *her* to write something.

The third and last such manifesto, as far as I can recall, was composed and circulated in 1919, soon after we moved to the Ranch, a mile down Painter from our old house. It was successful, but Anne and I realized intuitively that it was time to change our tactics, as members of the clan. We made two or three copies, and on a small hand press this time, a toy someone had sent us. Typographically it might have some current value as a rare document, considering what fetches high prices at book auctions. Visually it was blurred, staggering sideways, and in fact something to make any good printer wince, which is what my father may well have done. In content, however, it held our most impassioned plea to date . . . or at least the one uppermost in our spirits at that time.

We felt a new freedom, at the Ranch. Everything was big and wide and unfenced, or so it seemed after the increasingly cramped city lot on Painter. (As we grew taller and our numbers increased, that place had shrunk almost audibly.) The walls bulged and snapped. The hedges in the back yard leaned outward, and the two orange trees seemed to shrivel and look poorly. Our bedrooms, once so spacious, felt stifling. Even Grandmother admitted she would gladly exchange her palatial one-room apartment downstairs in Whittier for the brighter quarters in the country at the Ranch. . . . We could run wild in the orange orchards to our south and east, and speed our bikes wildly up and down the two miles of Painter Extension, then almost as innocent of traffic as we were. Father could enlist us to hold the far end of his measuring string down the tree rows, where he planted beans and corn and tomatoes with an extravagant enthusiasm. There was, along the quiet road, an elegant hedge of hundreds of roses of every variety, planted there by the Lolly Willowes who sold us her wild tangle. In other words, it was very difficult for Anne and me to leave this paradise, especially on Sunday, the one day of the week Rex did not have to publish the *News*.

We discussed our problem with Margie Thayer. We huddled first in the chassis of an old electric automobile which Rex had installed in the back yard as a playhouse for us. He had bought it for five dollars, I think, removed its wheels, and carted it from the junkyard on his trailer, a vehicle he acquired as soon as the contract for the Ranch was signed, as essential to the Rancher's Life. The Hired Man of the Moment had helped him unload the high romantic-looking carcass, and it rode out the rest of its life between the Big House and what we called the Cook House. There were no batteries, of course, but it was still elegant, and the steering shaft still revolved at a touch, and there was still plate glass in the windows. The upholstery on the one wide seat was soft, and the two tiny jump seats were adequate, and although we felt almost too old for a playhouse, the Electric made a fine office for a weekly short-lived scandal sheet we were then publishing.

The manifesto took shape, and nobody seemed aware of our increasing preoccupation with it. We were three articulate children—Margie and I just eleven, and Anne nine—and we took it for granted that we always got A in English, still untroubled about the unfairness of such an academic decision, based as it was on the cold fact that our parents spoke with more and better-ordered words than could the family of Gracie, although Gracie was much brighter than we.

We actually composed this final manifesto, and edited it, and rewrote with active pain. We felt that it must be the most powerful plea in our lives. It said, with the usual "We, the undersigned," of course: "WE do not wish to go to Sunday School any more. WE want to go to church the way you do, on Christmas, Easter, perhaps now and then. WE feel too old now for the Sunday School classes. WE feel that staying home on Sunday mornings and working hard to help Father and perhaps helping with the laundry will bring us closer to God. Please do not spoil the best day of the week for us, in those dressed-up clothes and all that. It would spare Father two trips into Whittier, and we would feel more religious at the Ranch, working hard in the open air."

It was signed, when it finally came bobbling off the little press, by Anne and me because we needed it most, but not by

Margie, who had a few creative doubts about the prose. Then we got Rose's signature: she was the foulest-mouthed of any cook we ever had, but with the heart-of-gold of the classic whore, and she ruled our kitchen for a couple of noisy turbulent years. We knew Grandmother would be impossible to approach on such a heathenish and impudent proposition, and Charles was living at the *News* since we moved down Painter, and was not available. We finally went across the street and conned the two adolescent Erich girls into putting their names at the bottom, although they were an unknown quantity to the people the whole thing was aimed at.

As far as I could ever tell, the paper was read privately by Rex and Edith, discussed with possible hilarity, and then firmly agreed to. It released Father from a most boring interruption to his Sundays behind the hoe (and the table). It obviated for Mother the routine of checking us for clean fingernails and panties, buttons done nicely, polish on shoes, of every Sunday safari up Painter to St. Matthias and the flutings of our dedicated teachers. Rose liked it because her lover Billy came out earlier and she could disappear with him into the Cook House. The whole thing was blissful. I could hazard that even the chickens laid more eggs, once Anne and I were released from that increasing bondage of the Sunday school pattern that had for such eons, like seven years, been followed by my father and mother.

How kind they were, to read our words and give them due thought! And how fortunate we may have been, that never again did we try! As we grew older we certainly, and in our different ways, made a few flat statements about our own actions, if not our parents', but that last inky broadsheet was, judiciously or by sheer instinct, the end of our atavistic approach to meeting a problem in the printed form. As the seed is planted . . . as the twig is bent. . . .